Selling Local

Jennifer Meta Robinson *and* James Robert Farmer

Selling
Local

WHY LOCAL FOOD MOVEMENTS MATTER

INDIANA UNIVERSITY PRESS

This book is a publication of

Indiana University Press
Office of Scholarly Publishing
Herman B Wells Library 350
1320 East 10th Street
Bloomington, Indiana 47405 USA

iupress.indiana.edu

The paper used in this publication meets the minimum requirements of the American National Standard for Information Sciences—Permanence of Paper for Printed Library Materials, ANSI Z39.48–1992.

Manufactured in the United States of America

Library of Congress Cataloging-in-Publication Data

Names: Robinson, Jennifer Meta, [date], author. |
    Farmer, James R. (James Robert), author.
Title: Selling local : why local food movements matter /
    Jennifer Meta Robinson and James R. Farmer.
Description: Bloomington, Indiana : Indiana University Press,
    [2017] | Includes bibliographical references and index.
Identifiers: LCCN 2017004284 (print) | LCCN 2017007339 (ebook) |
    ISBN 9780253026989 (pb : alk. paper) | ISBN 9780253027092 (eb)
Subjects: LCSH: Local foods—United States. | Farmers' markets—United
    States. | Community-supported agriculture—United States.
Classification: LCC HD9005 .R63 2017 (print) | LCC
    HD9005 (ebook) | DDC 381/.41—dc23
LC record available at https://lccn.loc.gov/2017004284

1 2 3 4 5   22 21 20 19 18 17

For

Jeff Hartenfeld, a farmer

Sara, Samuel, Caroline, and Collin Farmer

Eating is an agricultural act.
—Wendell Berry

CONTENTS

ACKNOWLEDGMENTS

We thank, foremost, the many farmers and patrons of local food who have shared their time and expertise with us in conversations across the country, at local markets and farms and throughout numerous research projects. We appreciate your observations and thoughtfulness about the journey so far, knowing that life continues to emerge in surprising ways. Special thanks to the people of south-central Indiana and Huntington, West Virginia, for extending their worlds to us. We thank Justin Rawlins for his thoughtful editorial assistance and manuscript preparation and Kevin Naaman for his help with sources. Thanks to Sarah Mincey for essential consultation on theory and Sara Minard, Bridget Masur, Natalie Woodcock, Eric Knackmuhs, Angela Babb, and Megan Betz for able research assistance. Thanks to Sobremesa Farm, Evening Song Farm, and Joseph Donnermeyer for sharing maps and images. Thanks to Steven McFadden for sharing his history of CSAs. Jennifer Roebuck and Dan Schlapbach were generous, as always, with wonderful photographs and good advice.

We are grateful for research funding from Indiana University—the College of Arts and Sciences; the Department of Recreation, Park, and Tourism Studies; the School of Public Health; and the Vincent and Elinor Ostrom Workshop in Political Theory and Policy Analysis—as well as the Indiana Clinical and Translational Sciences Institute, the Indiana State Department of Agriculture, and the United States Department of Agriculture.

We appreciate the faith Gary Dunham and Indiana University Press have placed in the project. Gary's clear-sightedness about salient audiences has helped guide the book to this final form. Thanks to Nancy Lightfoot for shepherding the project and to Jill R. Hughes for her clarifying copyediting.

From Jennifer

Many thanks to Bobbi, Rosie, J. D., Grant, and Farmers Anonymous for letting me listen in—you know who you are! Appreciation to the members of Indiana University Faculty Writing Groups and to Mary Magoulick for writing companionship. And thanks, as always, to Jeff Hartenfeld for helping me keep it real.

From James

Thanks to several farmers who are always willing to listen, critique, and explain—Tim Alexander, Rick Dalessandro, Lance Alexander—and to Tony Terhaar. And thank you to Jennifer, for her constant mentorship and teaching.

INTRODUCTION

After decades of wanting food in greater quantities, cheaper, and standardized, Americans now increasingly look for quality and crafting. Grocery giants like Walmart and Target have responded by offering "simple" and "organic" food displayed in folksy crates with seals of organizational approval, while only blocks away a farmer may drop his tailgate on a pickup full of sweet corn at a four-way stop. Meanwhile, easy-up tents are likely to unfurl over multigenerational farmers' markets once or twice a week in any given city or town. No longer peopled by women and old men, markets see sons shopping with their fathers as mother and daughter farmers share produce stands while buskers, students, political activists, photographers, and journalists ply their arts in the aisles. Ostrich, bison, goat, mutton, and every cut of the familiar chicken, pork, and beef come with dazzling endorsements of their local provenance: free-range, cage-free, local, non-GMO, grass-fed, heirloom, biodynamic, natural, organic, community-supported, cooperative, nonprofit. Mac 'n' "cheez" out of a box may still taste like home cooking to some, and canned-soup casserole may be the pinnacle of culinary adventurousness for others, but chances are, even someone who grew up on those mid-century delicacies is changing what she or he wants to eat and where it comes from.

This book is about is about local food and why it matters. Food organizes our relationship to the world in important ways. "Eating is an agricultural act," says Wendell Berry,[1] and our decisions about what we eat change how food is grown, the people who grow it, and the world we live in. Food has become central to the current cultural movement about making and accountability that is sweeping the country. Like its cousins in upcycling, artisan, small-batch, handmade, vintage, craft, and other labor-intensive endeavors, the movement arises concurrently with vast technological advances, population migrations, financial precariousness, and unprecedented environmental change. It responds to a sense of deterioration, alienation, injustice, insecurity, and xenophobia that plagues many Americans and offers a promising way forward—connecting people with places in ways that express their relationships and responsibilities, histories and hopes.[2]

This book is about both the *idea* of selling local—its appeal and promise—and the *practical* ways that gets done in the dynamic context of the twenty-first century. As the pieces come into focus, we can understand food's special capacity to blur distinctions between producers and consumers and to expand our sense of global citizenship. The responsibility for food that is healthful, just, and environmentally sound becomes a shared responsibility of an integrated world.

Trends

Country music superstar Willie Nelson once commented that growing up poor in Texas during the Great Depression meant local food was all they had to eat. True enough. For millennia, people ate mostly what was available to hand—fresh, stored, and traded. However, with the mass production of industrialization and improvements in transportation during the nineteenth and twentieth centuries, food production and consumption became centralized, homogenous, and fragmented. As cities expanded, farms were forced outside of population centers. In the 1920s, grocery stores replaced produce markets in major cities. At mid-century, women—the conventional home cooks—increasingly worked outside the home, and "convenience" became the watchword of food preparation: one-ingredient cakes, TV dinners, frozen vegetables that cooked right in the plastic bag. Improvements in refrigeration and shipping meant we could get pineapples "jet fresh" from Hawaii and "tea and oranges that come all the way from China" as a popular Leonard Cohen song put it. Soon, we thought, entire meals would come in pill form.

One popular way to tell the story of the local revolution is that Americans started taking food back around the time Alice Waters created a restaurant in Berkeley, California, that sourced its ingredients from its own garden. That was in 1971. Now restaurants go so far as to feature locally grown, locally ground polenta served in handmade bowls thrown by a nearby potter. Neighborhood potluck dinners, too, may include venison stew or steaks from beef raised locally. An ancient institution occurring worldwide—along the Silk Road in Kashgar, China; in Timbuktu, Mali, and Marrakesh, Morocco, in Africa; and in the Aztec cities of Tenochtitlan and Tlatelolco in Mexico, among other far-flung places—European-style markets were established in the colonial cities of Boston in 1634, Hartford in 1643, New York in 1686, and Philadelphia in 1693. New Orleans had a market as early as 1779 and Cincinnati, on the frontier, in 1801. The early boom in farmers' markets continued well into the 1800s until they began to fade under the pressure of economic and cultural forces. By the mid-1850s, farmers' markets began to decline so that by 1900 only half of the municipal areas in the United States still had one.[3] By 1979 agricultural giant California was home to only a half dozen markets, with only a single steady farmers' market in all of Southern California.[4]

Compare this decline to today. By 2010 California had more than 729 markets, with over 80 in Los Angeles County alone. Other states with high numbers included New York with 520, Michigan with 349, and Illinois with 305. Even Alaska, with its small population and short growing season, saw 46 percent more markets in a single year, bringing that state's 2011 grand total to 35.[5] Between 1994 and 2012, US farmers' markets increased in total numbers by more than 450 percent.[6] Across the country, farmers' markets now number over 8,000, a figure that continues to grow annually. Numbers such as these make farmers' markets the fastest-growing, though still small, segment of the US food economy and an important tool for the prosperity and well-being of communities.

Similarly, community supported agriculture (CSA) programs have taken off in recent decades. This new innovation on agricultural tradition dissolves the usual producer-consumer dichotomy by creating a formal partnership by which a farm becomes "either legally or spiritually, the community's farm."[7] Shareholders buy into some of the risks of the farm, typically at the beginning of a growing season; participate in its production and care; and receive a share of its bounty in return—maybe a great quantity in bumper years and not much at all in lean ones. Either way, the connection gets made: customers connect with a farm, and growers defray some of uncertainties by stabilizing their customer base and acquiring working capital. In addition, communities gain the security of a short-distance and highly accountable food system that supports local businesses.

CSAs first took hold in the United States in the mid-1980s in New England. One lineage, sometimes debated, can be traced to Japan in the mid-1960s when mothers concerned with the loss of farmland and the importation of food contracted with community-based farms.[8] The other significant lineage comes from German and Swiss cooperatives in the mid-1960s designed to fund and support the full cost of having agriculture that was ecologically sound and socially equitable.[9] From the earliest US examples in 1986—Indian Line Farm in Massachusetts and Temple-Wilton Community Farm in New Hampshire—the CSA model of sharing risks and rewards has grown to over twelve thousand programs nationwide.[10]

Recently, food hubs—which aggregate farm products from small producers into quantities suitable for larger institutions, such as restaurants, hospitals, and schools—and other innovative strategies have expanded the ways in which local food can be distributed. Today, more than three hundred regional food hubs operate in the United States.[11] They vary in business structure—nonprofits, cooperatives, for-profits, or multi-structured—but each offers a host of benefits to farmers, customers, and communities.[12] Currently, the federal government as well as state, county, and community organizations, including extension services, are actively supporting food hub development through grants, research, and state and regional initiatives.[13]

All of this energy comes in the context of explosive global population growth. Thirty-six metropolitan areas now qualify as "megacities" of over ten million residents, and a continued growth rate of over 1 percent per year will see eight billion humans by 2024.[14] Ironically, however, productivity-based critiques of local food tend to depopulate the rich human experience of food. They reduce food to calories-in and calories-out, necessary but insufficient as they are—effectively decentering the experiences of farmers and eaters and neglecting the elaborated foodways that help to make us human. Buying and selling local must be considered in these contexts, however. And we have found that, as simple and nearby as it sounds, "local" itself holds answers to this conundrum. The term productively bundles together complications and apparent contradictions for those seeking to reclaim independence of agency without renouncing a shared stake in the commons. Its meaning in use reveals an ideology that enacts, reveals, and recasts relations of power among people. If we can "sell" the idea of local, in it we can find the levers we need for scaling up production to meet future needs.

Perspectives

Our perspectives on local food come from both lived experience and scholarly engagement. We have both lived on small farms in the United States—growing, selling, and eating their bounty and buying from our neighbors who do the same. And we have both studied the people who make these farms run and those who rely on them for food. The result is a unique collaboration. We use our various experiences and disciplinary lenses to jump-start our understanding of the theory and practice of local food. By talking with the people of local food, and surveying them and watching them at work, we hope to give them fair voice and to explore the possibilities represented by the local ideology.

Jennifer Meta Robinson started experimenting with food politics in college when she became a vegetarian and joined a student farming cooperative. Her co-op job included compost duty—driving the group's old, half-ton pickup truck behind the dining halls every week to pick up trash barrels brimming with vegetable matter. In other roles at other co-ops, she bought apples and cider by the carload at local orchards and sprouted five-gallon buckets of mung, lentil, alfalfa, and sunflower seeds for student-run kitchens. When she left college after two years, she moved to rural Kentucky, built what now would be called an off-grid tiny house, and grew a few vegetables in her backwoods garden. At the same time, she became the manager of a small cooperative grocery store, which had monthly deliveries from the larger Federation of Ohio River Co-ops. The only types of organic produce available wholesale at that time were carrots, potatoes, and onions. After four years of such free-ranging, Jennifer returned to her studies at the nearby state university and, several degrees later, is now a professor of practice in the Department of Anthropology at Indiana University, where she teaches courses in communication and culture. She lives on the farm that her husband, Jeff Hartenfeld, established in 1977 as an organic specialty crop business that now sells primarily through a nearby farmers' market. In 2007 Jennifer and Jeff wrote *The Farmers' Market Book: Growing Food, Cultivating Community*, in which they describe in detail why farmers' markets in the United States have boomed in recent years. Jennifer also publishes and speaks widely about teaching and learning in higher education. She served as president of the International Society for the Scholarship of Teaching and Learning (2008–2011) and co-edits the Indiana University Press book series Scholarship of Teaching and Learning. Her concerns for sustainability and education have come together in such publications as *Teaching Environmental Literacy across the Curriculum*, which she co-edited with Heather Reynolds and Eduardo Brondízio in 2010.

James R. Farmer grew up surrounded by farms in east-central Indiana's Wayne County, showing cows and hogs in 4-H, dairy judging in Future Farmers of America (FFA) contests, and working on neighboring farms. While farming has always been his ideal occupation, he does the next best thing—he studies it. James is an assistant professor of human ecology in the School of Public Health at Indiana University, where he focuses his scholarship and service on community food systems, sustainable agriculture, and natural resource sustainability. James formerly owned a CSA in Brown County, Indiana, was a high school agriculture teacher, and advised Miller Farm, the student-run agriculture living-and-learning cooperative at Earlham College. His recently completed studies include Assessing Local Foods in Indiana: Farmers' Markets and Community Supported Agriculture; Overcoming the Market Barriers to Organic Production in West Virginia; Infusion or Assimilation: Barriers to the Integration of Local Food Systems across the Community; Community Orchards: Institutional Organization and Participant Outcomes; and Specialty Crops and High Tunnels: Evaluating Success and Building Future Capacity. His work on farmers' markets and CSAs has been presented at national conferences and regional and state meetings as well as state and local extension programs. He is an associate editor for the *Natural Areas Journal* and a reviewer for several other scholarly publications, including the *Journal of Agriculture, Food Systems, and Community Development*; the *Journal of Hunger and Environmental Nutrition*; and *Sustainability*.

This book combines our experiences and our research in various places around the country, bringing them to life through in-depth examples based in two towns—Bloomington, Indiana, in the Midwest, and Huntington, West Virginia, in central Appalachia. These innovative exemplars underscore the idea that food operates as a system that includes not only individual growers and eaters—who are, of course, all of us—but also communities, technologies, and the natural environment. Together, these elements offer some counterintuitive and thought-provoking contrasts to suggest why local food has grown so prodigiously and how it can be sustained in the future. Through those examples and many others, we show how the major mechanisms in local food—especially farmers' markets, community supported agriculture, food hubs, and digital networks—affect people.

We are building on Thomas A. Lyson's work on "civic agriculture," which describes the beneficial links between social and economic development when communities participate in local food.[15] Writing in 2004, Lyson was an early observer of the phenomenon before it came to much attention by state and federal agencies or many scholars. He observes that a "you food" rhetoric manages to infiltrate some of the most standardized fast-food chain restaurants, with consumers "'demanding' food products tailored to their individual tastes and preferences," even while industrial giants further entrench themselves in globalization, mechanization, and economies of scale. Burger King might promise that you can "have it your way," but industry practices in fact "transformed from a more locally interdependent system of production and consumption to a more globally oriented system where production was uncoupled from consumption."[16] Our perspective here is much in concert with Lyson's description of a civic agriculture that trumps strict economic determinism with pragmatic environmental sustainability, community building, ecological holism and process, developmental and equity orientations to decision making, dispersed economic power, and democratic political processes.[17] Coming more than a decade later, we add to Lyson's foundational discussion the significant diversification of iconic local food venues into a host of creative variations and offshoots. Moreover, *Selling Local* offers a more embodied approach to the people and places of community-based food, accounting for the realities they experience and that fundamentally contribute to local culture, economy, and environment.

While *Selling Local* is based on evidence of practice, its main focus is not how to work a farm or get into direct marketing. Many excellent publications exist on those subjects, including *CSA: Organizing a Successful CSA*, by Cathy Roth and Elizabeth Keen; *The New Farmers' Market: Farm Fresh Ideas for Producers, Managers and Communities*, by Vance Corum, Marcie Rosenzweig, and Eric Gibson; *Making Your Small Farm Profitable*, by Ron Macher and Howard W. Kerr Jr.; and the periodical *Growing for Market*.[18] These publications present practical advice to growers on what to grow; how to start, manage, and promote a direct-market farming business; and how to increase market share. In addition, the United States Department of Agriculture (USDA) regularly updates its instruction guides on its Agricultural Marketing Service site: https://www.ams.usda.gov.

Selling Local strategically develops comparative case studies in order to propose transferrable models of viable local food systems. Other books provide excellent concentration on a focused case or theoretical framework; for example, gender (Julie M. Parsons, *Gender, Class and Food: Families, Bodies, and Health*), economics (Remy Herrera and Kin Chi Lau, eds., *The Struggle for Food Sovereignty: Alternative Development and the Renewal of Peasant Societies Today*), global dispersion (James Farrer, ed., *The Globalization of Asian Cuisines*), public planning (Daniel Kemmis, *The Good City and the Good Life*, which examines farmers' markets as one model for urban planning), public health (Julie Guthman, *Weighing In: Obesity, Food Justice, and the Limits of Capitalism*, which brings to light the importance of looking beyond caloric intake and physical activity as the only explanatory measures connecting food and health), ecology (Gary Stephenson, *Farmers' Markets: Success, Failure, and Management Ecology*, which examines ecological management, mostly in the Oregon region), and race (Alison Hope Alkon, *Black, White, and Green*, which analyzes race and ethnicity in two San Francisco area markets).[19]

And some organize around a single food, region, or venue. Comprehensive examinations of a single food include Sarah Bowen's *Divided Spirits: Tequila, Mezcal, and the Politics of Production*, Antonio

Sustainability Defined

Figure I.1. Sustainability implicates overlapping areas of human-environment interaction. This Venn diagram is commonly used to describe the interdependence of these factors essential to sustainability. It is general enough to apply to areas with diverse economic, social, and ecological conditions while still posing sustainable development as a global objective.

Mattozzi and Zachary Nowak's *Inventing the Pizzeria: A History of Pizza Making in Naples*, and Gary Allen's *Sausage: A Global History*. Many other books look at doughnuts, lamb, dumplings, carrots, and so on. The city of Chicago has its own "food biography" (Daniel Block and Howard Rosing's *Chicago: A Food Biography*), markets and CSAs have their own books; among them are *The Farmers' Market Book: Growing Food, Cultivating Community*, by Jennifer Meta Robinson and J. A. Hartenfeld, and *Farms of Tomorrow Revisited: Community Supported Farms—Farm Supported Communities*, by Trauger Groh and Steven McFadden.[20]

    Although *Selling Local* is informed by the authors' personal experience in order to build a transferrable theory, other popular publications provide vivid memoirs or character studies to enliven local food issues. Barbara Kingsolver's memoir *Animal, Vegetable, Miracle* has been widely heralded for introducing food politics to newcomers, and Novella Carpenter's *Farm City: The Education of an Urban Farmer* profiles her experience raising vegetables and animals in her city yard in Oakland, California. In addition, books like Mary Carpenter and Quentin Carpenter's *The Dane County Farmers' Market: A Personal History* compiles a multifaceted portrait of the Madison, Wisconsin, market through numerous profiles of key people involved.[21]

Several unifying themes weave throughout this book. One is sustainability—of human effort, finances, and environment. Indeed, environmental sustainability has been defined as long-term "thriving within our means," and it can be achieved by balancing environmental health, economic prosperity, and social equity.[22] Proponents of local food often think of this movement as an important component of sustainability. During an era of climate change, it can help stabilize regional economies, both urban and rural, increase access to healthy foods, lower environmental consequences, and draw people into cooperative association with each other.

Another theme emphasizes making and sharing culture. Food is a particularly good medium for knowing ourselves and how we relate to the world around us—understanding our *culture*—because it is so central to sustaining life. Food creates bonds and distinctions among us that give shape to our lives. When people shop local food at centralized venues like farmers' markets, they get drawn into contact with others—and then that same food helps them to navigate the social world.

Finally, systems thinking serves as an organizing theme throughout the book. Systems thinking about food connects people, practices, and places. It helps us to analyze institutions and design new ones. It asks us to consider the interconnected nature of life and reflect on how our choices affect the world.

The Chapters

Chapter 1 asks the question "Why Local and Why Now?" The multifaceted, counterintuitive answer offers a theoretical foundation for the detailed discussion in the following chapters. The word "local" sounds neighborly and nearby, but multimodal research suggests a bundled set of meanings with internal complications and contradictions. For those who use and care about local, its connotations are not only about proximity, as a lay definition of the word suggests, but also about reclaiming independent agency without renouncing a stake in shared common goods and resources. This chapter develops a theory of localism that is rooted in food politics, practices, and aspirations and that makes sense of apparent paradoxes.

Chapter 2, "Understanding Farmers' Markets," provides an overview of farmers' markets, just one piece of a locally based agricultural system that includes CSAs, wholesale exchanges, food hubs, and other distribution schemes. Markets can be an especially stable sector because they are regular, visible, local, and *peopled*. That means they are especially well suited to help stabilize local economies, both urban and rural; increase access to healthy foods; lower environmental consequences; provide recreation; and draw people into association with one another. They can foster a sense of community that rests on belonging, responsibility, and reciprocity. The chapter introduces some of the main categories of farmers' markets and summarizes research on customer demographics and market experiences. The information it provides allows market vendors, advocates, and administrators to build intentionally more robust and diverse markets that support community well-being.

Chapter 3, "Understanding Community Supported Agriculture," outlines the appeal of CSAs to farmers and shareholders. It looks at CSA demographics around the country and the factors involved in making this relatively new addition to local food successful, considering both their management and the systemic barriers to participation that are implicit in common models. The chapter concludes with alternative approaches and innovations that broaden the accessibility of CSAs, remedying the exclusionary aspects that limit their growth and civic success.

Chapter 4, "What's Next in Local Food?," describes the emergence of major new outreach and aggregation systems, innovations in local, that will serve more people, broaden the impact, and help sustain the success of local food. These developments support new markets for small farmers and allow larger, institutional-type buyers to purchase locally. The chapter introduces several exemplars and discusses the factors involved in their commercial, communication, and community success. The distinction between recreation and leisure is used to explain both the local grower and the local eater. These lenses can support the growth of local food systems and their use in emergency relief, food hubs, urban agriculture, and expansion of the commons into this area. Finally, this chapter focuses on both mainstream and alternative innovations that hold promise for future needs.

Chapter 5, "Growing Capacity," identifies some of the major challenges in scaling up production of local food. We know American farmers are aging. In recent years, their average age rose to fifty-eight while their overall numbers fell.[23] At the same time, new farms tend to be diversified and smaller, with younger operators and more off-farm jobs to support them. Nationwide, midsize farms are getting squeezed out, with most farms either very large or very small in terms of output. Promising trends show an increase in women farmers and minority farmers, but these groups also face particular challenges, especially in acquiring land, an agricultural education, and a sense of community. The chapter explores the difficulties experienced by some new farmers and outlines the new educational opportunities and supportive policy groups putting local food in a good position to scale up.

Chapter 6, "A Systems Approach to Local Food," proposes a new framework for shifting our understanding of food production, from a simple hierarchical structure to an integrated system. It uses case studies to create a model that represents complex phenomena in an abstract but simplified way, stepping back from the details to explain, essentially, how the world of food works.[24] Expressed as a model, our theories of the world can be tested and refined against other examples, getting closer to accurate with each revision. Our model for local food proposes a map of relevant factors—as an explanation of how food systems work and as a realistic guide for how to support sustainable food in diverse human communities in ways that foster the ecological systems within which we live. The two case studies we have focused on show that a model can explain why counterintuitive situations sometimes succeed and thereby aid civic planning.

The conclusion identifies major lessons for the future of local food. By understanding that we are embedded in systems, together we can enter into design and action with broad goals for the well-being of people and the sustainability of the environment in mind.

Eating is an agricultural act we all share. Our common need for food blurs distinctions among people and expands our sense of relationship and responsibility for the production of healthful and environmentally sound sustenance. By beginning with the best information from research and experience, we can recommend practices that will support farmers, community activists, and educators as they work toward a sustainable and humane future. College students and instructors in fields like agriculture, anthropology, environmental studies, food studies, geography, natural resource management, recreation, sociology, sustainability, and tourism will find this introduction to selling local to be timely and comprehensive. Selling *local*—the food and the idea—offers a way to resolve common disconnects between growers and eaters, farmers and scholars, practitioners and policy makers.

Because of its current popularity, the topic of selling locally is something of a moving target: traditional sensibilities of place and belonging are being innovatively advanced by new communication technologies, such as social networking, just-in-time ordering, and geographic information system (GIS) technology. Getting beyond breaking news stories and personality-filled features, *Selling Local* offers a lasting foundation that transcends the moment and will continue to be useful as new trends and theories of local food emerge. Let us begin by asking why local and why now?

Notes

1. Wendell Berry, *What Are People For? Essays by Wendell Berry* (Berkeley: Counterpoint, 2010), 145.

2. Jennifer Meta Robinson, "Making the Land Connection: Local Food Farms and Sustainability of Place," in *The Greening of Everyday Life: Challenging Practices, Imaging Possibilities*, edited by Jens Kersten and John M. Meyer (Oxford: Oxford University Press, 2016); Thomas A. Lyson, *Civic Agriculture: Reconnecting Farm, Food, and Community* (Boston: Tufts University Press, 2004).

3. Jennifer Meta Robinson and J. A. Hartenfeld, *The Farmers' Market Book: Growing Food, Cultivating Community* (Bloomington: Indiana University Press,

2007), 36–45; Tracey Deutsch, *Building a Housewife's Paradise: Gender, Politics, and American Grocery Stores in the Twentieth Century* (Chapel Hill: University of North Carolina Press, 2010).

4. Russ Parsons, "The Idea That Shook the World," *Los Angeles Times*, May 24, 2006, http://articles.latimes.com/2006/may/24/food/fo-farmer24.

5. Sam Jones, "More Than 1,000 New Farmers Markets Recorded across Country as USDA Directory Reveals 17 Percent Growth," United States Department of Agriculture, http://www.usda.gov/wps/portal/usda/usdahome?contentid=2011/08/0338.xml.

6. United States Department of Agriculture (hereafter, USDA), "Local Food Research and Development," http://www.ams.usda.gov/AMSv1.0/FoodHubs.

7. USDA, "Community Supported Agriculture," *USDA National Agricultural Library*, http://www.nal.usda.gov/afsic/pubs/csa/csa.shtml.

8. Steven McFadden, "Community Farms in the 21st Century: Poised for Another Wave of Growth?," Rodale Institute, http://newfarm.rodaleinstitute.org/features/0104/csa-history/part1.shtml.

9. Ibid.

10. Ibid.; Local Harvest, "Community Supported Agriculture," http://www.localharvest.org/csa.

11. National Good Food Network, "Food Hub Center," http://www.ngfn.org/resources/food-hubs.

12. Todd M. Schmit et al., "Assessing the Economic Impacts of Regional Food Hubs: The Case of Regional Access," Northeast SARE, 2013, http://www.nesare.org/Dig-Deeper/Useful-resources/SARE-Project-Products/Northeast-SARE-Project-Products/Assessing-the-Economic-Impacts-of-Regional-Food-Hubs-the-Case-of-Regional-Access; Clare Thompson, "Food Hubs: How Small Farmers Get to Market," *Grist*, http://grist.org/locavore/food-hubs-how-small-farmers-get-to-market.

13. James Matson, Martha Sullins, and Chris Cook, "The Role of Food Hubs in Local Food Marketing," USDA Rural Development Service Report 73, January 2013, http://www.rd.usda.gov/files/sr73.pdf.

14. United Nations, "UN Projects World Population to Reach 8.5 Billion by 2030, Driven by Growth in Developing Countries," Sustainable Development blog, July 29, 2015; United Nations, Department of Economic and Social Affairs, *World Urbanization Prospects: The 2014 Revision* (New York: United Nations, 2014), https://esa.un.org/unpd/wup/Publications/Files/WUP2014-Highlights.pdf.

15. Lyson, *Civic Agriculture*.

16. Ibid., 2–5.

17. Ibid., 70–78.

18. Cathy Roth and Elizabeth Keen, *CSA: Organizing a Successful CSA*, 1999, https://www.uvm.edu/~susagctr/resources/CSA.pdf; Vance Corum, Marcie Rosenzweig, and Eric Gibson, *The New Farmers' Market: Farm Fresh Ideas for Producers, Managers and Communities* (Auburn, CA: New World Publishing, 2001); Ron Macher and Howard W. Kerr Jr., *Making Your Small Farm Profitable* (North Adams, MA: Storey Books, 1999); *Growing for Market* (growingformarket.com).

19. Julie M. Parsons, *Gender, Class and Food: Families, Bodies and Health* (New York: Palgrave Macmillan, 2015); Remy Herrera and Kin Chi Lau, eds., *The Struggle for Food Sovereignty: Alternative Development and the Renewal of Peasant Societies Today* (London: Pluto Press, 2015); James Farrer, ed. *The Globalization of Asian Cuisines* (New York: Palgrave Macmillan, 2015); Daniel Kemmis, *The Good City and the Good Life* (Boston: Houghton Mifflin, 1995); Julie Guthman, *Weighing In: Obesity, Food Justice, and the Limits of Capitalism* (Berkeley: University of California Press, 2011); Gary Stephenson, *Farmers' Markets: Success, Failure, and Management Ecology* (Amherst, NY: Cambria Press, 2008).

20. Sarah Bowen, *Divided Spirits: Tequila, Mezcal, and the Politics of Production* (Berkeley: University of California Press, 2015); Antonio Mattozzi, *Inventing the Pizzeria: A History of Pizza Making in Naples*, ed. and trans. Zachary Nowak (London: Bloomsbury Academic, 2015); Gary Allen, *Sausage: A Global History* (London: Reaktion, 2015); Daniel Block and Howard Rosing, *Chicago: A Food Biography* (Lanham, MD: Rowman and Littlefield, 2015), Robinson and Hartenfeld, *Farmers' Market Book*; and Trauger Groh and Steven McFadden, *Farms of Tomorrow Revisited: Community Supported Farms—Farm Supported Communities* (Kimberton, PA: Biodynamic Farming and Gardening Association, 1998).

21. Barbara Kingsolver, *Animal, Vegetable, Miracle* (New York: HarperCollins, 2007); Novella Carpenter, *Farm City: The Education of an Urban Farmer* (New York: Penguin, 2010); Mary Carpenter and Quentin Carpenter, *The Dane County Farmers' Market: A Personal History* (Madison: University of Wisconsin Press, 2003).

22. Indiana University Office of Sustainability, "Sustainability Defined," http://sustain.indiana.edu/overview/sustainability.php.

23. USDA, "Farm Demographics—US Farmers by Gender, Age, Race, Ethnicity, and More," 2012 Census Highlights, May 2014, https://www.agcensus.usda.gov/Publications/2012/Online_Resources/Highlights/Farm_Demographics. The Agricultural Census of 2012 showed that the total number of principal operators had dropped 4.3 percent from 2007. This is the most recent census available at our time of publication.

24. Timothy Wilson and David Gilbert, "Affective Forecasting," *Advances in Experimental Social Psychology* 35 (2003): 345–411; Barbara Crawford and Rebecca C. Jordan, "Inquiry, Models, and Complex Reasoning to Transform

Learning in Environmental Education," in *Transdisciplinary Research in Environmental Education*, edited by Marianne E. Krasny and Justin Dillon (Ithaca, NY: Cornell University Press, 2013); Amanda E. Sorensen et al., "Model-Based Reasoning to Foster Environmental and Socio-scientific Literacy in Higher Education," *Journal of Environmental Studies and Sciences* 6, no. 2 (2015): 287–94.

Selling Local

ONE

Why Local and Why Now?

"Local" has emerged as one of the hottest food and cultural concepts in the United States in the nascent twenty-first century. Many people choose to buy local, read books written or published or bound locally, wear clothing made from homespun fiber or fashioned nearby, ride locally made bicycles, recreate locally, and build homes with locally sourced materials. Three-quarters of Americans say that they are highly influenced by labels that indicate food is "locally grown."[1] Food industry giants that regularly source from around the world, such as members of the National Restaurant Association, the largest food service trade organization, and Walmart, the largest US grocer, identify "locally grown" as a top food trend in recent years.[2] The term's ubiquity alone begs examination.

Benefits and Constraints

Our research—individually over the past two decades and more recently in collaboration—has involved hundreds of interviews, visits, and observations, and thousands of surveys with locally oriented farmers and customers in the United States. Our focus has been especially on people associated with farmers' markets and CSAs in the Midwest and in the central Appalachian regions, but our own work and our reading of other scholars has ranged far beyond. We can identify several root reasons for the increase in interest in local food.

Economic Factors

Local food venues help to provide a measure of economic stability to a community. Farmers' markets, for example, which are essentially an assemblage of small businesses, tend to boost nearby commercial enterprises: a study in Ontario, Canada, found that 50 percent of market customers also shopped at other businesses while en route to or from a market.[3] Other communities in the United States, Canada, New Zealand, and Australia have also recognized that farmers' markets can be tourist attractions that draw outside money into local economies. They promote markets as a way to experience a community's unique agrarian surroundings, history, climate, and cuisine.[4] Studies in Athens, Ohio, and the North Carolina Highlands, among other places, have found that their farmers' markets can attract up to half of their customers from outside the immediate area.[5] CSAs, too, strengthen the rural economy, stabilizing farmers' incomes by creating ongoing purchasing relationships with consumers nearby. Similarly, food aggregation hubs, a new addition to local systems, help to build capacity by allowing farmers to grow more and sell more. Moreover, while the United States continues to produce prodigious amounts of commodity crops (such as corn, soybeans, wheat, and pork bellies), the country also benefits from the diversification of the local economy that occurs with demand for specialty agricultural products. Because these marketing arrangements decrease the likelihood that farmers will subdivide or sell their property, they also help preserve agricultural land and the force of people who know how to farm it.

A limitation of local food, however, is the perception, and sometimes the fact, that its cost is higher. For example, the public perceives farmers' markets to have higher prices than supermarkets, and enrollment in CSAs often requires a big cash outlay. These impressions remain even though prices for in-season produce can be cheaper, some markets now accept government food subsidies, and some CSAs now offer lower-price subscription payments. Surveys show that farmers' market and CSA customers tend to have higher incomes and more formal education than the general population of the area.[6]

On the farmers' side, the economic balance sheet is always a challenge: "I can grow or raise just about anything that we have the climate and soils for—it is the market that is the problem," says Tim Nickels, a fourth-generation farmer in western Kentucky. Although he can produce plenty of peaches and sweet corn, he has to find enough people to buy them at prices that cover his costs in doing business, which are especially high as he works on transitioning to more environmentally sustainable methods. Similarly, Paul Alexander, a local produce farmer in southern Indiana, feels challenged by having to be both farmer and marketer, doing the physical labor of reclaiming long fallow fields while simultaneously building a clientele. Those fields have a twenty-five-year seedbed of grasses and other undesirables that Alexander must battle in order to give his vegetable cash crops a chance. At the same time, he worries that the local population is too sparse to absorb all he can grow.

Social Factors

Such economic factors complement an array of social benefits that local food venues provide for communities, including developing social vitality, local culture and values, and human capabilities.[7] The social nature of markets and CSAs supports new friendships, strengthens old acquaintances, and can enhance a feeling of belonging among vendors and consumers. Aggregation hubs—when they welcome small, local growers and identify their sources as such—support the same kinds of social belonging. Food hubs, though, are new developments in the local food infrastructure—aggregating, storing, processing, and distributing regionally to larger retail, commercial, and institutional customers—so research on them has begun only recently. Hubs that welcome small, locally oriented growers clearly provide a model for access to larger buyers. Still, the public nature of all of these venues means that local crops, crafts, and cuisines can be connected to the identities, creativities, heritages, and collective memory of those who live in a particular region.[8]

On the other hand, local food venues may seem to be inaccessible to people whose ethnicity, class, social position, and cultural preparation for the market experience differs from the majority of those participating.[9] In addition, people with physical disabilities may find the exertion of an open-air shopping excursion at a farmers' market or a pick-your-own farm prohibitive. Thus, certain sectors of the population can be more prepared for and more privileged in local food experiences.

An additional social factor hinges on the homespun notion of having fun on the farm, also known as *agrileisure*. Many families know firsthand the pleasure gained from picking strawberries, pumpkins, apples, or Christmas trees at a local farm, and the USDA has long promoted recreation as both an outcome of the agriculture experience and a means to diversify farm income. Coining the term, Ben Amsden and Jesse McEntee describe agrileisure as emerging "from the intersection of agriculture, recreation and leisure, and social change."[10] The hybrid word binds the "supply and demand sides of farm-based recreation and tourism with the processes of economic diversification, community development, and environmental and ecological sustainability."[11] In other words, the leisure gained by consumers of agricultural activities—such as regular market shopping, food security gleaning, CSA barbeques, and nose-to-tail cooking lessons—supports the viability of farms and farmers while also fundamentally transforming the economic, social, and ecological world we share. Agri*leisure* participants, including regular farmers' market and CSA shoppers, act as engaged community members with a keen interest in food, agriculture, community development, or the social experience. Agri*tourists*, on the other hand, are often one-time visitors who enjoy a hayride, overnight farm stay, or walk through a corn maze but who have no ongoing or "internally compelling love" for connecting to the agricultural world.

The central appeal of agriculture, of course, is its emphasis on consumption—food. Indeed, Daniel Thomas Cook argues that the pleasure of consumption alone makes it a leisure activity.[12] The selection, preparation, and consumption of food in ways that strengthen families and friendships and perpetuate traditions are social *activities* often resulting in the pleasing, intuitively worthwhile, and faithful *states of mind* associated with recreation and leisure, respectively. James Farmer's studies have found that some customers shop at farmers' markets for recreation even more than for food.[13] And Kallina Gallardo and her colleagues found that the entertainment and festive atmosphere at farmers' markets significantly affect consumers' choice of which market to shop.[14] Further connecting the dots between the socioeconomic features of the farmers' market and the academic notions of research and leisure, leisure scholar Amanda Johnson says that when farmers' market customers buy for leisure, they also help to build and expand community.[15] In short, the pleasurable act of eating, especially when associated with the lively contexts in which local food is found, results

Figure 1.1. The meats available at this Bloomington, Indiana, farmers' market stand evoke food and farming traditions. *Photograph by Jennifer Meta Robinson*

Figure 1.2. This stand markets its production methods so that customers know how their food was raised and can judge how well it aligns with their values. *Photograph by Jennifer Meta Robinson*

in powerful feelings that all health, welfare, and community advocates should appreciate and cultivate.

These connections are so powerful that they can be called "serious leisure"—when one remedies a lack of fulfillment in ordinary occupations (e.g., being a lawyer, homemaker, teacher, clerk) with leisure activities that are more meaningful, substantial, and engrossing to them (e.g., fly fishing, garage band guitar, fantasy football).[16] Local food fans carry on serious leisure when they become deeply engaged with the styles and activities involved—visiting markets on vacation, timing entertaining to CSA deliveries, visiting a u-pick orchard to get peaches for drying, carrying special market totes, wearing a favorite market outfit. Food powerfully knits together discretion, necessity, pleasure, consumption, and context. So the discretionary time and effort spent on serious leisure with food (canning one's own tomatoes, learning to bake bread, sourcing local food for a holiday meal, buying a mechanized apple peeler or cherry pitter) is impossible to disentangle from the necessity of what seems a simple chore of feeding one's self and family. The pleasure and metaphysical sustenance of a Saturday's u-pick apples baked into a fancy pie can "seriously" outweigh the convenient cheapness of one found in the frozen food aisle. These complex intersections help explain why people choose to eat locally, even with the extra time necessary for shopping, cooking, and eating this way.[17]

Environmental Factors

Regional production and distribution mean fewer goods are shipped long-distance. Typically, the shorter supply chain reduces fuel consumption and transportation pollution. In addition, produce grown for nearby consumption requires less emphasis on shelf life, which translates to fewer chemical additives, preservatives, and refrigeration costs. Overall, local food can be an important way to reduce agriculture's carbon footprint.[18]

Local production also promotes more sensitivity to local and regional biodiversity.[19] The demand for standardization by multinational food corporations, restaurant chains, and supermarket conglomerates has resulted in some crops being grown ubiquitously (e.g., wheat, soybeans, and corn throughout the Midwest) and in areas not naturally

Figure 1.3. Making use of place-based knowledge, this vendor markets wild edibles of the south-central Indiana landscape. *Photograph by Jennifer Meta Robinson*

suited to them (e.g., rice in California's dry Central Valley), while others (e.g., Aquadulce Fava Beans or Red Garnet Amaranth) become scarce. This homogenization process has caused many large-scale farmers to monocrop in only one or two high-yield crops that often require large amounts of synthetic pesticides, fertilizers, and preservatives, with their deleterious environmental consequences.[20] Selling locally, on the other hand, small-scale operators often find their marketing niche by providing items that are not readily accessible at chain supermarkets.[21] Moreover, CSAs that actively involve their shareholders in the process of growing and producing their own food foster knowledge of and affinity for the local landscape, potentially spreading conservation ethics to more people as they become inspired to plug into their local "foodshed."[22]

However, the environmental benefits of buying and selling local can be overstated. The costs and consequences of buying locally but *out of season* can be substantial. Winter lettuce that is field-grown in California but shipped to New York City may be more environmentally sound than choosing lettuce that is sourced closer to Manhattan but grown in a heated greenhouse.[23] On the other hand, flying pineapples from Hawaii or melons from Argentina in January may never make environmental sense. In addition, sometimes smaller-scale growing can be less efficient than larger operations—by requiring more land or chemical inputs to grow a given quantity of food.[24] To decide if local is environmentally sound requires considering seasonality and efficiencies of scale.

What Counts as Local?

On the surface, localism seems to be all about proximity—what is sourced nearby has more appeal than what is transported from far away. But defining local in terms of distance turns out not to be very definitive, even among its advocates. Noted author Barbara Kingsolver and her family experimented with eating locally for a year by growing their own food or purchasing it from a single county of Virginia farmers, an experience she chronicled in her popular book *Animal, Vegetable, Miracle: A Year of Food Life*. In wider practice, the use of the term varies. The US Food, Conservation, and Energy Act (2008) defined local as products originating within 400 miles or within state lines. On the other hand, Washington, DC, is home to numerous FRESHFARM farmers' markets that define local as grown in "the Chesapeake Bay *watershed* region (including the states of DE, MD, PA, WV, and VA, and within a 200-mile radius of Washington, DC)."[25] Vendors in the Bloomington, Indiana, market are eligible if they grow anywhere within state lines, which may be as much as 200 miles away, but they are ineligible if they grow their produce just 55 miles away in the state of Illinois. New York City's Union Square Greenmarket locates "our Region" within "a circle extending 120 miles to the south, 170 miles east and west, and 250 miles north of New York City."[26] The national organization Business Alliance for Local Living Economies defines a business as local if the owner lives within 25 miles of it, if it is not publicly traded, and if the owner has sole control over its operations. Proximity, then, clearly provides part, but only part, of what it means to be local.

The lived experience of local also differs significantly from these institutional definitions. For an advocate's view of what the word means and what its practice values, let us turn to a passionate and evocative explanation from a ten-year local grower we will call Sage Goodell.[27] After several years of farming internships and a failed cooperative farming venture, Goodell moved with her husband and two small sons to a small farm in Indiana. There, they grow produce for their CSA and year-round farmers' market sales. Goodell's story is worth more detail, but for our purposes here, her description of her profession provides useful insights into a perspective shared by many local growers. Her comments constitute a verbal performance that, as Richard Bauman notes, strikes a cadence in tone that sets it apart from ordinary speech and, in doing so, instantiates social life through language.[28] Her comments imbue the term "local" with the lived experience of human life—with work, family, food culture, social life, economics, science, affect, and language. In her performance, "local" reflects the multidimensional integration of human experience with its surroundings—both human and nonhuman—even while it seeks to tease factors apart. Jennifer Robinson asked Goodell if it would be appropriate to describe her farm work using adjectives like "local," "small," "alternative," and "sustainable." Instead, Goodell says:

> We call this thing that we are doing *farmer*. We are working hard to create a new definition for farmer. We are working hard to replace the image of big tractors and acres of corn with an image of farm diversity, creative thinker, healthy people, healthy land, life not death, vibrant, nutritious, living food, good land steward, responsible caretaker of this earth. Rather than a worn-out, sick "farmer" sitting in an air-conditioned tractor spraying toxic chemicals on a field, you see a robust, energetic, inspired, loving farmer on her hands

and knees hand-weeding the carrots. Rather than going to Kroger and buying lifeless, tasteless, chemical-laden produce, you go to the farmers' market and shake hands with the person who grew your vegetables, harvesting them the day before and sharing with you the latest news on the farm. You develop a relationship with this farmer. She thinks of you as she harvests produce each week. She thinks of you at supper on market day, knowing you have gratitude as you nourish yourself with her produce. You have a relationship with the farmer that grows your food. This is the new definition of farmer.

Sage Goodell's act of self-definition, here, articulates seven notable facets of the ideology of local that enrich a lay sense referencing only distance.

1. Local Is Temporal

Local does not reference only spatial relations but also indicates time. Freshness is frequently cited as one of the most desirable qualities of local food in the fieldwork described in this book and nationwide. This is what Goodell refers to when she says her goal is to produce "vibrant, nutritious, living food." Picked so recently, it may still be alive. She mentions "harvesting [produce] the day before and sharing with you the latest news on the farm." The food she grows, like news, loses an essential quality over time. In surveys from across the United States, shoppers at farmers' markets, the marquee sites of local food, overwhelmingly respond that they shop there for the freshness of the food. For example, a recent survey of individuals living (1) in a low-income urban neighborhood and (2) on the rural-urban fringe of Bloomington, Indiana, cited freshness and quality as the primary value affecting their food purchasing decisions.[29] So Goodell's comments set up a temporal relation that connects people and their actions. Many shoppers have a problematic sense of what fresh means. They may not understand how long farmed food takes to be readied for purchase nor how long it remains edible. They may misunderstand that a small flock of chickens like Goodell's will take several days or a week to lay all the eggs sold in a single market morning, or that her garlic crop may be harvested all at once and sold over months, or that her meat is better after aging and is more practical when frozen so that she can sell it over many months. In addition, she employs a generational sort of temporality, agricultural practices dying away with the conventional farmers while the "robust, energetic, inspired, loving" next-generation farmers flourish. She assumes positive change over time rather than looking with simple nostalgia for cues from the past. Both senses of time—field-to-table and generational—collapse conventional measures. Local is about time, and time is about knowing.

2. Local Is Healthful

Some 88 percent of consumers believe that fresh is healthful and, by extension, local is healthful.[30] Customers often assume that because local is closer to the source, it is therefore healthier. However, some processes of aging render food not only tastier but also more nutritious, as with the healthful biotics in aged sauerkraut and blue cheese. In defining herself and her work, Goodell describes a generational trajectory of improvement in healthfulness and sets local in opposition to conventional agriculture. She describes a shift away from conventional agricultural methods that involve "spraying toxic chemicals" for "lifeless, tasteless, chemical-laden produce" and toward intensive methods that produce healthful food, "life not death, vibrant, nutritious, living food." Local, then, is as much about change as tradition: she looks forward to newly generated, living knowledge of health, not back to the best practices of the recent past.

3. Local Implicates Scale

The definition Goodell encodes "local" with involves a certain scale in addition to distance, time, and healthfulness. She sets the scale of "big tractors and acres of corn" and rote, straight-line work against "an image of farm diversity, creative thinker . . . on her hands and knees hand-weeding the carrots." Artisanal, or "small batch," is a term now used liberally to describe high-touch production of whiskey, cigars, ice cream, preserves, pet chow, and other "crafted" goods. We have observed local farmers work areas small enough to harvest their market crop barefoot. With such scale, local conveys vibrant qualities beyond nutritional values. Indeed, food grown nearby but processed at large scale can lose the value it might gain from its proximity to origin, according to the ideology of local. For example, a jam company that buys fruits and distributes it nationally is not considered truly local even to those living nearby the processing plant.

On the other hand, the scale of local handling can sometimes remediate industrial food. Dylan Clark, an anthropologist at the University of Toronto, describes how ideological repositioning can make previously rotten food edible. He describes a symbolic cleansing process by which members of a punk subculture transform food from inedible to palatable, by removing it from the capitalist, misogynist, and racist associations of mainstream food systems through such practices as shoplifting, dumpster diving, or cooperative meals.[31] Local food follows this sort of symbolic cleansing, for example, when a scrupulously health-oriented shopper decides to purchase sticky cinnamon rolls from the baker at a farmers' market that he would not eat if they were mass-produced by a baking giant like Dolly Madison or Hostess. Essentially, the positive associations of being small-scale overwhelm the negative qualities of industrial production even when the same major ingredients (white flour, white sugar, and imported cinnamon) are used.

Scale, by definition, of course, is relative. And "processing" can be considered so encompassing as to be unavoidable—most of what we eat having been necessarily or optionally plucked, winnowed, washed, or cooked in an effort to alter it for taste, nutrition, and cultural resonance. Even picking an apple off a tree starts a sequence that can arguably be called processing, albeit one with unusually vast import. The most ambitious local or slow food advocates would struggle to make bread made from homegrown wheat, leaven it with wild yeasts, and bake it in a mud oven that is fired with nearby deadfall wood. But scale still matters: industrialized frozen cheese food sprinkled over GMO corn pasta purchased in aisle 17 and heated with oil from the far side of the world remains a preposterous alternative for all of its twenty-first-century American mundaneness. Both present straw men for easy critique.

It is difficult to say if a farm can be too big to be local. A certain capacity is necessary for income, and as the local phenomenon expands into new markets and settings, people want more of it. At the same time that both the number and size of large farms are increasing nationwide, very small, niche, and micro farms are multiplying.[32] Niche farms, as the adjective indicates, position a farm within a specific retail marketplace, such as cut flowers, shiitake mushrooms, freshwater shrimp, pastured pork, or grass-fed beef. Niche farms can occupy a large or small space, but their crop selection is limited. Alternatively, a micro farm indicates a small size, from urban or suburban lot to about four acres. Micro farms generally have diverse offerings of various crops and livestock that fill the area available with appropriately scaled animals, production practices, equipment, and infrastructure.[33] Many new farms with local aspirations are both micro in scale and niche in their market—maintaining a desired lifestyle while maximizing profitability through reduced investment and a high rate of return. People tend to think of the quintessential locally oriented farm as small; however, we will need more of them, more large acreage farms, and probably greater production capacity on both of the above to meet the growing demand in most areas of the country.

4. Local Means Accountability

Importantly, the small scale of local food suggests a level of accountability—knowing and being known—that mass production does not. Goodell contrasts the traditional supermarket experience with going "to the farmers' market to shake hands with the person who grew your vegetables." That tangibility, an actual touch, enacts a "relationship," a bond of exchange, a shaking of hands that may perform a greeting, a thank-you, or a contract. Farmers' markets and CSAs are based on the principle that producers are available to vouch for their products, to stand beside them and be ready to speak about quality and production processes. When Goodell discovered one summer that her farm was included in a regional boil-water order, issued by health departments when drinking water becomes, or is suspected to be, contaminated by pathogens, she immediately discarded all the produce she had already picked and washed that week for the farmers' market. Although the contamination was not visible to the naked eye, she had no doubt that her responsibility to her customers was to protect their

Figure 1.4. The city's sign and the farmer's sign suggest different theories about how to motivate behavior. *Photograph by Jennifer Meta Robinson*

health by taking a loss in her income and effort that week. In a time of frequent recalls of mass-produced food in the United States, the high touch quality of local food helps to provide its meaning and value.[34]

5. Local Implies Environmental Stewardship

Also clear in Goodell's comments is that local implicates environmental stewardship (of land, animals, ecosystems), what she calls being a "responsible caretaker of this earth," which includes laboring "down in the soil on my hands and knees, in the dirt." More of the earth's resources are dedicated to agriculture than any other human activity. Sustainable caretaking of the environment and ecology on which agriculture depends is essential to the long-term production of foodstuffs for the expanding world population. At the same time, the general American approach to "progress" operates on a myth of human independence from the natural environment. It often overwhelms the regenerative processes available in healthy ecosystems: Goodell contrasts the debilitating effects of conventional farming, sometimes being toxic and causing sickness, with a general vibrancy of natural methods. Local food offers practical solutions in shorter transport distances, less fuel consumption, and less pollution, and many local food farmers strive to live with a small environmental footprint.

6. Local Fosters Systems Thinking

In another conversation, Goodell described her work as "growing nutritious food the smart way" to benefit all, because "we are all in this thing together." Her approach to land stewardship constitutes an "intimate relationship," a "marriage" of sorts. The stewardship that local drives toward is integrative. Goodell talks about health, vibrancy, goodness, robustness, inspiration, gratitude. She also talks about relationships in a system: "You develop a relationship with this farmer. She thinks of you as she harvests produce each week. She thinks of you at supper on market day, knowing you have gratitude as you nourish yourself with her produce. You have a relationship with the farmer that grows your food. This is the new definition of farmer."

Figure 1.5. Hand-spun and -dyed alpaca yarn for sale at the Bloomington Community Farmer's Market. *Photograph by Jennifer Meta Robinson*

Goodell sees food as a system of relationships among many actors impacting social, environmental, and economic systems. Industrial-scale food production, so good at producing quantities of calories, does not always do so justly or healthfully. As a small farmer in a community of small farmers who have very little profit margin or income security, Goodell knows this acutely. Her comments repopulate the food system with farmers, customers, and communities. She evokes the human element through mention of performative events like market days, suppers, and harvests. And she introduces human concerns through affective responses, such as gratitude, and physical requirements, such as nourishment. By clearly peopling the food system, she invites a reconciliation of both food security (having enough food) and food sovereignty (having agency over food and culture). In this way, she is thinking about systems, what she calls relationships. Her thought experiment about being "farmer" imagines people and their everyday practices in intentional relationships to social, physical, economic, and environmental spheres. The work of food happens beyond the reach of any single individual. It may occur at the level of the collective, at the level of the system.

7. Local Is Oppositional

While mainstream American culture values quantity and convenience per dollar, the local movement proposes the small, slow, nonstandard, and intensive. Goodell defines her work against capitalistic norms. She sets corporate agriculture with its productivity ideal to "feed the world" against localism's values of small-scale accountability and performative competence. Despite these oppositions, she also drives toward a unifying holism. By defining her local work in terms of an Other ("replacing," this "not" that, "rather than"), she enables expression of dissent, sets goals to advocate for, and alters hierarchies. In speaking, she is also acting. The rich farmer with air-conditioned tractors is demoted, and the poor one on her hands and knees is elevated. The flawless and bountiful are toxic while the small and laborious are vibrant. Working hard has value, and convenience is suspect. Acres of played-out land are less desirable than a small plot to nurture. Local thus becomes an alternative system of valuation, one that implicitly and explicitly critiques capitalist ideologies, environmental practices, and social formulations.

Freed from a strict spatial definition that only reductively renders the spirit of the movement, local food in its many dimensions can become an activist tool for change—it's not just about space but also about time, health, human scale, accountability, stewardship of environmental systems, and change. It puts people inside a system with many actors who have an important impact, which means, essentially, that people matter. Local food operations are sometimes criticized for being "boutique," producing small and perishable quantities, or adding luxuries unnecessary beyond staple diets (think golden raspberries or free-range chickens) that are accessible only to those with relative economic privilege. In fact, local food and subsistence-level lifestyles are far from exclusive propositions. Poor people can and do grow their own food, share it with others, and serve it in ways that provide pleasure. A little pork in the beans, some herbs on the potatoes, some branch water to fill the stew pot, a particular crispiness to the cracklin' are all tried-and-true recipes that make the best of making do. While the white middle class may seem to have pioneered the local food movement, the skills, knowledge, and even the heirloom seeds themselves were preserved largely by marginalized groups while the middle class opted for Betty Crocker box-egeneity. The humble heirloom apple and tomato varieties so coveted today in local food venues were kept alive by people growing beyond the industrial food system. Foods that seem unessential to industrial palates, frivolous extras even, may in fact serve important roles in connecting people to their national, ethnic, or class origins (e.g., collards for some families of Southern African Americans, water spinach for some Vietnamese immigrants, wild rice for some Native Americans); or allowing them to practice and preserve social connections and religious traditions (e.g., turkey for Thanksgiving, corn on the cob for the Fourth of July, gumbo for Mardi Gras, horseradish for Passover); or adding simply a tasty zip of pleasure (cayenne peppers, rosemary, lemongrass). As a technology of life, a heritage of self-sufficiency, a medium of creativity and agency, food emancipates and empowers. While many people continue to want and need the convenience of a meal-in-a-pouch, others are claiming agency through local, heritage, and "slow" foods they can grow themselves in the backyard, a window box, or a community garden plot. Such enrichments define humankind—the animal that regularly invents, reflects, and embellishes beyond mere necessity.

Local food is sometimes parodied as a precious and irrelevant upper-middle-class affectation. Most hilariously, Carrie Bronstein's and Fred Armisen's characters on the IFC television series *Portlandia* (2011–present) pore over the biographical details of the chicken they are ordering for dinner at a hipster café, worrying whether "Collin" had feathered friends back on the free-range organic farm on which he was raised. However, local food, like other maker movements, allows participation by a broad socioeconomic base. Affluent people may have the luxury of time to explore labor-intensive projects, but as they co-opt "old fashioned" or low-income handcrafting, they also support a market, a form of social capital, and an information buzz that renews the availability of these techniques and items for anyone who values quality, community, and sustenance. Thus, anyone with a bucket's worth of dirt and a one-dollar packet of seeds can grow their own tomatoes on the fire escape or back porch.

Nonetheless, anxiety can accompany such incremental changes. Can we really change the world one organic grape or bowl of local peas at a time? In our age of ironic distance, everyone's behavior is impeachable sometimes, and many people are keenly aware that buying a bag of organic produce at Walmart does not a movement make. Still, using consumerism for political impact has a long history in the United States that includes the Boston Tea Party, the abolitionists' abstention from Southern sugar, and produce boycotts in support of labor unions and workers' conditions.

In its many dimensions, then, local food can become an activist tool for change: a watermark, a yardstick, a design experiment that calls for adjustments in how we chart future directions. In calling herself a farmer, Sage Goodell links herself to others who are also farmers. By naming herself "farmer," she claims the agency necessary to define herself, to do so in opposition to others' assumptions, and to change her position in the social order. She claims a new vision of her profession, defining herself through language and practice. Like others in local food, she puts the world back together, keeping the human element in food even as the scale of industrial agriculture factors it out in order to meet productivity demands for a growing global population. The multidimensionality of local initiatives—farmers' markets, CSAs, urban farming, farm-to-school food distribution, clothing, dyeing, books, business, bikes, and so on—move co-optation beyond the easy reach of industrial mechanization, keeping power pluralistic, fragmented, and everywhere enacted through small everyday practices. Buying and selling local offers alternatives to the seductive ubiquity of global capitalism's systems and values. Making one's life over in local, common agricultural ways has long been an American expression of dissent from social mores, industrialization, displacement of populations, and devaluation of labor. It reflects an abiding American ambivalence toward modernity.

Local remains rhetorically ambiguous. It's a fiddly notion that must be puzzled out differently by different people according to the contexts in which they find themselves. Local food calls attention to the inconvenience of food; the necessities of its production, acquisition, processing, and consumption; and the lives and labors of those who make it happen. It gives actors in the system faces and stations as well as physical bodies and their limitations. It offers ways to reconnect people in place, to be known so that we can be accountable and accounted to, to navigate the present toward a future of environmental and social sustainability. Indeed, a challenge for the local in a global age is to understand that what is nearby is not always what is close, alike, or familiar. Things nearby may have roots and ramifications in faraway places, and what seems far away may have great impact and import at home. Our sense of being inhabitants of a small planet, a mostly closed system of reciprocal impacts, has increased with the globalization of goods, services, and economies. But our show of responsibility to others within these systems remains rudimentary. As people and goods become more far-flung from their roots, the desire for connectedness and community become more intense. Learning to think in terms of our many relationships has implications for our sense of who we are, where we are, and the world we find ourselves in, which are local, indeed, to each of us.

Notes

1. Cascade Harvest Coalition, "Marketing Research and Strategy for Growing Sales Opportunities at Puget Sound Farmers Markets," 2015, http://www.cascadeharvest.org/programs/farmers-markets. Accessed November 27, 2016, http://webcache.googleusercontent.com/search?q=cache:SBcoX7GHf7wJ:www.cascadeharvest.org/files/u1/Final_USDA_WSDA_FM_Report_09.pdf+&cd=1&hl=en&ct=clnk&gl=us

2. National Restaurant Association, "What's Hot in 2015? Discover New Menu Trends," December 3, 2014, http://www.restaurant.org/News-Research/News/What-s-Hot-in-2015-culinary-forecast-predicts-top; Anne D'Innocenzio, "Walmart to Purchase Produce Directly from Local Growers," *Huffington Post*, June 3, 2013, http://www.huffingtonpost.com/2013/06/03/walmart-produce-fruit-vegetables_n_3378575.html. Accessed November 27,

2016, https://web.archive.org/web/20151104034517/http://www.huffington
post.com/2013/06/03/walmart-produce-fruit-vegetables_n_3378575.html

3. Harry Cummings, Gailin Kora, and Don Murray, "Farmers' Markets in
Ontario and Their Economic Impact 1998," *AgriNews Interactive,* http://www
.agrinewsinteractive.com/features/farmersmarkets/farmersmarkets.html.

4. Jacinthe Bessière, "Local Development and Heritage: Traditional Food
and Cuisine as Tourist Attractions in Rural Areas," *Sociologia Ruralis* 38, no.
1 (1998): 21–34; Anne-Marie Hede and Robyn Stokes, "Network Analysis of
Tourism Events: An Approach to Improve Marketing Practices for Sustainable
Tourism," *Journal of Travel and Tourism Marketing* 26, no. 7 (2009): 656–69.

5. Gina T. Gerbasi, "Athens Farmers' Market: Evolving Dynamics and Hidden Benefits to a Southeast Ohio Rural Community," *Focus on Geography* 49, no.
2 (2006): 1–6; Melissa Weddle et al., "Farmers' Market Consumers in NC and
IN: 600 Miles but Little Difference in Who Is Shopping," paper presented at
Leisure Research Symposium, Charlotte, North Carolina, October 14–16, 2014.

6. James R. Farmer et al., "A Tale of Four Farmers Markets: Recreation and
Leisure as a Catalyst for Sustainability," *Journal of Park and Recreation Administration* 29, no. 3 (2011): 11–23.

7. David Conner et al., "Locally Grown Foods and Farmers Markets: Consumer Attitudes and Behaviors," *Sustainability* 2, no. 3 (2010): 742–56; Cummings et al., "Farmers' Markets in Ontario"; Cheryl Brown and Stacy Miller,
"The Impacts of Local Markets: A Review of Research on Farmers Markets and
Community Supported Agriculture (CSA)," *American Journal of Agricultural Economics* 90, no. 5 (2008): 1298–1302.

8. Mary Ann McGrath, John F. Sherry, and Deborah D. Heisley, "An Ethnographic Study of an Urban Periodic Marketplace: Lessons from the Midville
Farmers' Market," *Journal of Retailing* 69, no. 3 (1993): 280–319; Gerbasi, "Athens
Farmers' Market"; Bessière, "Local Development and Heritage"; Cummings et
al., "Farmers' Markets in Ontario."

9. Robinson and Hartenfeld, *Farmers' Market Book*, 215–25.

10. Benjamin Amsden and Jesse McEntee, "Agrileisure: Re-imagining the
Relationship between Agriculture, Leisure, and Social Change," *Leisure/Loi-
sir* 35, no. 1 (2011): 37–38. The terms "recreation" and "leisure" are often used
synonymously, but scholars differentiate them. Recreation is activity one does
for fun, enjoyment, amusement, or pleasure, according to Thomas Yukic (*Fundamentals of Recreation*, 2nd ed. [New York: Harper and Row, 1970]). Leisure,
on the other hand, means "living in relative freedom from the external com-
pulsive forces of one's culture and physical environment so as to be able to act
from internally compelling love in ways which are personally pleasing, intuitively worthwhile, and provide a basis for faith" (Geoffrey Godbey, *Leisure in*

Your Life: An Exploration, 2nd ed. [State College, PA: Venture, 1985], 9). For our purposes, recreation refers to the *activities* providing enjoyment, and leisure is the *state of mind* one hopes to gain by these recreational pursuits.

11. Amsden and McEntee, "Agrileisure," 37–38.

12. Daniel Cook, "Problematizing Consumption, Community, and Leisure: Some Thoughts on Moving beyond Essentialist Thinking," *Leisure/loisir* 30 (2016): 455–66.

13. Farmer et al., "Tale of Four Farmers Markets."

14. Karina Gallardo et al., "The Use of Electronic Payment Machines at Farmers Markets: Results from a Choice Experiment Study," *International Food and Agribusiness Management Review* 18 (2015): 79–104.

15. Amanda J. Johnson, "'It's more than a shopping trip': Leisure and Consumption in a Farmers' Market," *Annals of Leisure Research* 16 (2013): 4, 315–31.

16. Robert Stebbins, *A Perspective for Our Time: Serious Leisure* (New Brunswick, NJ: Transaction Publishers, 2008).

17. Carmen Byker, Nick Rose, and Elana Serrano, "The Benefits, Challenges, and Strategies of Adults Following a Local Food Diet," *Journal of Agriculture, Food Systems, and Community Development* 1, no. 1 (2010): 125–37.

18. Helen La Trobe, "Farmers' Markets: Consuming Local Rural Produce," *International Journal of Consumer Studies* 25, no. 3 (2001): 181–92.

19. Gilbert Gillespie et al., "Farmers' Markets as Keystones in Rebuilding Local and Regional Food Systems," in *Remaking the North American Food System: Strategies for Sustainability*, edited by C. Clare Hinrichs and Thomas A. Lyson, 65–83 (Lincoln: University of Nebraska Press, 2007).

20. La Trobe, "Farmers' Markets."

21. Vivian Carro-Figueroa and Amy Guptill, "Emerging Farmers' Markets and the Globalization of Food Retailing: A Perspective from Puerto Rico," in *Remaking the North American Food System: Strategies for Sustainability*, edited by C. Clare Hinrichs and Thomas A. Lyson, 260–76 (Lincoln: University of Nebraska Press, 2007).

22. Laura B. DeLind, "Of Bodies, Place, and Culture: Re-situating Local Food," *Journal of Agricultural and Environmental Ethics* 19, no. 2 (2006): 121–46.

23. Stephen Budiansky, "Math Lessons for Locavores," *New York Times*, August 19, 2010, http://www.nytimes.com/2010/08/20/opinion/20budiansky .html.

24. Steven Sexton, "The Inefficiency of Local Food," *Freakonomics*, November 14, 2011, http://freakonomics.com/2011/11/14/the-inefficiency-of-local -food.

25. Barbara Kingsolver, *Animal, Vegetable, Miracle: A Year of Food Life* (New York: HarperCollins, 2007); FRESHFARM Markets, "Join FRESHFARM Mar-

kets," http://freshfarmmarkets.org/farmers_markets/sell_at_our_markets
.php.

26. Greenmarket GrowNYC, http://www.grownyc.org/files/gmkt
/questionnaire/farmer.pdf, 1–2.

27. Jennifer's conversations with Goodell have continued since 2013, in informal discussions, formal interviews, and electronic correspondence. Because our subject in this book implicates people's means of livelihood and their social relationships in relatively small communities, we take seriously any unintentional impact on them. In some instances, qualitative research ethics indicate a level of care beyond what informed consent allows. Thus, in order to protect them from inadvertent disclosure of information, we have changed the names of some of our interlocutors in this book, even those who, like Goodell, have consented to be identified. The goal is to keep identities anonymous while still allowing an accurate account of the social world as argued by Karen Kaiser in "Protecting Respondent Confidentiality in Qualitative Research" (*Qualitative Health Research* 19, no. 11 [2009]: 1632–41).

28. Richard Bauman and Charles Briggs, "Poetics and Performance as Critical Perspectives on Language and Social Life," *Annual Review of Anthropology* 19 (1990): 59–88.

29. James R. Farmer et al., "Use of Local Foods to Bolster Food Security of Urban Individuals and Those Living in the Rural Fringe," *Journal of Community Health* (forthcoming).

30. Cascade Harvest Coalition, "Marketing Research and Strategy."

31. Dylan Clark, "The Raw and the Rotten: Punk Cuisine," *Ethnology* 43, no. 1 (2004): 19–31.

32. USDA, "Commodity Areas: Definition of Specialty Crops," 2013, http://www.ams.usda.gov/AMSv1.0/scbgpdefinitions.

33. MicroFarmLiving, "How to Earn a Green Living on a Micro Farm," 2016, http://microfarmliving.com.

34. The US government compiles lists of recalled foods from several of its agencies and posts them at "Your Online Resource for Recalls," *Consumer Protection Safety Division*, http://www.recalls.gov/food.html.

TWO

Understanding Farmers' Markets

I think when you buy local it's healthier, fresher, tastes better,
all around better.
　—farmers' market customer

Farmers' markets are booming. Fresh meats and produce, local
sources, bargain purchases, unusual varieties, friendly conversation,
and a lively atmosphere mean shopping can be an enjoyable event
rather than a dreaded chore for many Americans. Popular trends in
health that emphasize fruits, vegetables, and organic production con-
verge with the photogenic images of markets that spread across the
media. More markets are springing up across the country, and customer counts are rising. But not all *potential* customers shop at markets, and only a fraction of the food dollars actually spent there go
directly to farmers. Some people may perceive markets to be inconvenient, expensive, or exclusive enough not to bother. Those who do attend can often choose from several markets nearby. What drives some
customers to a market? What keeps others away? Why are some markets more successful than others? How can vendors capture more of
the local food dollars? Beyond the often-heard wisdom to "know your
farmer, know your food," local food success also means that we must
"know our customer, know our market."

When Michelle Obama made fresh and local food the central cause
of her public health agenda as First Lady, she joined a groundswell of interest in sourcing food beyond the commercial superpowers. Her con-
version of a section of the White House lawn into a vegetable garden,
tended in part by visiting schoolchildren, and her visit to a Washington,
DC, farmers' market tapped powerful symbols.[1] Through her efforts,
we have the image of one of the most powerful families on earth sourcing food as close to the ground as possible, able to stay in visual, if not

daily, touch with its progress. Even the president's family, it would appear, wanted the farm-to-table assurance of quality, accountability, and security that government-mandated labeling does not offer.

A lower-profile and more practical public similarly seeks alternatives to corporate food aggregation, processing, distribution, and health claims. They, too, back farmers' markets—and other direct-market accountability plans such as CSAs, farm-to-school, certified local, and cruelty-free campaigns. In a do-it-yourself movement fanned by massive food recalls, many people use farmers' markets to source not only food itself but also the people and practices around it. Some customers become so invested in freshness and accountability and so equate quality of life with certain qualities of food that farmers' markets become vital to their weekly routine. A few go so far as to use markets as educational institutions, learning how to grow their own—purchasing seeds, plants, and soil amendments; picking up cultivation tips and problem solving with more experienced growers; and, on occasion, vending their overflow fruits and vegetables at a market themselves. Even casual market customers make the connection between food production and consumption and between personal and environmental health.

What many studies show and many savvy public planners know is that the benefits of farmers' markets extend beyond individuals and families to local communities by boosting local economies, supporting the small business ventures of local farmers, strengthening community affiliation through open-access activities, and reducing environmental impact through shorter farm-to-table distances.[2] Farmers' market vendors, too, can strengthen the link between their goods and such desirable associations when they are aware of these trends.

Know Your Customer

Many customers value the local. More than simple access to tasty, nutritious, and even organic food, they like markets as a way to support the local economy and local farmers by eating locally. A survey of over 700 Indiana residents, including 321 market customers, finds that people value food that "doesn't have to travel far," "didn't come from

Table 2.1. Customer Priorities for Shopping at a Farmers' Market

Category	Prompt from Questionnaire	FM Mean Scores (n = 321)
Environment	I believe consuming food produced locally is better for the environment.	*4.40*
Nutrition	The nutritional value of a food is an important part of my purchasing decisions.	*4.37*
Local Economy	I give preference to food purchase decisions that support the local economy.	*4.36*
Local Farmers	I give preference to food purchase decisions that support local farmers.	*4.34*
Fresh Food	I give preference to foods that were picked just a few days before my purchase.	*4.31*
Seasonal	I give preference to eating foods that are in season, for example, tomatoes in July–October.	*4.24*
Fewer Chemicals	I give preference to foods that are grown with few chemical applications.	*4.22*
Hormone-Free	I give preference to animal products that are free from growth hormones.	*4.10*
Humane	I give preference to animal products that have been derived in a humane manner.	*4.03*
Organic	Purchasing organically grown food is very important to me.	*4.02*
Local—100 miles	I give preference to purchasing foods that come from within 100 miles of my location.	*3.99*
Whole Foods	I generally purchase whole foods rather than processed foods.	*3.90*
Costs of Food	The expense of fresh local produce deters me from purchasing it as often as I would like.	*2.93*

Notes: Based on a Likert-style scale: 1 = strongly disagree; 2 = disagree, 3 = neutral, 4 = agree, 5 = strongly agree. *Italics* indicate a significant (.05 level) difference between the two groups.

Source: James R. Farmer et al. "Agrileisure: Farmers' Markets, CSAs, and the Privilege in Eating Local." *Journal of Leisure Research* 46, no. 3 (2014): 320.

miles away," or was "grown nearby."[3] These priorities intersect with concern for practices that foster communities. One participant and his family shop locally at markets for the mutual benefit of being "best for us and the community." Another customer specifically associates money spent locally with people in his community: "I like supporting the local economy and the local growers of the food." And another customer goes further to recognize an ethical dimension to making viable the lives of people on whose labor one depends, remarking that purchasing local foods is one's "social responsibility in supporting people near us who are, you know, doing that work."

The Indiana local food participants also indicate a strong concern for the environment and their belief that buying locally is more ecologically sustainable.[4] Increasingly, consumers turn to markets as they become aware of the negative impacts of conventional agriculture, including petrochemical herbicides, pesticides, and fertilizers; loss of environmental resilience; and the use of fossil fuels for hauling crops and animal products to far-off points of sale.[5] Environmental concerns received the highest score among the thirteen values tested among participants in the Indiana survey. Other studies associate environmental values with ethical food choices, with both contributing to customers' perceptions of healthier food.

Customers in the Indiana study noted several specific environmental benefits. The local nature of food at farmers' markets appealed to those looking for "energy conservation," who said things such as "It doesn't have to travel far and use resources" and "It doesn't take as many fossil fuels to get them to my table." Other customers assumed that markets contribute to both "energy conservation and environmental awareness." Some also valued the "sustainability" of food at markets: "I like the sustainability of it, that it didn't come from miles away to my table, that it was grown nearby."

Vendors whose practices align with these customer values can make them apparent through signs, websites, and over-the-table conversations. One market vendor notes on his sign that he sells "the nearest locally grown produce" grown on his "Urban Homestead" just a few blocks away. Another posts pictures of the Brown's gas generator affixed to her van that stretches gas mileage and reduces CO_2 emis-

Figure 2.1. A Midwestern vendor growing just blocks from the farmers' market proclaims his produce to be from an "Urban Homestead. The Nearest Locally Grown Produce." *Photograph by Jennifer Meta Robinson*

sions. And at a Santa Monica market, farmers post their tilling, disking, hoeing, and pruning as sustainable practices.

Surveys typically put the average age of farmers' market customers in their early fifties.[6] Most are women—as many as 66 percent,[7] which perhaps reflects the persistence of women's responsibility for food in the home. Some 73 percent of farmers' market customers report being married or partnered, while almost a quarter are single and only 2.6 percent widowed, much lower than the national average of 6 percent, perhaps because of the difficulty some older people have of navigating markets.[8] The average household size of market shoppers, at 2.46 people, is slightly lower than the national average of 2.6, with 71.7

percent of market customers not having children at home.[9] One might infer from these numbers that deals like five-for-the-price-of-four cantaloupes may not reel in potential buyers—even if they could carry them all to the car.

One of the more consistently documented factors in customer participation is that they frequent markets close to where they live. There are now market tourists who make a point of stopping by markets on their travels for preserves, honey, soap, and other products amenable to hotel rooms or time in the car trunk. But more than half of customers at most markets travel only five miles or less, and 80 percent travel ten miles or less.[10] Vendors, meanwhile, must also take into account factors besides distance or convenience to sell the quantities they have at the prices they want. In an extreme example, one vendor drives six hours from her farm in Vermont to New York City's downtown Union Square Market, because she finds the markets closer to home too saturated with organic meat and thus too difficult to penetrate. Moreover, a densely populated area like New York has a better chance of supporting multiple markets with higher customer counts. This proximity factor can present significantly different cultures, experiences, and expectations between customers and vendors.

Because customers are unlikely to make even a modest trek on a regular basis, the crowd at a market tends to reflect those who live nearby, although nationally the majority of customers are vastly Caucasian.[11] The average household income for market customers varies by area; however, studies put the national median household income at $52,762.[12] In recent years the USDA has offered grants to help markets draw more customers with lower incomes. These grants subsidize the cost of the machines necessary for processing national Supplemental Nutrition Assistance Program (SNAP) credits, commonly referred to as food stamps.[13] In 2010, customers using SNAP cards made more than 453,000 purchases at markets, with an average purchase of $16, and totaling $7.5 million nationally.[14] Independently funded bonus incentives are available at some markets that double the value of SNAP credits. These programs are essentially grants that benefit farmers, by broadening the local food purchasing base; customers, by making fresh and nutritious food accessible to them, even in "food desert" areas where

Figure 2.2. A grower in Bloomington, Indiana, features midwestern favorites alongside cosmopolitan fare, including radishes, mustard, purslane, bok choi, and tofu from homegrown soybeans. *Photograph by James R. Farmer*

full-service groceries are scarce; and society as a whole, by providing healthy food to its vulnerable populations.

Indeed, most customers say they attend markets for their fresh, tasty, and nutritious food.[15] Strollers filled with bags of peaches and flats of vegetable starts while toddlers walk alongside clutching honey sticks or fists of warm kettle corn are not an uncommon sight at markets. Customers with wagons of watermelons and sweet corn are among the many who value "variety" and "whole foods."

Price is a less important factor (as low as sixth in one study) for many who shop at farmers' markets, though perhaps it figures more prominently for those who decide *not* to frequent them.[16] A study of Indiana market customers identified access to food with greater nutritional value as a high priority for most market customers. Many of them seem to recognize a convergence of factors that make food from farmers' markets more desirable: "I think when you buy local it's healthier, fresher, tastes better, all around better."[17] Many customers believe the "healthier, fresher, tastes better" convergence is more likely in food picked within days of purchase and markets, of course, are prime venues for such food. Even when customers do not understand the labor or timing involved in market sales, that a vendor didn't "get up awfully early" on market morning to pick a truckload of cantaloupe, or that the garlic didn't grow in braids on its own, they recognize that a farmers' market is the place to find the freshest produce.

In addition to their own tasty and healthy eating, however, market customers also tend to care about the communal and ethical dimensions of market food. These appear in studies as regard for the environment, support for local farmers, support for the local economy, desire to eat seasonally, and access to information about growing practices.[18] When asked, many customers express concern with how their food is produced: buying locally "helps us know where our food is coming from, like the food that we actually put in our meals and then put into our bodies. We like that."[19] These customers may seek out foods produced without hormones, with fewer chemicals, humanely, organically, or with environmentally friendly means.[20] They look for labels, signs, and other indicators (such as farm name, pamphlets, photos, bug damage) that the food is free-range, certified organic, no-spray, sustainable, grass-fed, grain-fed, or some other promise that concerns them. Short of readily available information, they may look for less reliable indicators of quality: Do long hair and overalls mean the beef was raised humanely? Does religious plain dress mean organic? If they do not talk with farmers to get details, customers may rely on the appearance of the farmers' market as a whole as a proxy for certain production practices, simply assuming that all the food there is grown to certain standards.[21]

The term "organic" undergoes particular regulation by the US government, yet some customers apply the label quite loosely, assuming that all food sold at farmers' markets is "organically" or "naturally" produced. Making things even more confusing is that "organic" labels of various sorts are prevalent at many markets. Farmers selling under five thousand dollars a year in gross organic sales qualify as exempt from inspection and can call their food "organic" if their practices com

Figure 2.3. Three young market patrons take a break near the music tent to enjoy fresh-popped kettle corn. *Photograph by James R. Farmer*

ply with the rules, even though they cannot display the official "USDA organic" seal. As early as 2006, 47 percent of farmers' markets nationwide sold some organic products, and consumer demand for organics continues to grow.[22] More recently, all-organic markets, or those aspiring to be, are becoming increasingly common, and some markets with large groups of customers interested in ethical, environmental, and health standards in their food choices have centralized information about production practices. The Santa Monica Organic Farmers Market in California does not require farmers to be on hand to vend, but it makes information about production practices available through a centrally located kiosk. This analog version of their online database lists information about production-related practices such as weed control (e.g., hand-weeding, tractor cultivation, hoes, goats); pest control (e.g., fly bait for the olive fruit fly, cloth bags, Bacillus thuringiensis [or BT], beneficial insects, "both natural and introduced"); fertilizers (e.g., liquid nitrogen); size, flavor, ripeness or appearance controls (e.g., pruning, thinning); and soil fertility (e.g., compost, manure, gypsum).[23] The database also lists information about each farm and its farmers, including acres cultivated, years farming, and history.

Other markets encourage vendors to post signs at their stands. Those signs take many forms and are opportunities for plenty of personality to show through. One farmer uses a large poster board with color snapshots of lively chickens free-ranging on her farm, which bears her family's name. Another farmer uses a vinyl banner that prominently incorporates the word "LIFE." Another displays an antique toy bull in cast iron to announce the kind of produce packed into coolers on the truck behind him. Still another seems to try to hit as many buzzwords as possible for homemade vinegar: "organic," "vegan," "indigenous," "fermented," "tasty," "affordable," "primal." Signs and pamphlets using unregulated but descriptive terms abound—"chemical-free," "local," "hormone-free," "antibiotic-free," "pasture-raised," "free-range," and so on. As unspecified as they may be, these terms are evocative. They help customers choose produce that might otherwise be indistinguishable from what is at the grocery store around the corner. Posting details about production no doubt helps some customers navigate their options, but perhaps the most thorough information is provided by growers staffing their stands.

Customers also like fun. Although it appears unevenly in research data on markets, recreation figures large for customers at markets, who mention it nearly as frequently as "food" in interviews.[24] It must be said, however, that the number of people citing this motivation probably correlates with how much "recreation" they actually find at their local markets. Markets run by municipal parks and recreation departments or by people who realize the value added by music, road races, buskers, cultural festivals, and such will probably draw more recreation-oriented customers and feel more recreation-like. Smaller markets with a handful of vendors and no obvious "entertainment" may feel to newcomers more akin to regular shopping.

On the other hand, not every farmer wants to wear a funny hat. Non-farm events may seem to detract from the focus on local food— some people attend mostly to chat, and some customers inflate the attendance numbers and clog the aisles with the whole family tagging along. More people in the market means more sales. Maybe not immediately and maybe not 100 percent, but more people in the market broadens the potential customer base. Besides, most people recognize that fun is good!

Know Your Market

The United States gained over 6,600 markets between 1994 and 2015, for a total of 8,669 at last tally.[25] That growth continues to gain momentum, adding almost 1,000 new markets between 2011 and 2013 alone. No one knows how long this growth will continue, but certainly not all of these new markets will persist.[26] While the boom lasts, farmers in some areas have ample choices for markets to participate in. Moreover, longer-lived markets tend to have better customer counts and higher vendor income, so it is important for vendors to choose their markets wisely in order to contribute to their success.[27] With a day or more to pick, prep, and pack for market; travel and sales time; and then hours or days to unpack, stow, and organize for the coming week, markets eat up time. Vendors have to weigh location, frequency, customer base, organization, and many other significant factors as they choose a market. And the markets themselves come in a multitude of variations. Here are just a few examples.[28]

The Crossroads Market

In season, a truck with strawberries, sweet corn, cantaloupes, mums, or poinsettias parks at a prominent crossroads. Potential cus-

Figure 2.4. The Bloomington Community Farmers' Market in Bloomington, Indiana. *Photograph by Dan Schlapbach and Jennifer Roebuck*

tomers have a chance to look over the offerings as they slow for the intersection. The person selling may have had a surplus of produce or may have been able to acquire a quantity of the fruits of someone else's labor. The produce may be fresh, local, and a regular feature of the growing season. Or it may be leftover or trucked in, a one-off opportunity. Customers may be able to comparison shop or bargain the price, but mostly this is a "carpe diem et caveat emptor" (seize the day but buyer beware) kind of event.

The Proprietary Market

Farm-based markets can be as straightforward as selling surplus from the kitchen garden on a card table at the end of the drive, with a little cup or lockbox for payment on the honor system. Or they can be as elaborate as post-and-beam tasting rooms featuring wines from

Figure 2.5. Shoppers enjoy the community and friends at a farmers' market.
Photograph by Jennifer Meta Robinson

the surrounding vineyard that are complemented with produce from surrounding farms. These markets are on private ground and set their own rules. In one rural hamlet, a church decided to open its parking lot to a farmers' market on Friday nights. About a dozen vendors assembled during the market's first season, and with a few hundred parishioners invested in its success, the market was surprisingly worthwhile for them. Based in the faith community and poised to add to its congregation, this market is open to the public but also within the control of the church leadership. It represents a win-win-win opportunity for the church, the neighborhood, and the growers.

The Small Farmer-Organized Market

About a dozen vendors pull into a community center parking lot on a Friday afternoon: colorful umbrellas, a guitar duo, hand-knitted hats, and twiggy walking sticks mix in with the summer squash, tomatoes, and flowers. Farmers pull in early to set up—first come, first choice of space. Still, regulars tend to gravitate to the same spots each week—under a tree, say, or nearest to the customer parking lot. There might be a new lamb there or a box of puppies. Rules and red tape stay at a minimum, and only enthusiastic volunteers work the information stand. Tradition, consensus, or just the loudest voice may determine whether a website is created, what the logo on the big vinyl sign will be, whether competition among vendors selling dried wreaths or peaches is desirable, whether this lot with bathrooms nearby is better than the grassy lot near the interstate exchange, and so on. One of the volunteers or maybe the founding farmer collects fees as little as five dollars, or maybe there is no fee at all. If the crowd is small or a vendor just doesn't make much money this week, the fee may be waived entirely and almost certainly good advice on how to improve sales will be forthcoming. This small market may be the only one in town, perhaps, with roots many decades deep, or it may be a new alternative to a larger one sponsored by the city or the chamber of commerce. It may have spun off from a larger market, moving to a more promising time slot or offering only local produce, only in-state, only organic, or only certain vendors. The small market may have as good or better parking, bathroom facilities, produce variety, music, cooking demos, public visibility, and customer loyalty as the larger one. Or at least they can work toward that parity.

The Public Grower-Vendor Market

Regular as Saturday morning, 100 to 150 vendors file into their designated spaces under fixed awnings to create the most popular recrea-

tion event in the city. Every vendor is also a grower. Six thousand to
ten thousand customers rendezvous with their favorite foods, family,
and friends in what is, the rest of the week, a parking lot. Newcomers
find their way for a first visit, assisted by vendor maps and professional
signage and lured by special events like a thirty-tuba band, the annual
salsa-contest tasting, juried crafts at the monthly market for handmade
goods, and the Asian Fest's tai chi and cooking demonstrations. Or
perhaps they come to staff the political and civic tables along the designated Info Alley. Buskers set up for thirty-minute sets at dedicated
spots. The crowd is sometimes so dense that parking can be scarce and
more retiring customers opt out. The market master makes sure all
the trucks are in their assigned spaces by 7:00 AM, the eggs and meats
are refrigerated, the single-day vendors are situated and paid up, and
all the displays are within the market's guidelines. She may drop by
the community radio booth to give a live report of the best of the day's
offerings. Full- and part-time staff, and maybe a few unpaid interns,
check in with each vendor and pass out the monthly vendor newsletter and the latest revisions to the policies. A volunteer board of vendors and customers advises the market management: Do baskets made
only by twining wild grapevines violate the prohibition on crafts during the summer months, or does milk aggregated for processing violate the grower-vendor principle? A state weights and measures inspec-
tor comes by once a month to certify scales, and the food bank pulls
in a large truck for donations at the close of day. If a vendor thinks a
neighbor's melons are too early to be believed or that a competitor's
maple syrup is too cheap to be real, she knows the market staff will in-
vestigate her challenge. And vendors who are questioned know they
can use an appeals process. With each day they attend, farmers accumulate points that plug into formulas that reward recent participation
along with longevity and a dose of luck when the vendors draw their
season-long spaces during a winter lottery. The space allocation system
is labyrinthine but transparent and better by most counts than the old
days when farmers slept in their trucks to be sure to get in. These days,
in another measure to extend dignity to the profession of farming, vendors are even granted up to four "vacation" days without losing points.
They often use them for illness, funerals, and other life events that are

left to the farmers' discretion but deserve our collective respect. The rules are many but fair and transparent, designed for a smooth show-case of the beauty and bounty of the region.

The City Renewal Market

Not all market vendors bear the same relationship to what they sell, and not all customers want the same features in their market pro-duce. City renewal markets offer the diverse offerings and low costs available by aggregating products, the human touch of direct-to-con-sumer marketing, the partnership possibilities of CSAs, and the de-pendability of retail storefronts.[29] An urban market on prime down-town turf draws maybe forty thousand customers to its seven days of lively shopping each week. Merchants keep permanent storefronts stocked with kitchenware, T-shirts, handmade ceramics, gourmet cof-fee, artisan bread, specialty butchers' cuts, and other offerings that are available daily, year-round. Looking more like farmers, some ven-dors have stalls heaped with Florida oranges, Texas grapefruits, Cali-fornia almonds, Alaska crab, and Ontario herbs that fulfill the promise that "a trip to the market is like a trip around the world," as one mar-ket advertises. At one hundred years old or more, many of the urban markets that had become entirely wholesale or largely derelict now figure in neighborhood revitalization plans, and that includes reserv-ing—and promoting—space for local food, usually for a day or two a week. Representatives of family farms may bring the kids along to learn the trade, arrange for interns to work with the public, and make the family's income for the week. With enormous management re-quirements, including year-round facilities and rental services, such a market may have more than a dozen staff who address public rela-tions and customer needs, install tenants, and cultivate a lively com-mercial atmosphere intended to provide large-scale economic benefits to the surrounding area. While the true local farmers can get lost in the sheer volume of global commerce at this type of venue, the vendors at these big markets are not necessarily different from those at some smaller ones. Without a strict policy requiring vendors to be growers, some people selling at a market are more like stand operators, aggre-gators, or entrepreneurs who assemble a range of offerings from different farms to sell at wholesale or retail prices. Sometimes the rules allow vendors or farmers to work cooperatively with a rural neighbor to bring their goods to market, filling out their own stand in the process. Increasingly, cooperative and proprietary CSAs use all types of markets to distribute their weekly bundles, selling the extras to any comers and doing a little advertising for new shareholders on the side.

With the increase in the number and types of farmers' markets around the country, both customers and vendors often have options. Some vendors decide to drive past nearby but smaller or more rural markets to reach ones where customers will pay more or appreciate unusual varieties of basil, cucumbers, or melons that they grew up with in, say, Armenia or Thailand. Marketing directly to customers, rather than through wholesalers, means that farmer-vendors can charge full retail price; diversify their crops and reduce waste with sales of smaller quantities; and do what amounts to ongoing market research in conversations with customers about the varieties, quantities, packaging, and other features they want. Some markets attract customers who want the best deal on a crate of tomatoes while others are satisfied with higher prices for their pick of unusual heirloom varieties that some might call "ugly." Farmers must invest their time in a market, or markets, that meet their needs and offer the best returns. Factors that farmers typically consider include driving time and location, competition from other markets and vendors, cost to participate, and the prices customers are willing to pay. Also important are market organization, policies, and infrastructure.

Markets may look like ancient festivals that effortlessly sprung up in a parking lot one morning a week, and customers may believe that farming goodfolk naturally create an orderly, civil space. Behind the scenes, however, successful markets always have some principles of organization as the five example markets suggest. The bigger the market, the more organization is necessary. Vendors can look to the rules for participation, fairness in their application, and the atmosphere and orderliness they provide. Staffing that is adequate to the market's size, solid advertising and outreach efforts, reasonable fees, and good income potential become important factors, too. Many different kinds of markets can work, but policies that are unwieldy or partisan may cause them to fracture or collapse altogether. Spinning off from a frustrating

Table 2.2. Informative USDA Sources for Agriculture and Income

Agricultural Marketing Service	A compendium of reports, programs, and services on topics including farmers' markets and local food marketing.	http://www.ams.usda.gov
Farmers Market Coalition	Compiles resources, networking, programming, and advocacy for managers and growers.	https://farmersmarketcoalition.org
Census of Agriculture	Conducted every five years. Participation is required by law.	http://www.agcensus.usda.gov
Economic Research Service	Crunches data and issues reports on agricultural issues.	http://www.ers.usda.gov

market to make a fresh start with a new one is not necessarily undesirable, but it can potentially confuse customers and create unnecessary competition between markets.

The first impulse may be to join a market with little administrative structure, few rules, and minimal or no fees. However, when vendors enter no formal agreement, there may also be no oversight of who can sell, no requirements for sellers participating in production, little equity in space allocation, and uneven resolution of disputes. If no fees are collected, then there may be no funds for advertising and improvements. The organization of a market will always affect its rules.[30] In the least structured arrangement of a crossroads market, no formal organization governs the producers and their participation. The proprietary market and the city renewal market act as businesses that set the rules for their tenants. The small farmer-organized market involves an unofficial association of producers that collects fees and sets guidelines but is not legally organized or incorporated. Finally, the large, public grower-vendor market is one model that creates or uses an existing legal entity with attendant bylaws and tax status and staffing or grounds provided or underwritten by municipal, county, or state government. A market vendor must decide whether the level of structure is adequate to the size of the market she wants to join and whether it will allow her to reach her goals for participating. Ideally, the size of a market somehow balances the local population of potential customers; the number and type of small farms in the area; the vitality of its soils, climate, and altitude; and other factors.[31]

Staffing is one of the most recognized factors in vendor satisfaction, higher sales, and the overall success of a market.[32] A market manager, sometimes called the market master, is generally the person who oversees the operations of a market. The manager may be assisted by additional staff on the day of the event. Markets with more than thirty vendors consistently employ a paid manager and additional employees with at least some of them working year-round.[33] Larger markets also tend to use site maps, vending plans, and boards of directors or advisors, all of which the staff participates in.[34] As a result, larger markets may cost more to sustain and create more competition among vendors, but at forty vendors or more, they also tend to indicate higher average incomes for farmers. A national study in 2006 found that markets of fewer than ten vendors had median monthly sales of $500 per vendor, while markets of more than forty vendors had median sales of $750. Interestingly, markets in the middle, with ten to thirty-nine vendors, had the lowest monthly incomes, perhaps because customer traffic did not sufficiently outweigh competition among vendors.[35]

Paid or unpaid, the market manager performs important functions for the market, including managing budgets, enforcing rules and regulations, mediating disputes, and maintaining working relationships with adjacent property owners and businesses and with municipal offices such as those for parking, vendor licensing, and health.[36] Managers also spend their time on such tasks as market setup and breakdown, sign posting, fee collection, equipment inventory and maintenance, information booth staffing, traffic direction, vendor recruitment, tax preparation, and market safety.[37] The market manager may also assign vendor spaces and keep records of vendor and customer attendance.[38] Some of the manager's most important functions include maintaining fairness and good relations among vendors. In some cases, the market manager advises vendors on how to design and merchandise their produce.[39] The market manager can provide a consistent, long-range perspective for planning and improvement and can spearhead fund-raising and grant-seeking efforts. In general, the responsibilities of a manager should be appropriate to the size of a market, becoming more complex as the market size increases but not burdening a small market with unnecessary procedures and regulations.[40]

Additionally, a manager or her staff may contribute to the overall success of the market by promoting it to sponsors, media outlets, and the public through special events, websites, press releases, social media updates, and relationships with civic and governmental groups and organizations.[41] Efforts to market the market pay off. Market managers most commonly use signs, banners, newspapers, brochures, and flyers to get word out about their markets. Less frequently they use print and electronic newsletters and direct mailings or radio and television spots.[42] According to one study, 18 percent of customers learned about their farmers' market through a newspaper story or advertisement.[43] Creative and energetic market managers bring in new customers by allying with community events like the annual road race for breast cancer, Latino pride day, and various contests. They may open areas of the market to local musicians, the high school theater troupe, and buskers of all sorts. They may have a public information area for political parties, environmental groups, legislative activists, community nonprofits, and the like. The presence of all these groups not only adds liveliness to the market but also spreads word through new networks of the friends, family, and supporters of the various causes. A market's profile in the community is an important measure of its health.

Farmers who are considering selling at markets should probably aim to get a realistic sense of the income possible from participating in them, particularly if they are choosing between a market that charges a flat fee versus one that requires a percentage of sales, or deciding between a season-long space rental versus one with higher day rates. In addition to visiting prospective markets to watch buying and selling patterns, prospective vendors can check national and regional averages at websites such as the USDA's Agricultural Marketing Service, especially its section "Farmers Markets and Direct-to-Consumer Marketing."[44] The site posts brief "fact sheets" and full reports from the annual National Farmers Market Survey and from the Census of Agriculture, which is conducted every five years. It is worth remembering that, despite best intentions, hard work, and commitment, most people will fall within the modest income ranges they list. As one farmer said, growing things is "the easy part." Rather, planning, selling, adapting to unexpected circumstances, and actually making a profit are hard.

Customers often have an inflated sense of vendors' incomes, but successful farmers are realistic folk. The annual median sales from a farmers' market, taking into account all markets tracked by the federal government in all regions of the country, was $2,222 in 2005, the last year of federal reporting available.[45] That amount ranged from the high mark of $5,552 in the mid-Atlantic region to a low of $1,200 in the North Central, or Midwestern, area. A more representative view comes into focus by looking at median *monthly* sales, which indicate that, nationally, vendors at all markets earn $468, with a high of only $875 in the Mid-Atlantic to a low of $245 in the Southwest. The report states, "Vendors at smaller markets earned higher revenue than vendors at larger markets, presumably because there was less competition for customers. . . . However, when the market size reached 40 or more vendors, the negative impact of competition appeared outweighed by increased sales volume from greater customer traffic."[46] In other words, larger markets may mean more competition, but they also tend to indicate higher average incomes for farmers. There are many reasons vendors may accept these low figures: they are building CSA accounts by networking through the market, bolstering financial stability by diversifying their crops and moving small quantities, supplementing other outlets at retail prices, supporting a desirable lifestyle, contributing to community and ecological sustainability, and so on. Each vendor has to decide on his or her tolerance level, but vendors can save time by being realistic from the start.

Some data counter these low figures, indicating that while many vendors struggle, there is a small percentage with significant annual sales at markets: "in the Far West and Mid-Atlantic regions, managers reported that almost 12 percent and slightly more than 15 percent of the vendors at their markets earned gross incomes of between twenty-five thousand and one hundred thousand dollars in 2005.[47] On the other hand, the same report found that annual vendor sales at all

US markets show that the North Central and Rocky Mountain regions had the lowest average annual vendor sales, with more than 80 percent of farmers' market vendors earning annual sales between one thousand and five thousand dollars.

The longevity of a market is one of the factors that can help vendors evaluate earning potential. Overall, younger markets tend to yield a lower monthly income per vendor.[48] As a market becomes more established, the vendor income should increase, with a dip in those that are ten to nineteen years old, especially if customer growth does not keep pace with greater numbers of vendors.[49] At twenty years and more, markets tend to generate more income for vendors, perhaps because they have settled into better locations and provide an appropriate array of produce.[50] Getting into a new market early may have advantages, especially if seniority figures into such issues as allocation of spaces or product assignment. Early entry also provides the opportunity for long-term relationships with customers, many of whom want to support local farmers more than they care to bolster the more abstract concept of a local economy.[51] A recognizable marketstand—through distinctive look and signage, prominent display of the farm name, information about the farm, the farmers, their practices, and their products—helps customers connect with the farmers they want to support. Distinctive farm names point to important farm characteristics— Stranger's Hill Organics, the Chile Woman, Linnea's Greenhouse.[52] Memorable displays may feature baskets, bowls, crates, colorful tablecloths, or tempting samples of goat cheese, maple syrup, or fermenting vinegar. Pictures of grazing cows, photogenic field-workers, and newborn piglets fill in the picture of who is behind the stand and give new market customers something to return to in coming weeks. Especially in markets where vendors have to move their stand each week or each year, such landmarks can mean the difference between a disoriented hunt and a satisfying circuit of recognition and discovery. All in all, it is good to help customers navigate their options.

For of course customers do have options. Across the country, direct-to-consumer sales have risen in recent years, but the vast majority of food dollars, as much as 99 percent, is still spent at conventional grocery stores.[53] Indeed, how can availability of only a few hours a week possibly compete with 24/7 shopping? Knowing the customer gives vendors and organizers more information to make sense of the buying habits of their patrons.

Those Who Don't

As lively and inviting as markets may be, consumers spend most of their food dollars at chain grocery stores. Even regular farmers' market customers may not relish the lack of climate control, difficult parking, remote bathrooms (or none at all), the lack of accommodations for people with less mobility, or the time of day or day of the week the market runs. In addition, prices at farmers' markets can seem high.[54] There is no two-dollar special on Wonder Bread at a farmers' market. Instead, the bread that is available may seem less familiar to market newcomers. It may boast unusual grains and feature ingredients called "whole," "slow," "free," or "wild." The processes, too, may be organized contrary to mainstream expectations: ground by hand, baked in a wood-fired oven, worked by a cooperative, and produced on a homestead. A loaf may also be pricy, perhaps six dollars or more per loaf. Organic, grass-fed, hormone-free beef that may be available at a market is simply in a different price bracket from that of ground chuck from the big Western feedlots. A single lumpy-looking heirloom tomato may come in at the same price as a pound of "perfect" specimens at a big chain grocery. Casual comparisons like these make farmers' markets look dauntingly expensive. The fact that crates of strawberries or peaches may be discounted at the end of market can only help those who have the flexibility to arrive at that time—and the desire and capacity to accommodate large quantities.

Finances and convenience figure as major impediments to participation for some potential customers.[55] And ethnicity, class, social position, and cultural preparation for the market experience may also seem prohibitive. Some people may find the varieties of food familiar or strange depending on their preexisting cultural associations. An heirloom tomato may appear to be either rotten or desirable depending on the associations a person has with it.[56] Foods like okra, collards, chiles, and certain mushrooms may be more regionally known and recognized. People with lower incomes may require public transportation and may not be able to carry heavy quantities of produce home with them. Those who do venture to unfamiliar neighborhoods may feel more secure when they can park nearby. But as many market-goers around the country know, parking can be at a premium. Contributing to these feelings, and perhaps more insidious, is the sense customers may have, reinforced by regulars or not, that they are out of place (see chapter 3). People who do not regularly shop at farmers' markets most commonly suggest a more convenient location, cheaper prices, non-Saturday market days, and more mainstream venues such as grocery stores.[57]

At first, markets may look largely alike, with people making transactions for colorful produce over folding tables. But each farmers' market has its own personality, its own rules and conventions. While even experienced market customers may not be immediately comfortable at a new market, newcomers are at a greater disadvantage; thus, the more transparent and welcoming a market or an individual stand can appear, the more easily customers can find their fit. Helpful maps and signs, web guides, newspaper coverage, first-timer days, staff who are helpful and visible, and a few tips about finding the best prices can go a long way. Is trying to bargain prices down a good idea, or does it seem to devalue the farmer's labor and the quality of her produce? Is buying before the opening time or after closing a good way to get the best deals, is it rude, or does it actually break rules? Is everyone selling here growing their own, or only those in certain sections of the building? Are artichokes really in season in Michigan this time of year? Without a little guidance, people simply may not know. Bringing a dog, walking counter to the foot traffic, wheeling mega-strollers, seeking wholesale prices, accepting food vouchers, and so on are matters of local practice. Purposefully reintroducing the ancient practice of selling goods at smaller, more personal markets will increase the crowds, the demand for local food, and the viability of small farming.

But some farmers, too, decide markets aren't for them. They don't relish associating with the sideshow acts. They feel they can sell more on their own farm, where customers are not juggling cups of coffee. They don't want customers' dogs—or touchy children—to contaminate the goods. They can make more money without standing in a parking lot in all kinds of weather. They can't spare the time to load and unload every week. Or, as the Nobel Prize-winning author William Faulkner said when he supported himself by working for the post office, they just don't care much to go out in public to chat with just anyone who has a price of a stamp—or a tomato.

Customers often feel that a particular market is *their* market and that a particular vendor is *their* mushroom man or honey lady or melon family. These connections are what make a local food system work. Customers may not know the farmer's name, but they often are proud and loyal to them. Bonds like these can transform a town or region into a community. The conventional food system has overwhelming power through its advertising budgets, government subsidies, and corporate agreements. With as many as half of new markets closing in three years, farmers' markets cannot survive simply by tapping the same customers over and over again. New customers need reliable, high-quality food and a well-rounded experience in a well-managed market to keep them, and thus the vendors, coming back.[58]

Farmers' markets are just one piece of an overall local agricultural system that includes CSAs, wholesale exchanges, food hubs, and other creative schemes. But markets can be an especially stable contribution because they are regular, visible, local, and *peopled*. That means they are especially well suited to help stabilize local economies both urban and rural, increase access to healthy foods, lower environmental consequences, provide recreation, and draw people into association with one another. They can be foundational to a sense of community that rests on belonging, responsibility, and reciprocity.

Notes

1. Kasie Coccaro, "The White House Kitchen Garden Summer Harvest," *Let's Move* (blog), May 28, 2013, http://www.letsmove.gov/blog/2013/05/28/whitehousekitchengardensummerharvest.

2. Helena Norberg-Hodge, Todd Merrifield, and Steven Gorelick, *Bringing the Food Economy Home: Local Alternatives to Global Agribusiness* (London: Zed

Books, 2002); Scott Sanders, *A Conservationist Manifesto* (Bloomington: Indiana University Press, 2009); Gill Seyfang, "Ecological Citizenship and Sustainable Consumption: Examining Local Organic Food Networks," *Journal of Rural Studies* 22, no. 4 (2006): 383–95.

3. James R. Farmer et al., "Agrileisure: Farmers' Markets, CSAs, and the Privilege in Eating Local," *Journal of Leisure Research* 46 no. 3 (2014): 320.

4. Ibid., 313–28.

5. Gilbert Gillespie et al., "Farmers' Markets as Keystones in Rebuilding Local and Regional Food Systems," in *Remaking the North American Food System: Strategies for Sustainability*, edited by C. Clare Hinrichs and Thomas A. Lyson, 65–83 (Lincoln: University of Nebraska Press, 2007); Cheryl Brown and Stacy Miller, "The Impacts of Local Markets: A Review of Research on Farmers Markets and Community Supported Agriculture (CSA)," *American Journal of Agricultural Economics* 90, no. 5 (2008): 1298–1302; Mary Hendrickson and William Heffernan, "Opening Spaces through Relocalization: Locating Potential Resistance in the Weaknesses of the Global Food System," *Sociologica Ruralis* 42 (2002): 347–69; Helen La Trobe, "Farmers' Markets: Consuming Local Rural Produce," *International Journal of Consumer Studies* 25, no. 3 (2001): 181–92.

6. See, for example, National Agricultural Statistics Service, "Iowa Farmers' Market Customer Summary," November 30, 2009, http://www.nass.usda .gov/Statistics_by_State/Iowa/Publications/Other_Surveys/2009Customer Summary.pdf.; Farmer et al., "Agrileisure," 7; Kerr Center for Sustainable Agriculture, "Farmers' Market CUSTOMER SURVEY (9/29/01)," http://www .kerrcenter.com/farmers_market/Customer_Survey.pdf. Accessed November 27, 2016, https://web.archive.org/web/20130704144348/http://kerrcenter.com /farmers_market/Customer_Survey.pdf.

7. See, for example, Farmer et al., "Agrileisure," 319; Mary Ann McGrath, John F. Sherry, and Deborah D. Heisley, "An Ethnographic Study of an Urban Periodic Marketplace: Lessons from the Midville Farmers' Market," *Journal of Retailing* 69, no. 3 (1993): 280–319.

8. US Census Bureau, "America's Families and Living Arrangements: 2011," http://www.census.gov/population/www/socdemo/hh-fam/cps2011.html; Farmer et al., "Agrileisure," 319.

9. Farmer et al., "Agrileisure," 319; US Census Bureau, "State and County QuickFacts," http://quickfacts.census.gov/qfd/states/00000.html.

10. Edward Ragland and Debra Tropp, *USDA National Farmers Market Manager Survey, 2006*, US Department of Agriculture, Agricultural Marketing Service, May 2009, http://dx.doi.org/10.9752/MS037.05-2009, 38.

11. For example, see Farmer et al., "Agrileisure," 320, in which 90.6 percent of patrons surveyed in Indiana self-identified as white.

12. US Census Bureau, "State and County QuickFacts"; Dan Charles, "On the Farmers Market Frontier, It's Not Just about Profit," *NPR*, August 30, 2012, http://www.npr.org/blogs/thesalt/2012/08/30/160303008/on-the-farmers-market-frontier-its-not-just-about-profit.

13. USDA, "SNAP Applicants and Recipients," http://www.fns.usda.gov/snap.

14. Sarah Gonzalez, "Farmers' Markets Grow by 17 percent in US," *Agri-pulse*, August 4, 2011, http://www.agri-pulse.com/Merrigan_Farmers_Markets_8052011.asp.

15. Farmer et al., "Agrileisure."

16. Ibid., 14.; Ragland and Tropp, *USDA National Farmers Market Manager Survey*, 34; Jennifer Meta Robinson and J. A. Hartenfeld, *The Farmers' Market Book: Growing Food, Cultivating Community* (Bloomington: Indiana University Press, 2007).

17. Farmer et al., "Agrileisure."

18. Cynthia A. Cone and Andrea Myhre, "Community-Supported Agriculture: A Sustainable Alternative to Industrial Agriculture?" *Human Organization* 59 (2000): 187–97; Hinrichs, "Embeddedness and Local Food Systems: Notes on Two Types of Direct Agricultural Markets," *Journal of Rural Studies* 16 (2000): 295–303; Laura B. DeLind, "Of Bodies, Place, and Culture: Re-situating Local Food," *Journal of Agricultural and Environmental Ethics* 19, no. 2 (2006): 121–46; David Conner, "Expressing Values in Agricultural Markets: An Economic Policy Perspective," *Agriculture and Human Values* 21 (2004): 27–35; David Conner, "Beyond Organic: Information Provision for Sustainable Agriculture in a Changing Market," *Journal of Food Distribution Research* 35, no. 1 (2004): 34–39; Rosie Cox et al., "Common Ground? Motivations for Participation in a Community-Supported Agriculture Scheme," *Local Environment* 13, no. 3 (2008): 203–18"; Ragland and Tropp, *USDA National Farmers Market Manager Survey,* 34; James R. Farmer et al., "A Tale of Four Farmers Markets: Recreation and Leisure as a Catalyst for Sustainability," *Journal of Park and Recreation Administration* 29, no. 3 (2011): 11–23; Farmer et al., "Agrileisure," 321.

19. Farmer et al., "Agrileisure," 313–28.

20. Ibid., 319.

21. Robinson and Hartenfeld, *Farmers' Market Book*, 105–126.

22. Ragland and Tropp, *USDA National Farmers Market Manager Survey*, 28; USDA, "Organic Market Overview," http://www.ers.usda.gov/topics/natural-resources-environment/organic-agriculture/organic-market-overview.aspx#.UdCGvzvVCSp.

23. Bacillus thuringiensis is a soil-dwelling bacterium, commonly used as a biological pesticide and well-known to organic gardeners.

24. Farmer et al., "Tale of Four Markets."

25. USDA, "Farmers Markets and Direct-to-Consumer Marketing," http://www.ams.usda.gov/services/local-regional/farmers-markets-and-direct-consumer-marketing.

26. Stephenson et al., "When Things Don't Work: Some Insights into Why Farmers' Markets Close," *Special Report Number 1073-E*, December 2006, http://smallfarms.oregonstate.edu/sites/default/files/small-farms-tech-report/eesc_1073.pdf.

27. Ragland and Tropp, *USDA National Farmers Market Manager Survey*, 44.

28. Center for Rural Pennsylvania, *Starting and Strengthening Farmers' Markets in Pennsylvania*, 2nd ed. (Harrisburg: Center for Rural Pennsylvania, 2002).

29. The city renewal model described here does not meet a strict definition of a farmers' market, because it includes merchants who buy and sell rather than produce goods. Ragland and Tropp define a farmers' market as one in which greater than 51 percent of total retail sales are marketed directly by growers to consumers (*USDA National Farmers Market Manager Survey*, 20). However, I include this version of a market in this inventory because, increasingly, commercial and city ventures make an effort to involve farmers. Many customers do not understand the differences between a more commercial market and a farmers' market and may not recognize the value of such distinctions. They can be as passionate about a city renewal market as others are about a farmer-driven market. In addition, the large and loyal crowds drawn to historic sites and heavily publicized urban markets may make participation worthwhile for farmers even when they make up just a small number of the vendors.

30. Center for Rural Pennsylvania, *Starting and Strengthening Farmers' Markets*; Gary Stephenson, Larry Lev, and Linda Brewer, "Understanding the Link between Farmers' Market Size and Management Organization," *Special Report Number 1082-E*, Oregon State University Extension Service, December 2007, http://dnr.alaska.gov/ag/FMM/013APPJMarketSizeMgmtOrganization.pdf.

31. Stephenson et al., "Understanding the Link," 15.

32. Theodore Morrow Spitzer and Hilary Baum, *Public Markets and Community Revitalization* (Washington: ULI–The Urban Land Institute and Project for Public Spaces, 1995), 67; Megan Elizabeth Hughes and Richard H. Mattson, "Farmers' Markets in Kansas: A Profile of Vendors and Market Organization," *Report of Progress 658*, Agricultural Experiment Station, Kansas State University, 1992, 5; Stephenson et al., "Understanding the Link," 62; Neil D. Hamilton, *Farmers' Markets Rules, Regulations, and Opportunities* (Fayetteville, AR: National Center for Agricultural Law Research and Information, 2002), 8.

33. Stephenson et al., "Understanding the Link."

34. Ibid.

35. Ragland and Tropp, *USDA National Farmers Market Manager Survey*, 41–43.

36. Spitzer and Baum, *Public Markets and Community Revitalization*, 69–70.

37. Stephenson et al., "Understanding the Link."

38. Ibid.; Spitzer and Baum, *Public Markets and Community Revitalization*, 69–70.

39. Spitzer and Baum, *Public Markets and Community Revitalization*, 69–70; "Richmond Indiana Farmers Market," http://www.richmondinfarmersmarket .com (site discontinued).

40. David Zimet, Timothy Hewitt, and George Henry, "Characteristics of Successful Vegetable Farmers' Retail Markets," *Proceedings of Florida State Horticulture Society* 99 (1986): 295; Hamilton, *Farmers' Markets Rules, Regulations*, 8–9.

41. Spitzer and Baum, *Public Markets and Community Revitalization*, 69–70.

42. Stephenson et al., "Understanding the Link," 16.

43. Farmer et al., "Supporting Specialty Crops and Local Food Systems in Indiana," Specialty Crops Block Grant final report, Indiana State Department of Agriculture, 2009, 31.

44. USDA, "Farmers Markets and Direct-to-Consumer Marketing."

45. Ragland and Tropp, *USDA National Farmers Market Manager Survey*, 43.

46. Ibid., 41.

47. Ibid.

48. Ibid., 44.

49. Ibid.

50. Ibid.

51. Farmer and his colleagues note: "A statistical difference in the data exists between farmers' market participants and CSA participants in the value of supporting the local farmer vs. supporting the local economy as a whole. This may be indicative of why many CSA subscribers were also often attendees at farmers' market (77.7%), but a much smaller percentage of farmers' market participants simultaneously subscribed to a CSA (7.2%). Rather than interpreting this finding to suggest that farmers' market consumers do not care as much about the local farmers' from whom they purchase their food, we interpret it to mean that farmers' markets may attract a cross-section of the general population that is more reflective of the mean, whereas CSAs attract a following with a special interest in knowing and committing to support of specific individuals." Farmer et al., "Agrileisure," 320.

52. Stranger's Hill Organics, http://www.strangershillorganics.com; the Chile Woman, http://www.thechilewoman.com; City of Bloomington, "About Linnea's Greenhouse," http://bloomington.in.gov/documents/viewDocument .php?document_id=7419.

53. Renée Johnson, Randy Alison Aussenberg, and Tadlock Cowan, *The Role of Local Food Systems in US Farm Policy*, Congressional Research Service, March 12, 2013, http://www.fas.org/sgp/crs/misc/R42155.pdf.

54. In a study of 712 individuals and their experience with farmers' markets, 15 percent, or 117, were non-local foods participants, not using markets or CSAs. Farmer et al., "Agrileisure," 318.

55. Ibid. The Farmer study of 712 individuals and their experience with farmers' markets included 15 percent, or 117, informants who did not participate in local foods venues like markets or CSAs (Farmer et al.). These nonparticipants tended to be women (63.2 percent) in their mid-fifties, with an average household size of 2.5 (though 54 percent without children), about half having college or graduate degrees, almost 60 percent married, and 88 percent Caucasian. The household income levels for nonparticipants were 14.6 percent at or above $90,000; with 9.4 percent ranging from $75,000 to $89,999; 10.3 percent ranging from $60,000 to $74,499; 9.4 percent ranging from $45,000 to $59,999; 20.5 percent ranging from $30,000 to $44,999; and 23.9 percent ranging from $0 to $29,999.

56. Jennifer A. Jordan, "The Heirloom Tomato as Cultural Object: Investigating Taste and Space," *Sociologia Ruralis*, 47, no. 1 (2007): 20–41.

57. Farmer et al., "Agrileisure," 321.

58. Lohr et al., *Mapping Competition Zones for Vendors and Customers in US Farmers Markets*, Agricultural Marketing Service, September 2011, http://www.ams.usda.gov/AMSv1.0/getfile?dDocName=STELPRDC5094336.

THREE

Understanding Community Supported Agriculture

> CSA is not just a clever, new approach to marketing. Community farming is about the necessary renewal of agriculture through its healthy linkage with the human community that depends upon farming for survival.
> —Steven McFadden

As defined by the US Department of Agriculture, a CSA "consists of a community of individuals who pledge support to a farm operation so that the farmland becomes, either legally or spiritually, the community's farm, with the growers and consumers providing mutual support and sharing the risks and benefits of food production."[1] The consensus emphasizes the collective, political, and economic nature of the arrangement, defining it as "an alternative, locally-based economic model of agriculture and food distribution" that involves a "network or association of individuals who have pledged to support one or more local farms, with growers and consumers sharing the risks and benefits of food production."[2] Our notion of a CSA most closely aligns with the one Indian Line Farm uses: an organization that "brings together community members and farmers in a relationship of mutual support based on an annual commitment to one another. . . . Members purchase a 'share' of the anticipated harvest and make payment in advance at an agreed upon price." In exchange, the farmers grow, raise, and care for bounty that subscribers share. As the Indian Line website says, "In short, the farmer and members become partners in the production, distribution and consumption of locally grown food."[3]

In 1985, Massachusetts-based Indian Line Farm and New Hampshire-based Temple-Wilton Community Farm pioneered CSAs in the United States, and in 1986 they marked their first CSA growing season.[4] Where did they come from? Many sources point to the Teiki movement in Japan in the mid-1970s, in which groups of women who, concerned about the agricultural chemicals used in food production, partnered with local farmers on an annual basis to procure food produced in a manner acceptable to them for feeding their families. While this story is often cited as the origin of CSAs in the United States, longtime CSA expert Steven McFadden points to even earlier developments. According to McFadden, Indian Line Farm and Temple-Wilton Community Farm more directly associated their work with the wide-ranging Austrian philosopher Rudolf Steiner (1861–1925). In addition to developing innovative educational and social reforms, Steiner advocated a theory of "biodynamic" farming that would address what he saw as the physical and metaphysical qualities of agriculture. He advocated practices for soil fertility and crop success with such mystical treatments as animal blood and planetary influences. By the 1970s, some of these theories had found their way into US alternative agriculture and, indeed, persist here today.[5] Perhaps Steiner's most important contribution to agricultural innovation, apart from attention to soil amendments, was to focus on farming as a system of relationships that incorporates farm owners, workers, consumers, and the land. According to McFadden, decisions at the Temple-Wilton Farm were driven by concerns for new models of property ownership and human relations and by the "needs of the land and of the people involved in this enterprise."

Yet an often-overlooked origin of the modern-day CSA stems from the work of Dr. Booker T. Whatley, an African American farmer and scholar who, according to Natasha Bowens, began promoting the concept of a community supported farm several years before the Indian Line and Temple-Wilton farms were established.[6] As documented by a 1982 interview in *Mother Earth News* magazine, Whatley advanced the possibility of making "$100,000 on 25 acres" using regenerative (sustainable) farming methods and through "membership" that built a community around the farm. Bowens traces Whatley's model for community supported agriculture to 1960s and 1970s Alabama and contends that his ideas were reaching as many as twenty thousand small farmers through subscriptions to Whatley's newsletter and training seminars. Much like the modern-day CSA, Whatley's model "enables the farmer to plan production, anticipate demand, and, of course, have a guaranteed market" by mostly catering to suburban and urban dwellers so that they can partake in "the privilege of coming to the farm and harvesting produce."

Today the CSA movement includes approximately twelve thousand farms and has outpaced farmers' markets in sheer numbers. CSAs have taken hold, in part, because they offer a proactive way for consumers to gain greater accountability for and control over the sources and methods of food production. More people want healthier, environmentally sound food. At the same time, farmers appreciate up-front capital to fund their season's expenses and ensure information and supply channels to customers. In addition, associating oneself officially with a farm also provides satisfying resonances with the recent American past for many people.

According to Melea Press and Eric Arnould, CSAs address the tension between a pastoral ideal and the desire for consumer amenities produced by industrialization.[7] They identify five key reasons why CSAs are well designed to resolve this uncomfortable contradiction.

1. CSAs offer food that is often produced sustainably and without chemical additives, providing an antithesis for conventional or industrial production.
2. CSAs allow individuals to join small groups and to engage with them meaningfully.
3. CSAs model a way to both connect with nature and embrace consumption.
4. CSAs offer both food security and food sovereignty, along with more adequate supplies of food and more meaningful choices regarding them than are offered by the industrial system.
5. CSAs continue a national narrative about successful American pastoralism.

They make a consistent next chapter in a story that begins with the American colonial farmer and continues to 1950s suburban home-ownership and 1970s back-to-the-land self-sufficiency. The CSA and urban agriculture movements of today allow people who are otherwise disconnected from food production to construct a plausible role for themselves in this central story of our nation.

After more than a quarter century of development in North America, the diffuse beginnings of CSAs mean continuing challenges in how to define and realize these partnerships in the context of twenty-first-century agrarian initiatives. Questions persist: What does the "community" part of community supported agriculture really mean? Is a CSA a marketing scheme, a shopping alternative, or a social movement? What are the benefits of subscribing? Who subscribes and who remains missing from the community? What is in store for the CSAs of tomorrow? This chapter critically considers the role of CSAs in a new resettling of America.

Community Ideal or Just Another Marketing Scheme

Steven McFadden, in *The Call of the Land: An Agrarian Primer for the 21st Century*, describes the philosophy of community supported agriculture as "an economic and social association among local households and farmers who share the responsibility of producing and delivering fresh food."[8] The ways that CSAs vary their emphasis and share responsibility between economics and socialities, consumers and farmers, results in different operational models. One way to consider their differences is on a typological continuum from *community ideal* to *marketing approach*. From an outside observer, CSAs may look quite similar; however, they vary greatly based on governance structure, true ownership design, and mission-driven ambitions.

The Biodynamic Association leans toward community building. It describes the ideal CSA as one in which farmers and shareholders collaborate "together on behalf of the Earth," sharing responsibilities such as general risks that are normally associated with farming (weather, pests, disease, etc.).[9] The Biodynamic Association describes these kinds of CSAs as being organized around three main groups of stakeholders: farmers, a core group, and consumers. Farmers generally complete all the agricultural activities without interference from the other two groups. The core group, comprised of farmers and consumers, handles the business side of the operation: marketing, share-payment collection, farmer payments, legal issues, special event organization, recruitment of new shareholders, and so on. Finally, the consumer group focuses entirely on buying shares and receiving the farm's bounty. This idealized CSA appeals for many reasons; foremost, it seeks to produce healthy, sustainably grown food. In addition, this model of the CSA supports community development, promotes health, fosters the local ecology, provides recreation and leisure pursuits, and offers education. Many CSAs do incorporate these attributes and aspirations; however, common also is the CSA that emphasizes its marketing approach, which focuses on the consumer(s) assuming greater risks and stabilizing finances through a pre-sourced distribution outlet. Often left out is the broader goal of the CSA movement: community development. In essence, the two examples described represent opposite ends of a continuum, with the biodynamic version of the CSA at one end and the marketing-oriented version at the opposite end.

Most CSAs are someplace in between. Tailored to both farmer and shareholder needs, they allow for more fluidity in style and structure than, say, farmers' markets and small groceries. CSAs include the traditional single-farmer model as well as those that have hybridized with farmers' markets; collaborations among several growers; size-based, weight-based or price-based shares; specialty-only shares of products like meat, dairy, organic fruit, or bread; and value-added bonuses. The remainder of this section provides examples of a variety of CSAs selling a diversity of products.

Among the most common variations on the CSA continuum are the single- and multi-farm providers. For example, Evenstar Farm in Eagle, Idaho, is a single farm that sells thirty shares for a season that runs from May through early October.[10] Both full and half shares are available, and shareholders acquire their produce at a 20–30 percent discount when compared to local food retailed at farmers' markets and grocery stores. The farm grows common vegetables, such as tomatoes, cabbage, squash, and collards, along with unique items like herbs and uncommon greens. This single-farm model is likely the most prevalent in North America; however, it is not without challenges. In particular, based as they are with a family or individual farmer, single-farm CSAs mean intensive concentration of all aspects of agribusiness—growing, marketing, distribution—on just a limited number of people. One illness, accident, or other setback in this case affects all of those doing the work of the farm and their collective income.

Alternatively, multi-farm CSAs work cooperatively, aiming to-gether toward the same goal.[11] Multi-farm CSAs have the latitude to distribute effort. For example, they may focus one grower on warm-season produce while another focuses on season extension and winter production. Or they may invite in specialist growers, such as those in vegetable, tree fruit, dairy, meat, and egg production, so that share-holders can access most of their local culinary ingredients from a single distribution location. Cooperation allows more products and more se-lective ones, and it can also mean distribution of other farm needs, including sharing labor, equipment, marketing, accounting, certifica-tion, maintenance, and so on. The Local Harvest CSA in New Hamp-shire, for example, cooperatively organizes six New Hampshire farms that together can serve three hundred shareholders from May through November.

While the vast majority of CSAs grow and distribute vegetables, other types that specialize in fruits, meat, eggs, and dairy products are increasingly popular. However, their focus can introduce more vul-nerability than in a diversified model. Until 2015, the Wayne-Egenolf, or WE, Farm was one of only a few meat CSAs in the Bloomington, In-diana, area, raising cattle, hogs, and poultry on 150 acres of leased pas-ture and forest. The farm's shareholders contracted for a share of meat produced from the farm. The shares were offered for three-month in-tervals at two levels—value and prime. They also sold products direct to consumers and retailers throughout the area. Also in the area, Maple Valley Farm, run by Larry and Tina Howard, raises grass-fed beef, lambs and goats and pasture-raised pigs, chickens, laying hens, and tur-keys. Not quite a CSA, the farm offers partnerships in their live herd. In essence, people can buy a "real ownership stake" by which they "own the livestock and get a predetermined portion of the entire animal (e.g., ¼ cow, ½ pig). You have control over the cuts and the entire por-tion of the animal is available for your consumption."[12] The intent, in this case, is for the farmers and the partners to more closely cooperate to "support consumer choice, environmental stewardship, farm sus-tainability, community, health and animal welfare" and a living wage.

Unlike a relatively straightforward regulatory situation for meat CSAs, those specializing in milk must negotiate additional in-state rules and regulations as well as processing guidelines and opportuni-

Table 3.1. Comparison of Traditional Produce CSAs with Cow/Herd Shares

	Traditional Produce CSAs	**Dairy Cow/Herd Shares**
Commitment	Financial commitment to the farm, prior to the growing season	Financial commitment to the farm/herd/cow can be started and terminated at most any time
Cost	Based on quantity of weekly allotment, associated with size and number of shares	Based on the individual shareholder's quantity of weekly allotment, associated with size and number of shares; original up-front share cost and weekly boarding/care fee.
Length of Time	Generally based on length of season	Runs indefinitely
Return on Investment	Weekly allotment of produce	Normally scheduled allotment of product (varies based on share type, product, etc.)
Ownership Status	Shareholder	Shareholder
Risk Involved	Loss of crops / return on investment	Loss of animals / return on investment
Major Differences	Share price must be paid anew with each season; CSAs generally represent a formal commitment for a set period of time.	Weekly fees also apply; termination opportunities; payment method—dairy, for example—generally does not need to be paid entirely up front, as the commitment extends for much longer or indefinitely.

ties. The crux of the complications for milk is healthfulness, or perceptions of healthfulness, when it is sold "raw." As of 2013, the purchase of raw milk was entirely illegal in ten states, legal as pet food in three states, and legal through herd shares in eleven states where state statute, policy, court decision, or ambiguity of state government policy influences enforcement. The sale of raw milk directly from the farm, in 2013, was legal in sixteen states, and ten states allow its sale in retail establishments.[13] Given that most state rules are set up to support off-the-farm processing at commercial dairies, and few small farms can warrant the construction of on-the-farm processing facilities for milk, dairy CSAs are commonly used for distribution of unprocessed milk. Groundwork Farms in Millheim, Pennsylvania, is positioned in a state that, with a proper permit, allows retail sales, farmers' market sales, and sales both on and off the farm.[14] They offer a dairy CSA share to complement their produce, herb, egg, and bread options.[15] Their shareholders sign up for a thirteen-week period or more to receive a variety of dairy products such as raw milk, cheese, yogurt, butter, and cream. Similarly, cow and herd shares can circumvent laws and policies prohibiting the retail sale of raw milk, because the customers are legally part owners of the animal or herd. Customer payments are credited to the care and boarding of the animal, and in exchange, customers receive a portion of the milk or other value-added product. While not entirely synonymous with CSAs, cow and herd shares also use a shareholder structure, and weekly allotments are generally provided (table 3.1). In addition, for both, the return on investment is a portion of the weekly bounty, and the risk of loss on investment is shared among producers and consumers. However, while CSAs contract for a share of the products of a farm or cooperative, animal shareholders hold a stake in the animals themselves.

The Farmers and the Shareholders

Spearheading a CSA has numerous benefits for the farmers as well as a host of challenges. CSAs provide economic stability through a committed community of shareholders; however, they demand a capacity for customer service, marketing, transparency, and resilience for when things go wrong.

From a farmer's perspective, the biggest advantage of a CSA is the economic stability it brings. Because subscribers pay for their shares up front—generally speaking, several months before they begin to receive the farm's bounty—they create a stable base of both capital and community. Farmers can then plan for those shares and diversify from them. The farmer can script the season's seeds, animals, inputs,

Figure 3.1. Two images show Evening Song Farm in Vermont before Hurricane Irene (*top*) and after the storm and flooding ravaged its topsoil (*bottom*). *Photographs by Ryan Wood-Beauchamp and Kara Fitzgerald*

and labor with greater knowledge of what will be needed to fulfill the farm's commitments. Additionally, they can engage the shareholders to inform crop selection, to provide labor for special projects, and to market the farm. However, such partnerships do not always come naturally. For example, in about 2010, parishioners at the First Presbyterian Church in Huntington, West Virginia, started the area's first CSA in order to gain better access to local produce. Taking this new idea for acquiring food with her, Sara Farmer, James's wife, went to the winter meeting of Huntington's Central City Farmers' Market to make a pitch to the farmers she hoped to recruit. Indeed, after the meeting, one farmer stuck around to inquire further about the idea even though the rest dismissed the scheme. After Sara and the farmer had several telephone conversations, and she made a personal visit to the farm, Lewis Bodimer, a longtime produce farmer and market vendor who raised produce across the river in Gallipolis, Ohio, agreed to give the CSA model a try. The final hurdle, however, was that Lewis and his wife, Rebecca, objected to taking an early season payment for produce delivered much later. Their ethical commitment to the principle of payment upon delivery nearly derailed the venture. The resulting compromise saw the up-front subscription funds held by the church for weekly distribution to the farmers. After that, recruitment of more shareholders was simple: the church posted an announcement on its Facebook page. Within seven days, parishioners at First Presbyterian and another nearby church had bought forty shares. What seemed to be a speculative enterprise continues to thrive today, a partnership of its committed community and forthright farmers.

A community committing to providing up-front capital for the season and assistance with marketing, then, is also sharing the risk of the farming operation. This is a risk that is acutely understood by farmers but probably less so by consumers, who are used to the seemingly bottomless supplies of an American marketplace sourced and aggregated from all over the world. In this way, CSAs differ markedly even from farmers' markets, a down-home form of aggregation that mitigates risk to consumers. CSA shareholders, knowingly or not, sign on to share not only in bounty but also in risk—of pests, mechanical mishaps, seed mistakes, physical injuries, and crop failures. Weather, the most notoriously uncontrollable of all farming inputs, can be too hot or too cold, too wet or too dry, too windy or too still, too steady or too volatile. While a complete crop failure is unlikely for a diversified farmer, the ever shifting combination of variables means crop yields are always a gamble. Farmers with less experience provide additional unknowns, even in years with the best growing conditions.

While some losses are unavoidable, few are as catastrophic as those experienced at Evening Song Farm in Cuttingsville, Vermont. When Hurricane Irene blew up the eastern US seaboard in 2011, it left a path of profound geological impact in its wake as torrents of rain were dumped on the Appalachian mountain hillsides in New England. Few farms likely suffered worse than Evening Song. Sitting along the swollen Mill River, Evening Song lost its high tunnel greenhouses and all crops planted in the fields to flooding. In fact, as dramatic photographs show, the river washed the farm's topsoil down to the underlying bedrock.

Obviously, Evening Song's CSA shareholders lost their investment that year. But the farmers, Kara Fitzgerald and Ryan Wood Beauchamp, lost something more profound: any potential of growing crops on this land for quite some time. According to the farmers' blog, they received help from shareholders, friends, family members, neighbors, local businesses, and other organizations from across the United States so that they could reconstruct greenhouses and a produce barn. In addition, they were offered use of farmland in the interim while they strategized their next steps, and forty tractor-trailer loads of paper fiber and fertilizer were donated by a local company (Resource Management Inc.) to help reestablish a cover of topsoil on the decimated field. Today, Evening Song Farm flourishes through the provisioning of food via their CSA, the local farmers' market, and sales to area businesses.[16] This story of Evening Song Farm's revival exemplifies the power of the *community* component in "CSA." In a short period of time, with the aid of the CSA and the broader community, Evening Song had moved from a private operation to a communal investment, an icon of perseverance.

Still, CSAs are not a panacea for farmers. In fact, running a CSA presents numerous challenges. In particular, specialized operations can introduce more vulnerability than in a diversified model. As a case in point, even though WE Farm was one of only a few meat CSAs in the Bloomington, Indiana, area, it struggled. Like many other CSA own-

ers, Laura Beth Wayne and Josh Egenolf marketed their personal dedi-
cation to the land, animals, plant life, soil, and community as much as
their meat. The WE website included a blog of farming delights and
challenges that shareholders responded to with enthusiasm. For example, Egenolf wrote on December 7, 2010:

> My hands, feet, and nose are shrouded in frost in little time. The
> calves backs are laced with icy crystals and they are bawling as I pass
> by, my truck dash so stiff with the cold I swear it will fracture like the
> San Andreas with the first pothole I come to in the road. It does not.
> I return 10 minutes later with a snow-capped bale of hay; they are
> glad to see me, as they have wallowed the final remains of their last
> bale for bedding. They dive tongue-first into their new prize, pull-
> ing tufts of dried fescue in by the mouthful. I go check their water
> tank. It is frozen solid. The fuse that powers the tank heater is out,
> but nature is little forgiving of such failures. With a new fuse and
> few hours of heat, the water will flow again. The calves will take that
> water, take that hay, and with some time and some good husbandry
> from us, convert it into food. Such a situation few get to experience,
> to misguided others it seems insufferable and cruel to these beasts,
> but to those of us choosing to slow down and appreciate it, it is ac-
> tually an incredible miracle. All flesh is grass, and is so in the most
> seemingly harsh situations. I am charged by the notion that I have
> the privilege to witness the miracle of creating flesh from grass, no
> from the sun and soil through grass and into beast, so that others
> might enjoy it as food and add it to their own being. I am privileged
> to witness, share, and husband such things. . . . I cannot thank you
> enough. In supporting our farm, our stewardship, and our family,
> you in turn support yourselves by making healthy the very commu-
> nity, landscape, body, and mind on which you depend. I am thank-
> ful you care enough to support a farm which is pro-local, pro-diver-
> sity, and pro-earthworm! I am comforted by such notions, and my
> heart is warmed.[17]

Under the prevailing spirit of mindfulness and uplift, one can detect
in this essay the enormous physical, social, and financial responsibilities that farming presents. Indeed, some five years later WE Farm sold
its animals and closed its website despite the community's enthusiastic
reception for its high-quality products.[18] With more than a million and
a half people in Indianapolis (sixty miles away) and one hundred thou-

sand residents in Bloomington (fifteen miles away), WE Farm seemed well positioned geographically to tap into the increased demand for naturally raised local food. But achieving "balance" in life and work, so that there is time for family and other pursuits, is a persistent challenge for small farmers, and other meat-based CSAs have also struggled. On their website Wayne writes, "We have to reevaluate how WE Farm fits into our lives. I truly believe that it will evolve and still be a part of our lives, it will just look a little different. The size and scale that we have been farming is not sustainable for our lives at this point. With two little ones and two full-time jobs, we have to take a step back."[19]

Navigating member turnover, accommodating consumer preferences, delivering high-quality products, and planning for the unexpected all create additional concerns on top of the basic job of growing food and the essential task of making a viable life. Current statistics suggest that turnover of CSA shareholders is between 25 and 70 percent each year.[20] Consequently, CSA operators must continuously market their organization and recruit members. These yearly fluctuations in membership come as a result of such issues as subscribers' perception of the quality of products; convenience of subscribing, ordering, and pickup; and lack of knowledge regarding the common products grown locally and in each season. Market research points to the importance of word-of-mouth recruitment of new shareholders. A recent study among members of nineteen different CSAs in Indiana found that nearly 60 percent of the subscribers were first-timers, with 100 percent of participants closely knowing another CSA shareholder and 93.1 percent having learned about their current CSA by word-of-mouth.[21]

Individuals subscribe to CSAs for many reasons, and figuring those out is fundamental to maintaining a successful member base. The most obvious reason is fresh food. According to one CSA subscriber, "I really liked the food, the vegetables, especially the fruit[;] it was really great," while another noted that he likes "the variety each week. There is something different each week, and she doesn't overload us with the any one item. So there is a lot of variety. I also like that I can actually call the farmer at any point if there is something wrong. So, it's very personal. I really like that. I like knowing the farmer." Beyond food, many subscribers want to support local farmers and the local economy.[22] Subscribers to CSAs value being able to develop a more intentional relationship with the farmer(s), to acquire an in-depth understanding of the farm and its practices, to gain a sense of community and belonging, and to participate in a growing trend among urban and suburban residents. Subscribers also value the fact that CSAs put them in a privileged position to acquire food items that are scarce in their area. Pasture-raised pork, free-range poultry, unusual squash, Southeast Asian greens, or other heirloom vegetables are examples in some areas. Finally, some CSA shareholders value the opportunity to cast a personal, consistent, and deep vote in support of their local food system.

Privilege and the CSA

It comes as no surprise, however, that CSA participation is not always easy. Subscribers leave CSAs for a number of reasons, including too much food, too little variety, too much variety, too many unfamiliar or unpalatable greens in the fall and spring "shoulder" seasons, and too little choice. This "too" variable presents a significant challenge at the core of CSAs. The seasonality of farming means long periods of less than optimal growing conditions that subscribers are not always prepared to endure. In the northern latitudes, the cooler months (mainly in April–June, but also September–November) can mean little variety and none of the big-draw vegetables like sweet corn and cantaloupes. The current industrial food model that provides consumers' unlimited choices of produce throughout the year has pushed American food palates to want diversity and to balk at the monotony of the season's staples. Being aware of this propensity and responding with a diversity of crops spaced appropriately throughout the growing season is fundamental to farmers' pleasing many shareholders. Animal-based CSAs, such as meat or dairy, do not have the same challenges as produce CSAs given the nature of the products, their position on the menu, and the longer shelf life, particularly when value is added.

Another variable affecting CSA shareholder stability and retention is the internal competition farmers face with their other distribution points. Our survey of CSA subscribers in the Midwest indicated that they sometimes received vegetables from the CSA that were inferior to what was available from the same growers at the farmers' market.

In addition, longer-term subscribers sometimes perceive a decrease in quality as the size of a CSA grows. While farmers must manage the CSA and their distribution systems effectively in order to maintain adequate income to sustain the farm and themselves, they must consider how their efforts to grow can affect shareholder satisfaction and, subsequently, retention. Otherwise, they can undermine the stability of the entire program.

CSAs have long been critiqued for issues of privilege and exclusivity. In particular, education, wealth, and race appear in current research in a confluence of some of the most significant barriers to expanding CSAs. Education is one important disparity that points to other inequalities that defuse the potential of CSAs. A recent study of CSAs and farmers' markets found, in part, that most customers had higher levels of educational achievement than the general population.[23] This Indiana-based study found that 85.6 percent of the CSA participants surveyed had a bachelor's degree, with 55.5 percent of them also having a graduate-level degree. Comparatively, only 22.7 percent of *all* Indiana residents in 2011 had a bachelor's degree, with 8.3 percent holding a graduate-level degree. This disparity indicates the link between educational attainment, which correlates with socioeconomic status, and access to these local food venues. This circumstance is relevant beyond Indiana in that, nationwide, 28 percent of adult citizens held bachelor's degree in the same period.[24] Additionally, another recent study by Thomas Macais confirms that CSA members around Burlington, Vermont, generally have a higher level of education—and higher socioeconomic status—than the general population.[25] What this means for the expansion of CSAs is that the distribution scheme is currently targeting only a fraction of the population that it could. What it means for social justice is that good food is mostly reaching those who already have access to excellent quality and quantities of comestibles.

More advanced education usually means greater income, which, when coupled together, supports greater access and customer participation.[26] Clare Hinrichs argues that the face-to-face interaction and the community framework of CSAs and other direct-market local food venues compound the social inequalities that exist in the marketplace, creating barriers to participation for both the less educated and less wealthy.[27] She argues that many CSAs and direct agricultural markets are comprised of "exclusive products and exclusive markets" that "involve social relations where the balance of power and privilege ultimately rests with well-to-do consumers."[28] Indeed, the theory of producer-to-consumer direct marketing rests on the premise that it provides an alternative to the one-size-fits-all mass production embraced by the dominant food system. However, as Hinrichs rightly notes, direct markets are not exempt from perpetuating inequity in income and access, even when they manage to shift the power around. As consumers with greater resources become empowered, an increasing number of marginalized consumers and break-even farmers may become disadvantaged.

In part, a class-bound system is supported by the strong role that social networks play in how CSAs are marketed and how people learn about the CSA in which they come to hold shares. According to our (2010) study in Indiana, one-third of subscribers learned about their CSA directly from a friend or coworker, while 14.6 percent learned about it through their social network via an email or Facebook. Additionally, 84.3 percent of CSA participants knew of a friend who also was a shareholder, with 49.2 percent knowing a coworker, and 48.2 percent knowing a family member who subscribed to a CSA. In total, 100 percent of CSA participants in the study had, at minimum, one other person they knew who also held a share in a CSA. This predominance of in-network growth is not surprising, because many CSAs use a grassroots, "organic" style of marketing that relies heavily on word-of-mouth and social networks to advertise and recruit shareholders.[29] However, it does mean that like breeds like, and CSAs are potentially attracting only people who are like those already subscribed.

With its outsized role in US social relations, race becomes a prevailing factor in participation and recruitment. CSA participants in our Indiana study were overwhelmingly white (95.3 percent), even though a lesser portion (86.8 percent) of the state's residents are white, according to the 2010 US Census. Participation in Indiana CSAs by people of color also showed important disparities: only 1.1 percent of participants identified as Asian, 0.7 percent as African American, and 0.7 percent as being of Hispanic descent. The census findings for the state population are 9.4 percent African American, 6.1 percent Hispanic or Latino, and

1.7 percent Asian. Scholars studying other locations have found similar rates of participation and note especially the underrepresentation of African Americans in these alternative food systems.[30] CSAs, and local food more generally, are far from race-neutral as currently practiced and require purposeful effort to make them inclusive.[31]

Income is a key variable as well to improving food security and access through local foods.[32] In our same Indiana study, 48.8 percent of CSA participants reported a household income at or above $90,000. Meanwhile, the median household income in Indiana that year was $47,697. Additionally, 81 percent of all CSA participants surveyed reported a household income at or above $45,000. In comparison, the median US household income level for 2010 was $51,914. John Polimeni and his colleagues conducted research that is one example among many that found similar patterns in participation. The researchers found that participants in Roxbury Biodynamic Farm's CSA operation in Kinderhook, New York, showed similarly disproportionate participation, with 74.1 percent of participants having a household income greater than $40,000.

These four intertwined variables of privilege—education, social network, race, and income—have been noted consistently in the research literature as factors that constrain participation in CSAs by a more diverse cross-section of the population.[33] Local and sustainable food advocates, too, are beginning to recognize the limitations of the current system and to address them by developing improvements on the classic CSA model.

While issues of privilege that shape much of the American experience likewise inform these and other alternative food venues, many innovative options for broadening participation in local food systems exist. CSAs, often perpetuating major economic and cultural challenges, also reveal that privilege. Their basis in social organization means that changes in CSAs can reflect and overcome significant exclusionary aspects of the larger culture. By addressing two or more variables at once, CSAs can evolve to be more than just another marketplace for the elite. CSAs of tomorrow, if they are to flourish, must adopt innovative strategies that invite new and different people to the table. Employing strategies such as alternative locations, fee structures, participant models, and educational venues will open accessibility and draw greater diversity, in greater numbers, to a local food experience that supports farms, farmers, communities, and public health.

CSAs of Tomorrow

Past CSAs relied upon small groups of individuals with convenient access to farms, who prioritized the support of local farms and food above other motives in food procurement. The result was good food for a privileged few, but most would argue that such selectiveness is the intent of the model. Rather, the earliest goals of *community-supported agriculture*, as Steven McFadden points out, were to bring *community* back into the food system while directly *supporting* the economic stability of small-scale farmers in the business of *agriculture*.[34]

Today farmers and community members collaborate to make CSAs more inclusive, accessible, and efficient by positioning them as part of the urban agriculture landscape and embedding them within existing institutions. Changes in federal food policy make that easier now by allowing small growers to accept government vouchers for food assistance, such as Supplemental Nutrition Assistance Program (SNAP) benefits. In addition, food security organizations are partnering with local farmers to move surplus food and donations into the distribution system. These changes offer new opportunities to decrease economic barriers to participation in local food systems and benefit, as farmers can directly market to a wider share of the general public. With such developments, CSAs present a promising venue not only for the distribution of local foods but also for the rebirth of civic agriculture.

Alternative Payment Systems

CSA farmers looking for ways to expand access to their goods and services might consider innovative options for payment, alternative locations, and community-based education. Likely the simplest mechanism a farm can incorporate to increase access is alternative payment options. The drawback to this method is that the farmer does not receive 100 percent of the capital for the CSA before the growing season.

However, an alternative payment scheme could be set up to allow several installments that begin in advance of the first delivery, continue through the height of the season, and end a month or more before the share season ends. Marlett Farm CSA, based on a small, sustainable farm in southern Indiana, offers two payment strategies for its shareholders. In the first option, payment for shares is received in full by March 1 for the season that begins in May. In the second option, payments come in four installments, forty dollars for a half share or eighty dollars for a full share, with the final installment being paid on July 1, six weeks before the end of the summer share season. Only 12.5 percent of the Marlett Farm CSA shareholders actually take advantage of the installment plan, with most paying in full by early March; however, having the installment option means participants with less flexibility to frontload their food costs can still participate.

A Progressive Fee

Another method for expanding low-income participants is through a progressive fee system that subsidizes shares for those who might otherwise not be able to afford to participate. This means, effectively, that those who *can* pay knowingly pay more so that those who *can't* pay less. For example, say a farm had budgeted their ten-week CSA at $160 for a half share that feeds two adults and $320 for a full share that feeds a family. Wanting to offer some shares at subsidized prices might mean raising those prices to $180 for a half share and $360 for a full share. Collecting the equivalent of fifty total full shares at the higher prices means this farm is able to offer an additional twenty-five subscriptions at a price as low as $80 instead of $180. The farm still covers its needs but also invites in more low-income shareholders. In order to be transparent, the farm then publicizes this subsidy program, detailing that $20 from each half share and $40 from each full share is used to assist individuals and families who can demonstrate a financial need. Such a plan may in turn attract full-price participants who highly value the community component of CSA.

Other methods for subsidizing low-income shares include sliding-scale payment systems, in which different subscribers pay different fees based on income; grants and donations from organized programs and generous benefactors; and collaborations with community organizations that help cover the farm's or the subscriber's unpaid costs.[35] In Eugene, Oregon, the Willamette Farm and Food Coalition works with several faith communities and multiple CSAs in order to assist individuals in the payment of their shares.[36]

Other CSAs organize a work-food exchange (also known as working share or volunteering). This kind of arrangement can benefit both customers and farmers. A recent study of West Virginia specialty fruit and vegetable growers found that one of their greatest challenges was finding enough farm labor.[37] This is a particular challenge for specialty crop farms because the labor tends to be more intensive and hands-on. Thus, some CSAs have instituted payment options that allow shareholders to exchange their work on the farm for the payment of their share. Often a farm accepting these arrangements must decide how many people they can use and prioritize applicants by financial need. Homestead Organics Farm Inc. and Gallatin Valley Botanicals, both of Montana, offer opportunities for CSA memberships through a work exchange. Gallatin offers a 50 percent discount for members who volunteer forty-five hours over the course of eighteen weeks, while Homestead offers a full share to participants with enough need and time for labor, effectively allowing an arrangement in which no money changes hands.[38]

Institutional CSAs

Though one of the greatest benefits of CSAs to farmers is the early full payment of CSA shares, a close second is knowing that they have a dedicated group of customers week after week. Recently, private and nonprofit organizations have organized access for their members by developing CSAs through institutional channels. A CSA at the University of Richmond (Virginia) offers one example. In this case, the CSA is organized by the institution, using a variety of farmers from the local area to put together the products the university's participants want. The university provides an established network of potential CSA shareholders, has the accounting system in place to make automatic payroll deductions and payments, and provides a centralized delivery point for the distribution of the weekly shares. The cost of the CSA share is $450, and University of Richmond employees can have the amount automatically deducted from their pay over a fourteen-week period, amounting to just $32.15 per week.[39] Though farmers do not receive a full payment for shares up front, they do know that payments will be regular and reliable.

Alternative Locations and Urban Growing

A major factor limiting participation in CSAs is the location of the pickup and drop-off points. What is convenient for farmers may not always be convenient for customers—particularly for those who live in areas not served by local farms. Much of the time CSAs offer on-the-farm pickup that generally is not on a public transportation line or is reachable only by a time-consuming route. Other times CSAs offer delivery points in suburban or urban areas that are convenient to more affluent clientele. A simple strategy for making CSAs more geographically accessible is by increasing the number of drop-off locations and locating them along public transportation lines.

The Genesee Valley Organic CSA of Rochester, New York, addresses these issues with a modified ride-share system that pairs new members who have transportation limitations with veteran CSA shareholders who have cars. The benefits to this arrangement are several. New members gain assistance with transportation needs. Veteran members can help orient new members to the policies, practices, and culture of a CSA.[40] Ride buddies can share recipes and other knowledge of food culture. Farmers gain a larger pool of subscribers, and finally, the community of local food becomes more diverse.

Educating in and for the CSA

During James's first year running a CSA, he sent out mid-summer evaluations asking for feedback about our produce. Among many favorable responses was one person's comment that he did not like lettuce, spinach, arugula, or, indeed, any spring greens. That customer's preference presented a bit of a problem at a time of year when little else grows in Indiana. Other customers were adamant that they wanted spinach salads with cucumbers or cilantro along with their tomatoes, both combinations presenting significant challenges in a climate that heats up early. These consumers, like many others, were accustomed to the US industrial food system that offers nearly everything most of the time. They had developed a homogenized palate that ignored the nuances of season, culture, and region.

Failing to accommodate local palates can also present a problem. For example, grits and sweet tea are quite common in the South, with stewed greens and shuck beans in central Appalachia, crab cakes in Maryland, and pasties (of the turnip variety) in northern Michigan. When a CSA's offerings diverge from the preferred local menu, customers can become disgruntled.

However, CSAs, and farmers' markets as well, offer a season-long opportunity to educate shoppers. Recipes for cooking and preserving, tips for quick cleaning, and sample home menus can be slipped into customers' or shareholders' baskets. Links to website forums that trade ideas among local consumers and post dates of workdays and potlucks on the farm are easy ways to share knowledge. Customers may welcome some advance notice for how their diet is going to diversify as the season progresses, perhaps beginning with a variety of greens such as spinach, lettuce, and kale; followed by early peas, collards, and kohlrabi; and then a little later by summer squash and zucchini; and winding up with tomatoes and peppers, pumpkins and popcorn. The challenge to making recommendations is that not all people cook, eat, or even enjoy the same items equally. If kohlrabi is apt to generate questions like "What's that alien life form in the refrigerator?" then the farmers' job is to educate potential customers before a season starts and shareholders throughout the long summer.

Many successful, education-oriented vendors and CSAs inform their consumers and shareholders by providing recipes for the week's share items along with common ingredients found in most kitchens. Advice on how to prepare both common and unique items fosters consumer happiness, return business, and positive word-of-mouth advertisement, particularly if a farm provides out-of-the-ordinary items.

Of course, the best-case scenario for increasing demographic diversity and accessibility for any CSA likely includes several of these strategies. The particular arrangements that are desirable will differ for each individual CSA and the population it serves, or could potentially serve. What we do know from the research and our own experience is that the more intentional one is in developing an inclusive CSA, the more likely one is to form a diverse and vibrant community.

In thirty short years, CSAs have become a valued venue in local food systems and a useful tool for economic stability on small farms. But they also have revealed that local food participates in the systemic inequities that pervade American culture. Can CSAs of the future move beyond marketing to fully embrace a role in building a diverse, socially just community? The willingness of CSAs to adopt alternative models for payment, location, and inclusion, and their willingness to share the successes among them, will help them have a significant impact in growing local foods across the landscape—urban, suburban, and rural alike. Redesigned, CSAs can be part of a movement "to extend basic, healthy linkages" across communities in ways that support the public's continued interest in knowing where their food comes from, how it is grown, and how they may engage in restoring both a sense of community and the healthfulness of the food system.[41]

Notes

1. USDA, "Community Supported Agriculture," *USDA National Agricultural Library*, http://www.nal.usda.gov/afsic/pubs/csa/csa.shtml.

2. Wikipedia, "Community-Supported Agriculture," http://en.wikipedia.org/wiki/Community-supported_agriculture.

3. Indian Line Farm, "Community Supported Agriculture at Indian Line Farm," http://www.indianlinefarm.com/csa.html.

4. Steven McFadden, "The History of Community Supported Agriculture, Part I," Rodale Institute, http://rodaleinstitute.org/the-history-of-community-supported-agriculture-part-i.

5. Ibid.

6. Natasha Bowens, "CSA Is Rooted in Black History," *Mother Earth News*, http://www.motherearthnews.com/organic-gardening/csas-rooted-in-black-history-zbcz1502.aspx.

7. Melea Press and Eric Arnould, "How Does Organizational Identification Form?" A Consumer Behavior Perspective," *Journal of Consumer Research* 38 (2011): 650–66.

8. Steven McFadden, *The Call of the Land: An Agrarian Primer for the 21st Century*, 2nd ed. (Bedford, MA: Norlights Press, 2011), 80.

9. Biodynamic Association, "Community Supported Agriculture: An Introduction to CSA," https://www.biodynamics.com/content/community-supported-agriculture-introduction-csa.

10. Evenstar Farm, "What Is a CSA?" http://www.evenstarfarm.net/whatIs.html.

11. Jill Perry and Scott Franzblau, *Local Harvest: A Multiform CSA Handbook* (Signature Book Printing, 2010), http://www.sare.org/Learning-Center/SARE-Project-Products/Northeast-SARE-Project-Products/Local-Harvest.

12. Maple Valley Farm, http://maplevalley.howardfamilyenterprise.com/index.php, November 2, 2016.

13. Farm-to-Consumer Legal Defense Fund, "Raw Milk Nation," http://www.farmtoconsumer.org/raw-milk-nation-interactive-map.

14. Ibid.

15. Groundwork Farms, "Prices and Shares," http://www.groundworkfarms.com/prices-and-share-descriptions.

16. Evening Song Farm Facebook Page, https://www.facebook.com/pages/Evening-Song-Farm/134669806604503.

17. WE Farm closed its website in fall 2015, and this page is no longer available.

18. A notice of WE Farm's closing is available on the webpage, "Last 'Market' Call!!" http://us3.campaign-archive2.com/?u=5675cf88530d6d486fca298bd&id=ec610f7b42. A legacy description of the farm resides at City of Bloomington, "About WE Farm: The Wayne-Egenolf Farm," https://bloomington.in.gov/documents/viewDocument.php?document_id=7437.

19. Laura Beth Egenolf, "Meat Sales and Family," *WE Farm: The Wayne-Egenolf Farm*, http://us3.campaign-archive2.com/?u=5675cf88530d6d486fca298bd&id=8394e67820.

20. North Carolina Cooperative Extension, "Community Supported Agriculture (CSA) Resource Guide for Farmers," http://growingsmallfarms.ces.ncsu.edu/growingsmallfarms-csaguide; Katherine L. Adam, "Community Gardening," ATTRA—National Sustainable Agriculture Information Service, 2011, www.attra.ncat.org/attra-pub/download.php?id=351; K. Brandon Lang, "Expanding Our Understanding of Community Supported Agriculture (CSA): An Examination of Member Satisfaction," *Journal of Sustainable Agriculture* 26, no. 2 (2005): 61–79.

21. Farmer et al., "Agrileisure: Farmers' Markets, CSAs, and the Privilege in Eating Local," *Journal of Leisure Research* 46, no. 3 (2014): 321.

22. Ibid.

23. Farmer et al., "Tale of Four Farmers Markets," 15.

24. United States Census Bureau, "State and County QuickFacts," http://quickfacts.census.gov/qfd/states/00000.html.

25. Thomas Macias, "Working toward a Just, Equitable, and Local Food System: The Social Impact of Community-Based Agriculture," *Social Science Quarterly* 89, no. 5 (2008): 1086–1101.

26. Bureau of Labor Statistics, "Employment Projections," http://www.bls.gov/emp/ep_chart_001.htm.

27. Clare C. Hinrichs, "Embeddedness and Local Food Systems: Notes on Two Types of Direct Agricultural Markets," *Journal of Rural Studies* 16 (2000): 295–303.

28. Laura B. DeLind, "Market Niches, 'Cul de sacs,' and Social Context: Alternative Systems of Food Production," *Culture and Agriculture* 13, no. 47 (1993): 7–12, 8; Hinrichs, "Embeddedness and Local Food Systems," 301.

29. Macais, "Working toward a Just, Equitable, and Local Food System."

30. Julie Guthman, "'If They Only Knew': Color Blindness and Universalism in California Alternative Food," *Professional Geographer* 60, no. 3 (2008): 387–97.

31. Mary E. Thomas, "'I Think It's Just Natural': The Spatiality of Racial Segregation at a US High School," *Environment and Planning* A 37, no. 7 (2005): 1233–48; Arun Saldanha, "Reontologising Race: The Machinic Geography of Phenotype," *Environment and Planning D: Society and Space* 24, no. 1 (2006): 9–24; Richard H. Schein, "Race and Landscape in the United States," in *Landscape and Race in the United States*, edited by Richard H. Schein, 1–21 (New York: Routledge, 2006); Guthman, "'If They Only Knew.'"

32. Community Food Security Coalition, "What Is Community Food Security Coalition?" http://foodsecurity.org/about-us.

33. Clare C. Hinrichs and Kathy S. Kremer, "Social Inclusion in a Midwest Local Food System Project," *Journal of Poverty* 6, no. 1 (2002): 65–90.

34. McFadden, *Call of the Land*.

35. Cristin B. Forbes and Alison H. Harmon, "Buying into Community Supported Agriculture: Strategies for Overcoming Income Barriers," *Journal of Hunger and Environmental Nutrition* 2, no. 2–3 (2008): 65–79.

36. Ibid.; Willamette Farm and Food Coalition, "Finding Local Food: Community Supported Agriculture (CSA) Programs," http://www.lanefood.org/csa-programs.php. Accessed November 27, 2016, https://web.archive.org/web/20160517132632/http://www.lanefood.org/csa-programs.php.

37. James R. Farmer et al., *Overcoming the Market Barriers to Organic Production in West Virginia* (Morgantown, WV: Downstream Strategies, 2013).

38. Forbes and Harmon, "Buying into Community Supported Agriculture."

39. University of Richmond, "Bountiful Benefit: New Benefit Allows Employees to Purchase Local Produce through Payroll Deductions," June 3, 2010,

http://news.richmond.edu/features/article/-/1631/new-benefit-allows
-employees-to-purchase-local-produce-through-payroll-deductions.html.; University of Richmond, "Employee Wellness," http://employeewellness
.richmond.edu.

40. Hunger Action Network of New York State, "Community Supported Agriculture," http://www.hungeractionnys.org/commfood_csa.htm. Accessed November 27, 2016, https://web.archive.org/web/20080703152526/http://www.hungeractionnys.org/commfood_csa.htm.

41. McFadden, "History of Community Supported Agriculture."

FOUR

What's Next in Local Food?

After its genesis with the 1960s back-to-the-landers, the local food movement saw slow evolution during the 1980s followed by vigorous growth beginning in the mid-1990s. This ascendance has transformed it from an alternative sideline to a small but mainline sector of the US food industry. Farmers' markets and CSAs now number about eight thousand and twelve thousand venues respectively. Cooperative groceries are joined by both specialty chains and conventional industry giants in the marketing of local and specialty food. The next wave of innovations will take place in this context of mainstreamed availability, increasingly urbanized populations, more ubiquitous communication technologies, and better popular understanding of food systems. So what does the future of local food look like? How well will it integrate into US culture beyond the cuisine of hipsters and urban foodies? What can we make of the emerging trends?

In 1989 Wendell Berry wrote about the prevailing disconnect between those who eat and those who grow food:

> Most urban shoppers would tell you that food is produced on farms. But most of them do not know what farms, or what kinds of farms, or where the farms are, or what knowledge of skills are involved in farming. They apparently have little doubt that farms will continue to produce, but they do not know how or over what obstacles. For them, then, food is pretty much an abstract idea—something they do not know or imagine—until it appears on the grocery shelf or on the table.[1]

This is the kind of disconnect, however, that the local movement is poised to bridge. By more precisely defining the theater of their food sourcing, people can more readily observe, assess, and redirect the impact of their choices. A couple of decades after Berry's comment was made, the origins and provenance of food have become important to many households, wholesalers, distributors, retailers, schools, and other food institutions. Indeed, "locally sourced meats and sea-food" and "locally grown produce" occupy the number one and two positions in the results of the 2015 "What's Hot" survey that the National Restaurant Association distributes to chefs across the United States. The related terms "environmental sustainability," "hyper-local sourcing," and "farm/estate branded items" help fill out the top ten. Although "local" remains far from capturing a major percentage of total sales, one definition of mainstream, it is now a growing part of the public conversation, acting as a catalyst for "causes as diverse as health, nutrition, and life-style, social justice and food security, land preservation, environmental conservation, community and economic development, and urban greening."[2] This popularity has prompted innovations that expand the movement in terms of who it reaches, the experiences available to them, and the services provided.

Technology

The growth and reach of local food movements have been facilitated since the mid-1990s by the internet. Its utility for community building, marketing and sales, and collective activity has enabled wide promotion of the locations, offerings, and value of farmers' markets and CSAs. It has generally helped elevate food issues in the popular consciousness by making it easy to spread emerging, upstart, and dissenting information. Because of the internet, scientific findings, food safety and contamination news, and even anecdotal evidence no longer rely on centralized news services. Although other factors are clearly in play, figure 4.1 shows that farmers' markets and adult use of the internet have grown at similar trajectories, and a similar correspondence would be expected with CSAs, which numbered only two in 1986 and today range from seventy-eight hundred to twelve thousand, depending on whose count.

Back-to-the-land may sound Luddite, but certain kinds of technology and innovation figure large in today's movement. Successful small farmers today seem to use technology in ways that allow them to balance a rough equation that accounts for labor, productivity, value of product, and lifestyle. Thus, they may value the hands-on, intensive

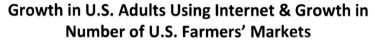

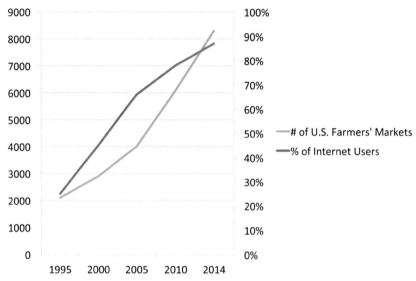

Figure 4.1. Growth in farmers' markets and internet use throughout the United States, 1995–2014. *Graph by James R. Farmer*

connection allowed by a walk-behind tractor but turn to the internet to research greenhouse designs or to learn how to combat buffalo gnats. They may run their own electrical lines and butcher their own chickens but also use the internet to submit USDA grant applications and crowd-source funding to start a school field-trip program. CSA farmers can carve out more time to enjoy country life by using Facebook or a blog to simplify outreach, offering enticing photographs and keeping its shareholders up-to-date on what is in season, alongside a website that can streamline recordkeeping with posted policies, sign-up forms, and payment functions.

Online farmers' markets and ordering systems assist farmers with marketing and planning, including indicating quantities and varieties to plant. Social networking sites like Facebook and Instagram allow for word to spread about produce pickup locations, a new CSA, a favorite band playing at a farmers' market, and mouthwatering "food porn" pictures. Less sexy information can be accessed, too, about new farm co-ops, greenhouse designs, grant opportunities, and outlets for specialty inputs such as heirloom seeds and honey bee starter kits. What was once insider knowledge that was passed down through families, neighbors, and formalized agricultural education programs is now widely available to any new, beginning, and want-to-be farmers.

Specialized applications for handheld devices, such as smartphones and tablets, have become information points for direct, locally produced food. Farmers and customers, both, can use these systems to spread the word. The app Farmstand, for example, uses a social media platform to "connect every community with locally grown food" and "make YOU the hero of your local farmers' market."[3] It maps over eighty-five hundred farmers' markets across the United States, providing pertinent details about their months of operation, hours, proximity, and offerings. Farmstand users can extend their local experience by finding markets when they are away on vacation or business trips. One Apple App Store reviewer called Farmstand "Facebook for farmers' markets." Users "can satisfy your inner Instagram lover by sharing photos, recipes and thoughts with other users and browsing their favorite produce."[4] Although the social component of Farmstand is still geographically uneven, patrons of some markets do post about favorite baked goods (think lemon squares), creative displays (bedding plants in the boot of a VW beetle), availability ("Got a hankering for jam/preserves? Go to here . . . go to here now!"), and showy offerings (colorful mixed greens). The app is also able to link with other social media platforms, including Twitter, Facebook, and Google+, and offers a blog. Several other apps are available that perform similar functions, including Fresh Food Finder, Harvest, Seasons, and Locavore.

Distribution software, too, has emerged to assist farmers and food hubs in getting products to market. Local Food Marketplace was originally developed for Eugene Local Foods, an Oregon food hub, in order to support sales and distribution planning and facilitation for food hubs selling retail and wholesale. According to Michael Morrow of the Hoosier Harvest Market in Greenfield, Indiana, the software allows farmers to log their available products on a weekly basis, which customers can then purchase online for a Thursday pickup or delivery. Such systems make obvious contributions to farmers' options for distribution and consumer opportunities for procuring local food, but they also reduce the farmer-consumer connection facilitated by more direct venues.

Another key development in electronic technology that propels the growth of local food is electronic banking. Until recently, the financial and logistical costs of accepting credit or debit cards by small-scale operations was prohibitive. However, the advent of mobile payment mechanisms for handheld devices allows farmers to take advantage of the cashless economy and tech-savvy culture. Producers can choose from multiple online transaction options, including Square and Intuit GoPayment. Among other fees, Square charges 2.75 percent plus fifteen cents per swipe or 3.5 percent and fifteen cents per keyed transaction while Intuit GoPayment charges 1.7 percent plus thirty cents per swiped transaction and 2.7 percent plus thirty cents per keyed transaction.[5] Although these charges either cut into a grower's profits or raise her prices, the possibility of ready money means customers may be willing to spend more. Research by Kallina Gallardo and her colleagues (2015) found that producers selling at farmers' markets reported a 35 percent increase in sales as a result of being able to process electronic banking transactions.[6] In addition, 42 percent of farmers' market customers they interviewed noted they would buy more because electronic payments were accepted. A quick walk through many farmers' markets reveals that growers are indeed investing in this kind of mobile technology in order to facilitate customer spending. One maple syrup vendor reports that customers who are short on cash for a single jar may instead buy an entire case after learning they can use a credit card.

Electronic banking transactions have become so ubiquitous that the US government now uses debit cards for SNAP, and those can in turn be accepted by farmers' markets and their vendors, after a registration process. The federal Farmers' Market Nutrition Program is an application of SNAP that allows for the use of Women Infants and Children (WIC) as well as the Commodity Supplemental Food Program (CSFP) for low-income seniors at farmers' markets. This infra-

Figure 4.2. Farmers at Sobremesa Farm, in Monroe County, Indiana, extend the season in their USDA-NRCS-EQIP-funded high tunnel. *Photograph by Robert Frew and Juan Carlos Arango*

structure has increased farmers' market participation among low-income individuals and partially relieves cost barriers to eating locally. According to the USDA Agricultural Marketing Services, this service had good early success that left room for significant growth: "Between fiscal years 2008 and 2009, for example, the total value of SNAP redemptions at farmers markets and farm stands nearly doubled, from over $2 million to over $4 million. . . . Of more than 193,000 retailers participating in SNAP in 2009, only one-half of 1 percent, or just over 900, were farmers markets or farm stands, even though the number of farmers markets in the United States exceeded 5,200 in that year."[7] By 2014, SNAP redemptions at farmers' markets exceeded $16.6 million.[8] Such growth will likely continue as individuals and markets invest in the infrastructure, such as wifi points and vendor information sessions that make possible the use of SNAP benefits and other electronic transactions.

Seasonality

While the local foods movement in most of the United States has been relegated to seasonal markets—specifically spring, summer, and fall—some venues now run year-round. This is a promising new trend related to both technology and know-how. Many food consumers might expect that local foods available in the winter would consist of an abridged list of root vegetables, brassicas, meat and dairy products, and eggs; however, supplies in the fringe and winter months is expanding. Between 2009–2011, the US saw a 17 percent growth in winter farmers' markets.[9] According to Larry Jones, an Indianapolis landlord who rented a commercial space to the Indy Winter Market, four hundred people showed up the first day the market opened. The second year, over one thousand customers attended the market on a weekly basis.[10] Such growth is typical nationwide. By December 2012, the USDA counted more than eighteen hundred winter markets running, nearly 24 percent of the total count of US farmers' markets that year.[11]

Such growth in winter markets is supported by the increased use of unheated high tunnels and greenhouses.[12] A high tunnel is an unheated, plastic-covered structure for growing plants, distinct from a low tunnel (a cover over a single row) or a heated greenhouse. The low-cost structure blocks wind and rain and buffers low temperatures.[13] Some tunnels are designed to withstand winter conditions and might be used all year; others are not, and the plastic covering is removed for the winter. Growers can extend the season in a high tunnel, leading to earlier, later, and more frequent harvests, thereby producing more vegetable crops year-round.[14] Nationally, ten thousand farms enjoy new high tunnels thanks to a cost-share program by the USDA through the Natural Resources Conservation Service (NRCS) Environmental Quality Incentives Program (EQIP).[15] In addition to these investments from the USDA, growers have personally invested significant amounts in high tunnels. There are examples of high tunnels making a pivotal difference in farms' ability to diversify. In these cases, high tunnels make possible a new abundance that in turn creates new markets for specialty crops. One such example comes from an Illinois NRCS district conservationist, who observed exactly this success with high tunnels in southern Illinois:

> A high tunnel is tiny in the grand scheme, but it has a big impact on how you run your farm. The USDA-NRCS helped 23 farms get high tunnels established. . . . Because of that help, there is now local, fresh food in months that it had not been available. Directly because of that, producers started a winter market in Carbondale. You had all these farmers with produce to sell—extra months that they could sell their product at a premium price. This was a neat thing to watch, especially in an economically depressed area where you really saw the impact. This was able to develop because of high tunnels.[16]

In addition to products available year-round, such as eggs, honey, dairy, and meats, and season-extended products that high tunnels allow, such as early tomatoes and late spinach, off-season local foods frequently feature products that have "value added." Dried-flower wreaths, jams and preserves, handmade paper, soup mixes, goat milk soap, beeswax candles, dried-fruit pies, and so on require more work and sometimes more ingredients than can be provided from any one farm but also are expected to sell at a higher price than less processed farm goods. As local meat finds greater demand, preserved meats and dairy, too, are appearing in off-season markets and CSAs. However, the increased demand for meat "is not necessarily being met due to supply chain issues—such as bottlenecks at processing, seasonality, and whole-animal utilization—in the local meat industry in general. The extent of the demand for local meat and consumer purchasing patterns remains largely unknown and requires considerably more research."[17]

Common Ground

The redistribution of land in cities from private to public assets and from developed to agricultural uses represents a major shift that reverses much of the resource management practice that has dominated the United States since the mid-nineteenth century. It reclaims blighted areas, such as brownfields, empty lots, and parking lots, for the collective good and fuels speculation about how much of their own food cities can provide.[18] Urban agriculture is transforming thousands of acres across urban areas found in cities such as Detroit, Milwaukee, Chicago, Baltimore, and those throughout northern Ohio, as well as elsewhere around the world, including Montreal, Canberra, and the Cape Town metropolitan areas.[19] As we write, the 2018 Farm Bill proposed to the US Congress contains a provision to make urban farming eligible for federal funding and other supports for the first time. Meanwhile, many rural growers struggle to access farmland without a family inheritance. In both kinds of location, we detect a reemergence of the notion of an agricultural commons.

Historically, a "commons" was an area that no single person owned but many had use of and responsibility for. Unlanded farmers would utilize the commons for grazing and cultivation purposes. They did not own the land itself, but worked it with responsibility for its continuing vitality nonetheless. Likewise, fishers harvest from the common fisheries of the sea, with an implicit responsibility to maintain sufficient stock and conditions for common use in the future. However, depletive extraction of resources from the commons is prevalent where respect, forethought, and communication for common good is not culturally significant or as legally robust. For example, if farmers in the arid mountain West are draining rivers and aquifers to irrigate hay fields, a "common pool resource" (water, in this case) is depleted by some at a detriment to others (downstream farmers, homeowners, recreationists, wildlife, etc.).

Interestingly, a farming commons appears to be regaining currency recently in the American agrarian scene. Access to farmland has long been a major constraint for beginning farmers and those seeking to expand their operations.[20] The most common acquisition mechanism for farmland is through inheritance, the family farm being passed from generation to generation. However, many new and beginning farmers, particularly those engaging in sustainable agriculture, are first-generation farmers who have no familial tie to land.[21] Small-scale farms selling locally, which often specialize in fresh foods, benefit from being located close to developed areas, because proximity to the customer base maximizes distribution potential and product freshness. Consequently, these farms are commonly located in areas prone to development and are therefore particularly vulnerable to development-driven elevation in land prices.[22] The cost of land makes farming-the-commons programs vitally important for increasing the number of US farmers and enhancing a community's food security.

Today people are creating more arrangements to link farmers to land in ways that fall outside of the usual scope of private owner-ship. Cooperative arrangements may depend on people pooling their money to purchase property together. Share-based models for coop-erative property are being piloted and are emerging, sometimes with CSAs and farms incorporated into them. Some models are improvised and some are codified with extensive legal apparatus. Some of the lon-gest-lasting cooperative arrangements from the 1970s have relied on contiguous rather than co-owned properties—those purchased with pooled funds and subsequently legally divided and deeded to differ-ent owners, sometimes with additional acres owned in common. This balance of separate and self-determining simultaneous with proximal and cooperative arrangements can form a core around which addi-tional purchases by like-minded people can congregate and consoli-date resources.[23]

In addition, arrangements stewarded by land trusts and managed by municipal park and recreation departments and community gardens and orchards are also emerging on donated and public land. Beyond preserving disappearing farmland and wildlife habitats, land trusts have opened some of the property they own outright to community gardeners and local farmers. For example, the Trust for Public Land purchased sixty-four community gardens in New York City that were going to be auctioned to private investors (possibly for development). These properties are now protected from development, and thirty-two of the parcels have been transferred to other like-minded groups, such as the Brooklyn-Queens Land Trust, after four million dollars in im-provements.[24] Other land trusts, too, are becoming directly involved in local food. In Maine, for example, the Brunswick-Topsham Land Trust and the Kennebec Estuary Land Trust have developed a "strong regional partnership to enhance the local food economy, raise aware-ness of the benefits of local food, and increase farmland conservation in the southern Midcoast region" of the state. Their goals are to (1) conserve farmland, (2) organize educational events on local food, (3) assess the need for a food hub, (4) assist local farmers' markets, (5) provide educational information to farmers and the public, and (6) market local food.[25]

Similarly, community gardens and orchards being established in and around cities offer common space to individuals who wish to grow but do not have access to land nor desire farming to be their vocation. Notably, some farmers' market vendors get their start on community garden lots. With roots in the "vacant lot cultivation associations" of the late 1800s, community gardens rose through the "children's school garden movement" (1890s–1920s), "civic gardening campaigns" (1890s–1920s), "War Gardens" (1917–1919), "depression-era gardens" (1931–1935), "victory gardens" (1941–1945), "community gardens" of the 1970s, and today's urban community gardens.[26] Today the American Community Gardening Association estimates that there are over eighteen thousand community gardens throughout the United States and Canada.[27] As described by Luke Drake and Laura Lawson, community gardens in North America generally fit into one of three models: individual plots in a communally maintained space, a large area that is gardened collectively, or a mixed design that has both individual plots and shared space.[28] The pursuit of a variety of goals lead to the development of community gardens, including the desire to acquire food and additional income or develop skills, cultural expression, recreation, relaxation, social interaction, and activism.[29] A 2009 report by the USDA Economic Service identified that of the forty-three million American households growing their own food, nearly one million were growing in community gardens.[30]

Community orchards, though less frequently found, are also increasing rapidly in numbers. Community orchards are those that are managed by a community of people for the community—not for private profit.[31] A major distinction between community gardens and orchards is the term commitment of the projects. While community gardens in essence are annual in nature, community orchards are perennial, long-term commitments thus requiring a far-sighted perspective on property availability, site selection, training, and care. Community gardens are typically plots of public ground leased annually, with the fruits of that plot going to the lessee. On the other hand, community orchards are long-term collective enterprises with the fruits of the orchard going to the community or participating volunteers.

Community orchards began in the early 1990s in England with citizens, municipalities, and civic groups working to rescue abandoned orchards that were at risk from neglect and development.[32] The English orchards are often times leased from private landowners. Alternatively, the US model generally includes the planting of orchards on public land, making them open to full public access. Municipal park and recreation departments are common collaborators with community members for orchard initiatives, along with granting agencies that help underwrite the costs of these community initiatives. As of 2013, there were thirty-seven urban orchard initiatives, with 73 percent of them being founded in 2007 or thereafter.[33] The vast majority of these initiatives, according to Kyle Clark and Kimberly Nicholas, focused on the planting and harvesting of tree fruit, while others are geared toward mapping "publicly accessible fruit trees."[34]

One such agency is the Fruit Tree Planting Foundation (FTPF) of Pittsburgh, Pennsylvania. FTPF is a nonprofit charity with a mission "to plant and help others plant a collective total of 18 billion fruit trees across the world (approximately 3 for every person alive) and encourage their growth under organic standards."[35] They support programs to plant trees at public schools, in city and community gardens, in low-income neighborhoods and international hunger relief locations, on Native American reservations, at health centers, and within animal sanctuaries. Other foundations that support the planting of community orchards include the Orchard Foundation and Project Orange Thumb.

In addition to the food harvested and gleaned from community gardens and orchards, environmental and social benefits abound. Areas that were once overgrown noxious weed patches or rubble fields are now being converted into spaces that support biodiversity, sequester carbon, help control water flowage into urban drainage systems, and support pollinators in urban environments. Community is being built alongside this construction of the garden or orchard. In such places, several beneficial outcomes have emerged from those involved in community gardening projects. Scholars have found that community gardens build denser networks of relations than would normally exist, while the setting builds social capital and performs as a commons.[36] In a study of community gardeners in the Greater St. Louis region, Kimberly Shinew and her colleagues found that both black and white gardeners tended to agree that "community gardening brings together people who wouldn't normally socialize together."[37] Furthermore, these spaces provide the opportunity to improve access to healthy food options, educate the participants on important public health issues, provide appropriate cultural learning, and strengthen a community's social capital.[38]

During the nineteenth and twentieth centuries, the United States transitioned from a commons approach in food production to one focused on private property rights and individual or corporate ownership. Today 65 percent of land in the forty-eight contiguous United States is privately owned, with the greatest concentration in the eastern half of the country and in and around cities.[39] Large-scale commons efforts are sparse. Yet as Americans have migrated from the farms and countryside to suburban and urban settings, the need for communally held and accessible land has grown. Today, with more than 80 percent of the US population living in cities, social movements for just, healthy, and sustainable foods; concerns about food contamination and recalls; and the desire for better control over food sources have urged a return to food production in the commons. In response, land trusts are increasingly making their protected fields available to farmers, while park and recreation departments and other municipal agencies are again entrusting public lands to the public for the cultivation of food. The commons are again being used in a manner most similar to methods still found in developing countries or as seen in the United States and Great Britain a century or more ago.

Urban Agriculture

While the idealized farm may consist of rolling pastures with meandering cattle, an old red barn, fields of waving grain, and orchards capping the ridges, farming is increasingly cropping up between high-rise buildings, on old brownfields, and in abandoned lots where classic arts-and-crafts-style homes once stood. Urban agriculture includes the acts of cultivating/producing, processing, and distributing food in or immediately around cities, towns, and villages.[40] According to the Urban Agriculture Network, its namesake is

> an industry that produces, processes, and markets food, fuel, and other outputs, largely in response to the daily demand of consumers within a town, city, or metropolis, on many types of privately and publicly held land and water bodies found throughout intra-urban and peri-urban areas. Typically urban agriculture applies intensive production methods, frequently using and reusing natural resources and urban wastes, to yield a diverse array of land-, water-, and air-based fauna and flora, contributing to the food security, health, livelihood, and environment of the individual, household, and community.[41]

Importantly, urban agriculture in the United Sates is not just about food. Rather, it emerges from a nexus of food, social change, and economic movements occurring in cities. From it emerge substantial sustainability benefits that enhance goods and services provided by the ecosystem. These benefits include a smaller carbon footprint for food, improved air quality, water filtration and runoff control, a cleaner and an enhanced urban environment, and, thus, better human health. According to Rich Pirog of the Leopold Center for Sustainable Agriculture, the typical American meal contains ingredients from about five different countries, not including the United States.[42] The same study found that, on average, local apples were transported only 61 miles, while the conventional equivalents were being delivered from 1,726 miles away. This change in distance means that food produced and consumed locally requires from four to seventeen times less fuel for shipping than conventional produce. In addition to lowering food miles, urban agriculture promotes improved carbon sequestration in plants and soil; improves hydrology by directing water from streets and storm sewers to capture systems and urban "fields"; promotes the absorption of ozone and particulates by plants, especially trees; decontaminates soils; and provides buffers that reduce noise pollution. Scaled up for the size of the population in urban areas, growing and consuming locally can quickly add up to substantial reductions in environmental impacts and offer an assortment of ecosystem services to compensate for other deleterious effects resulting from city life.

Social benefits also accrue from the urban agriculture movement. As in many environments, marginalized urban populations often face increased barriers to healthy food. Agriculture in cities is now being used as a social program to enhance food security and the sovereignty of urban dwellers through community based food distribution outlets, garden spaces for community members, neighborhood networking, and small business development. Alison Hope Alkon describes a survey of the West Oakland and North Berkeley farmers' markets that shows that about a third of all those surveyed indicated they see friends and neighbors at the market during nearly every visit.[43] Other scholars have found similar results, with nearly 100 percent of respondents to a twelve-market Indiana study indicating they have friends, family members, or neighbors who also shop at the market.[44] Important outcomes of this shared experience in this public space are community building and the development of social capital, which can be defined as "the relationships and networks that create the trust that undergirds civil society."[45] Research in New Orleans found that a city market there encouraged the development of social capital through (1) a shopping experience that provides transactions with a social component, (2) an environment where both vendors and customers feel a sense of community, and (3) an opportunity where a positive relationship between the market and the community is being developed.[46]

Some land for urban farms comes by way of owners who effectively release its use to the community, perhaps without titles, leases, or guarantees. When property prices rise or neighborhoods rebound, the owners may decide that a different use is more in their interest. It is not uncommon for urban growers to find that the land they have tended has been rezoned, put up for sale, or otherwise repurposed. While urban agriculture may not be a panacea to food security issues, it can be a powerful part of the solution to creating healthy, nutritious food options while also enhancing a sense of community.[47]

Agritourism

The past decade has also seen substantial growth in agritourism. In contrast to agrileisure, by which participants take pleasure and renewal through mundane experiences (see chapter 1), agritourism locates an opportunity for an exceptional experience on a working farm, ranch, orchard, or other agricultural venture. Agritourism benefits growers by allowing them to

- · diversify revenue sources,
- · establish alternative marketing outlets,
- · generate price premiums for farm products,
- · capitalize on the aesthetic value of agricultural land, and
- · share their passion, knowledge, and experience with others.[48]

Only a grower's creativity and tolerance (not all are interested!) limit the options for an agritourism enterprise, which include u-pick produce, wineries, produce stands and markets, farm stays, bed-and-breakfasts, corn mazes, pumpkin patches, school tours, farm weddings, and showcase festivals (think freshwater prawns, wine, maple syrup, horseradish, or garlic).

The 2007 USDA Agricultural Census found that more than 23,000 farms offered agritourism and recreation services valued at over $566 million. That grew by 2012 to over $700 million from about 34,500 farms.[49] Nearly 15 percent of those farms grossed more than $25,000 in sales related to the agritourism operation.[50] In North Carolina, for example, the number of farms operating agritourism enterprises grew by 82 percent between 2007 and 2012, a 843 percent increase in revenue.[51] Virginia saw a similar increase in trends during the same period, with revenues rising by 468 percent. Clearly, a concerted effort to build agritourism as a popular pursuit for customers will also help farms achieve economic stability through diversification. Moreover, tourism has the potential to educate the public and certainly increases the contact between the people and places of food in ways that can foster ongoing relationships.

Food Hubs

Given the current demand for local food, farmers have an unprecedented opportunity to scale up supply, and many of them have innovated accordingly. However, many obstacles still exist to increasing output, the production capacity of farms selling locally tends to be low, and many local farmers want to maintain direct-to-consumer sales networks and pragmatically sustainable operations. At the same time, the volume and consistency that wholesalers and other large clients—such as restaurants, grocers, schools, and hospitals—expect are unattainable for most small-scale farmers, especially new ones. However, new sales arrangements are emerging that can preserve the integrity of the diversified small farm while also increasing their economic viability. Aggregation points, cooperative processing, institutional buying, food hubs, and produce auctions are some of the important new distribution venues that will make local a viable food source for greater numbers of people. In addition, some farms participate in gleaning programs by which food banks and relief agencies conduct a final, free harvest from fields or orchards after the farmer is finished with them. All of these efforts represent the next phase of the movement, beyond farmers' markets and CSAs.

Our 2015 survey of farmers in south-central Indiana sought to identify individuals with an interest in aggregating crops for sales and distribution to local grocers, restaurants, and social service agencies serving marginalized populations. Among the farmer respondents, 36 percent indicated they wanted to expand or initiate direct sales to restaurants; however, only 4 percent indicated any interest in selling to a wholesaler such as a food hub or other type of commercial enterprise. This sort of disconnect—wanting to sell more but resisting aggregation and the lower prices it entails—hinges on the conception of what small farmers believe is viable for them: direct relationships with customers, diversification, and sales appropriate to their values and lifestyle. Nearly 80 percent of those surveyed noted they choose direct-to-consumer distribution venues because they are most appropriate for the scale/size of their farm. Still, a small but growing segment of local farmers shows interest in increasing their production in order to supply institutions.[52]

One option to handle such growth is food hubs. Food hubs offer an alternative aggregation point to auctions and can better serve some growers and customers. Historically, food hubs have been a means for small and midsize farmers to aggregate or process their offerings in large enough quantities to serve institutional buyers, restaurants,

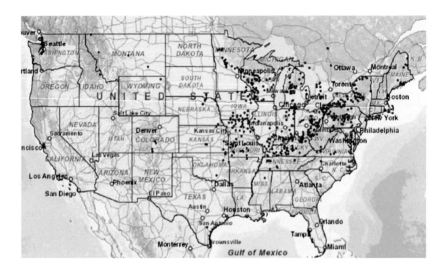

Figure 4.3. Map of current Amish settlements in the United States and Canada (as of May 31, 2015). *Map by Joseph Donnermeyer*

and wholesalers, but their prominence became sidelined during the scaling up of big agriculture during the latter half of the twentieth century. The USDA's definition of a food hub emphasizes qualities of local food that both growers and customers value, including account-ability, relationship, and regionalism: a hub "actively manages the ag-gregation, distribution and marketing of source-identified food prod-ucts primarily from local and regional producers to strengthen their ability to satisfy wholesale, retail, and institutional demand."[53] The USDA counts about three hundred hubs nationwide, with the vast ma-jority catering to farmers with annual sales under five hundred thou-sand dollars.[54] Food hubs provide critical infrastructure by distributing and marketing products to the mainstream and also by providing ser-vices such as consumer education and post-harvesting management.

Three business models dominate food hubs: for-profit privately held entities (40 percent), nonprofit businesses (30 percent), and cooper-atively owned enterprises (20 percent).[55] They may cater to individual customers, businesses, and institutions, or a mix of all three.

Model 1: Direct-to-Consumer Sales

The Wild Ramp in Huntington, West Virginia, opened its doors on July 12, 2012. A nonprofit organization, it relies on fourteen volunteers to fulfill its mission of operating "a year-round community-supported market that provides a viable economic outlet for local food producers while providing consumers access to locally grown agricultural products."[56] The Wild Ramp emerged from the collective action of a concerned and food-minded group wanting to support local farmers, acquire local food, and help foster a more sustainable community. Today the Wild Ramp provides twenty-five hundred square feet for local food sales and public educational programs on cooking, gardening, and environmental sustainability. In addition, community events foster relations between farmers and the general public. After a year the Wild Ramp moved to its current location in Central City, Huntington, adjacent to the daily retail farmers' market. In a city of less than fifty thousand, the Wild Ramp sold over six hundred thousand dollars of agricultural produce and artisanal goods on consignment between its opening in July 2012 and October 2014. Farmers receive 90 percent of the sale price they have predetermined for the fruits, vegetables, cheeses, meats, and other items, while the other 10 percent funds three paid employees. Over five hundred volunteer hours per month are also contributed by community members and farmers.

Model 2: Institutional Sales

Local Food Hub, in Charlottesville, Virginia, "partners with Virginia farmers to increase community access to local food" while providing support services, infrastructure, and market opportunities. Focusing on small farms, Local Food Hub connects local farms and farmers to retailers, restaurants, schools, and other institutions in order to directly distribute high-quality, fresh local food as a healthier alternative. They source from more than seventy farmers who are within one hundred miles of Charlottesville, with farms from one hundred to less than five acres in size. Some of the farms have organic certification, while others are practicing organic or conventional growing methods. Different from the Wild Ramp, Local Food Hub buys from farmers outright (at nearly $940,000 in 2014) and then sells to various institutional types. In 2014 Local Food Hub sold predominantly to retailers, restaurants, caterers, distributors, institutions of higher education, buying clubs, schools, and universities; however, their nonprofit and community-focused model allowed for 65 percent of their revenue generation to come from individual donations, grants, and special event fundraisers, while 27 percent came from product sales.[57]

Model 3: Hybrid Sales

The Iowa Food Hub in West Union, Iowa, caters to both individuals and institutions. Similar to the other hubs profiled, the Iowa Food Hub takes on the dual purpose of selling food and educating the community. "Working to connect farmers, families, and food grown close to home," Iowa Food Hub sources food within a 150-mile radius for wholesale, retail, and institutional demand.[58] Focusing on small to medium-size farms, the Iowa Food Hub works to enhance food access and equality, the development of local economies and job creation and retention, success of both beginning and established farmers, and food system research and education. The Iowa Food Hub hosts five primary activities, including their Food Box Program (much like an online farmers' market); delivery services for hire; new market development and research that focuses on schools, institutional buyers, and grocery stores; farm-to-school programs; and local food procurement and sales.

The common qualities of these three food hubs underscore their dual-purpose missions of food aggregation and distribution in conjunction with education and outreach. They directly benefit farmers and consumers with much-needed infrastructure to support the role of local foods in the redevelopment of the food system. In addition, their outreach and service efforts educate the community to build capacity for new foodways, developing the public's receptivity to food options, health and nutrition, and locally based economies.

Plain Communities and Community Produce Auctions

Traveling across parts of New York, Pennsylvania, Ohio, Indiana, Michigan, and twenty-three other states and the province of Ontario, one can happen upon thriving Amish communities whose numbers have more than doubled to a quarter million people since 1991.[59] These communities underpin their farms, families, sense of self, and community resilience with a lifestyle that harkens back to the old world but thrives in the twenty-first century. Their continuing focus on farming has led Amish communities to develop produce auctions throughout the Midwest as a means for aggregating and distributing their farming products and handcrafted goods. These auctions serve as a model for future development of the broader local food movement.

For example, the Davies County Produce Auction in southwestern Indiana operates at least three times each week during the height of the growing season. The morning starts with Amish farmers driving single-horse wagons to market with their ripe produce. They are joined by trucks and trailers with bins of cantaloupe, pallets of sweet corn, and cases of cucumbers, tomatoes, and broccoli. Buyers from roadside stands, food wholesalers, and restaurants dominate sales, with an occasional urban foodie or rural octogenarian making an appearance to satisfy a personal taste for farm-fresh food. Members of the Amish community run the Davies County Auction, with a cooperatively organized group of thirteen farmers and businessmen at the helm. According to the manager, the majority of auction buyers are farm-stand operators buying such quantities as 50–250 dozen ears of sweet corn, 400 pounds of tomatoes, or several dozen bushels of green beans. Other buyers resell the produce at area markets, and mom-and-pop-style restaurants also sometimes shop there.

A study of nine Pennsylvania produce auctions in Amish country shows that the main goals for these auctions are to provide quality produce to consumers while supporting the local community through profit making.[60] The research found that these auctions typically offer sweet corn, cantaloupe, watermelon, tomatoes, and pumpkins, as well as some specialized crops like asparagus and onions. They em-

ploy seven to ten people during the season and gross approximately
three and a half million dollars per auction. As with the Indiana auction, most of the buyers are roadside stand operators (40 percent), other
farmers (possibly to sell at their roadside stand) (27 percent), chain and
independent grocers (27 percent), and restaurants (6 percent) with the
occasional individual shoppers buying far smaller quantities. These
auctions, according to researchers Stephan Tubene and James Hanson,
appeal as "convenient shopping centers for sellers and buyers . . . of
fresh and locally grown produce not found in traditional wholesale
terminal markets; and by allowing exchange and networking among
farmers and buyers."

The possibility of expanding these auctions to more heterogeneous
groups has strong possibilities but must be considered in their full context. The University of Kentucky Extension Service details the risks
and benefits for selling at produce auctions.[61] Primary risks include
the price uncertainty that is inherent in an auction, along with the effects on price of procuring a critical mass of buyers and oversupply of
particular products. Benefits, on the other hand, include set days and
times, aggregation that draws large-quantity buyers, and a venue for
test-marketing varieties and lot sizes. In addition, this study found that
a third of Kentucky growers selling at auction sold 75 percent of what
they brought. Successful produce auctions, like farmers' markets and
multi-farm CSAs, require cooperation and community commitment
to make them viable options for growers.[62]

Emergency Relief

Farmers have long been recognized as important players in food
security. As early as 1917, Governor Joseph A. A. Burnquist of Minnesota remarked:

> Let the Minnesota slogan become "A Garden for Every Home." Let
> every loyal citizen become self-sustaining in food supply as far as
> possible, in order that out of Minnesota's surplus, means may be
> found for helping to feed a hungry world in the months to come.
> The army of food producers has quite as great an opportunity for
> national service as the army that goes to the front. The American
> people must this year feed not only themselves, but also millions of

dependents in other parts of the world. Special attention should be given to crops that may be canned, preserved, or dried. Cooperative purchase or purchase by municipalities of machinery for food preservation is recommended.[63]

Today, US farmers frequently work with community agencies that address food relief through gleaning programs, extra plantings, and farm-to-pantry efforts. For example, the state of Maine's "Mainers Feeding Mainers" program, facilitated by Good Shepherd Food Bank, has provided four million of pounds of Maine-grown food to residents since 2010. Toward their goal of getting "fresh and nutritionally balanced Maine-harvested food to Maine families in need," Good Shepherd contracts and purchases from nineteen local farmers who distribute directly to local food pantries while fourteen farmers distribute through the organization's warehouses.[64]

In southern Indiana, the Hoosier Hills Food Bank encourages farmers, and even home gardeners, to "plant a row for the hungry" to help increase the supply of local fresh fruits and vegetables flowing into the food pantry. The assumption is that just a little bit of extra work and expense can make a big difference to those in need. Hoosier Hills also works a gleaning program, in which food bank volunteers visit local farms after harvest to retrieve blemished produce that is otherwise nutritious and flavorful but would be left to waste. Over eighty volunteers worked with six different farms in 2014 to glean 150,000 pounds of fresh food. Additionally, Hoosier Hills, like other food banks, takes a truck to the farmers' market to collect unsold firsts at the end of each market day. The donated crates of cucumbers, heads of lettuce, baskets of zucchini, and so on ease food emergencies, reduce waste, and save farmer labor by providing an alternative to composting otherwise nutritious and desirable products. In 2014 the Hoosier Hills Food Bank collected 41,261 pounds of food from Bloomington market growers and patrons plus another 4,360 pounds from other sources, like Plant a Row.[65] Even a small market can make an important difference, however. At the Mercer Island Farmers' Market in Washington State, for example, the food bank collected over 2,000 pounds of donations that went on directly to support two area food relief agencies.[66]

CSAs, too, have taken steps to increase access to local food by low-income families. City Fresh in Cleveland specializes in low-income CSA shareholders. It works with twenty small farmers located within seventy miles of Cleveland to provide healthy in-season fruits, vegetables, grains, and value-added products to its more than six hundred weekly members. Different from most CSAs, City Fresh offers payment plans on a weekly basis instead of a full season at a time, limited income discounts, and fifteen different pickup locations. All of these features are designed to accommodate low-income participants. Meanwhile, City Fresh reports that eighty-one cents of every dollar goes directly back to the farmers, the remaining nineteen cents covering overhead costs. City Fresh's total return to farmers in 2014 was $115,000.[67] Following on City Fresh's success, Louisville-based Fresh Stops focuses on getting fresh local food into low-income urban neighborhoods. Its signature innovation involves having "families pool their money and SNAP benefits to purchase in bulk from local farmers on a sliding scale. Each family receives a 'share' of seasonal produce which feeds 2–4 people."[68] Today Fresh Stop offers nine locations across the Louisville metro area, working with thirty-seven farmers from Kentucky and other nearby states. Collectively they have sold over forty-six thousand pounds of food and infused more than $50,000 into local farms.

These trends indicate that the next step in local foods is moving beyond farmers' markets and CSAs into mainstreaming and creative advancements. The traditionally isolated activity of farming is likely to be substantially rewritten with the advent of cooperative enterprises and urban agriculture. Thus, understanding the interrelationships among farms, distributors, and consumers as they exist in broader systems is paramount as we design resilient food systems that enhance food security, steward vital ecosystem services, and continue to build community around a behavior that is essential to our existence.

Notes

1. Wendell Berry, "The Pleasures of Eating," in *Cooking, Eating, Thinking: Transformative Philosophies of Food*, edited by Deane W. Curtin and Lisa M. Heldke, 374–79 (Bloomington: Indiana University Press, 1992).

2. Robert King, Miguel Gomez, and Gigi DiGiacomo, "Can Local Food Go Mainstream?" *Choices Magazine*, http://www.choicesmagazine.org/magazine

/article.php?article=111; Peleg Kremer and Tracy DeLiberty, "Local Food Practices and Growing Potential: Mapping the Case of Philadelphia," *Applied Geography, 31* (2011): 1252–61.

3. Glenn Sidney and John Ford, "Farmstand," https://www.farmstandapp.com.

4. Rose Winer, "5 Best Apps to Guide You to Local Seasonal Produce," *Zester Daily,* http://zesterdaily.com/agriculture/5-best-apps-guide-local-season-produce.

5. Jennifer Van Grove, "How to Accept Credit Card Payments on Mobile Devices," *Mashable,* October 14, 2010, http://mashable.com/2010/10/14/accepting-mobile-payments.

6. Karina Gallardo et al., "The Use of Electronic Payment Machines at Farmers Markets: Results from a Choice Experiment Study," *International Food and Agribusiness Management Review* 18 (2015): 79–104.

7. Wendy Wasserman et al., *Supplemental Nutrition Assistance Program (SNAP) at Farmers Markets: A How- to Handbook*, US Department of Agriculture Agricultural Marketing Service. June 2010, 3.

8. Farmers Market Coalition, "Advocacy," http://farmersmarketcoalition.org/advocacy/snap.

9. Morrison, "Growth in Farmers' Markets Continues into Winter Months," *Indianapolis Business Journal,* February 19, 2011, http://www.ibj.com/articles/25401-growth-in-farmers-markets-continues-into-winter-months.

10. Ibid.

11. Arthur Neal, "Innovation Helps Fuel Growth for Winter Farmers Markets," *United States Department of Agriculture Blog,* December 5, 2012, http://blogs.usda.gov/2012/12/05/innovation-helps-fuel-growth-for-winter-farmers-markets.

12. Kaitlin Koch, "How to Purchase Local Michigan Food Year-Round," Michigan State University Extension, January 26, 2015, http://msue.anr.msu.edu/news/how_to_purchase_local_michigan_food_year_round.

13. David Conner et al., "Consumer Demand for Local Produce at Extended Season Farmers' Markets: Guiding Farmer Marketing Strategies," *Renewable Agriculture and Food Systems* 24, no. 4 (2009): 251–59.

14. Eric J. Belasco et al., "High Tunnels Are My Crop Insurance: An Assessment of Risk Management Tools for Small-Scale Specialty Crop Producers," *Agricultural and Resource Economics Review* 42, no. 2 (2013): 403–418.

15. Elanor Starmer, "High Tunnel Initiative Brings Local Foods to Detroit," *United States Department of Agriculture Blog,* February 20, 2014, http://blogs.usda.gov/2014/02/20/high-tunnel-initiative-brings-local-foods-to-detroit/#more-50193.

16. Cara Bergschneider, personal communication with Farmer Research Lab, February 17, 2015.

17. Hilary Torres, Rich Pirog, and Judith Barry, "Before We Seek Change, Is There a Demand for Local Meats?" MSU Center for Regional Food Systems (2014), http://foodsystems.msu.edu/uploads/files/Demand_for_Local_Meat_Review.pdf.

18. Sharanbir S. Grewal and Parwinder S. Grewal, "Can Cities Become Self-Reliant in Food?," *Cities* 29, no. 1 (2012): 1–11.

19. Growing Power, http://www.growingpower.org; Abalimi Bezekhaya, "What We Do," People's Garden Center, http://abalimi.org.za/about-abalimi/what-we-do; "Urban Agriculture," *Alternatives*, http://www.rooftopgardens.alternatives.ca/about/urban-agriculture; "The People's Potato Community Garden," *The People's Potato*, http://www.peoplespotato.com/community-garden.html; "Our Programs," *Mid-Ohio Foodbank*, https://www.midohiofoodbank.org/programs-services/our-programs/UFCO; "Turner Garden," *Urban Agriculture Australia*, http://www.urbanagriculture.org.au/turner-garde.; "D-Town Farm," *D-Town Farm*, http://www.d-townfarm.com/d-town-farmorg.html; "Homegrown Baltimore: Grow Local," Baltimore Office of Sustainability, http://www.baltimoresustainability.org/homegrown-baltimore-grow-local; "Home," *Michigan Urban Farming Initiative*, http://www.miufi.org.

20. Robert Potts et al., *The Changing Midwest Assessment Land Cover, Natural Resources, and People*, Gen. Tech. Rep. NC-250 (St. Paul, MN: US Department of Agriculture, Forest Service, North Central Research Station), http://www.nrs.fs.fed.us/pubs/3346; Claire Thompson, "Say It Ain't Soil: What's the True Value of Organic Farmland?" *Grist*, June 15, 2012, http://grist.org/sustainable farming/say-it-aint-soil-how-much-is-organic-farmland-worth.

21. Kathryn Ruhf and John Mitchell, "Programming and Support for Beginning Farmers," Proceedings from the 4th National Small Farm Conference, United States Department of Agriculture, 2005, 249.

22. USDA, *Census of Agriculture*, 2007, http://www.agcensus.usda.gov/index.php.

23. Jennifer Meta Robinson and J. A. Hartenfeld, *The Farmers' Market Book: Growing Food, Cultivating Community* (Bloomington: Indiana University Press, 2007).

24. The Trust for Public Land, "Community Gardens," http://www.tpl.org/our-work/parks-for-people/community-gardens.

25. Kennebec Estuary Land Trust, "Local Farms—Local Food," http://kennebecestuary.org/resources/local-farms-local-food.

26. Katherine L. Adam, "Community Gardening," ATTRA—National Sustainable Agriculture Information Service, 2011, www.attra.ncat.org/attra-pub/download.php?id=351.

27. American Community Gardening Association. "Frequently Asked Questions," https://communitygarden.org/resources/faq.

28. Luke Drake and Laura J. Lawson, "Results of a US and Canada Community Garden Survey: Shared Challenges in Garden Management amid Diverse Geographical and Organizational Contexts," *Agriculture and Human Values* 32, no. 2 (2015): 241–42.

29. Laura J. Lawson, "History and Development of Community Gardens: A Brief History of Urban Garden Programs in the United States," 2009, http://ljlawson.rutgers.edu/assets/pdf/UGPlecture.pdf. Accessed November 28, 2016, https://web.archive.org/web/20150421030631/http://ljlawson.rutgers.edu/assets/pdf/UGPlecture.pdf.

30. Steve Martinez et al., *Local Food Systems: Concepts, Impacts, and Issues*, USDA Economic Research Service, May 2010, https://www.ers.usda.gov/webdocs/publications/err97/7054_err97_1_.pdf.

31. Guy K. Ames, "Community Orchards," ATTRA—National Sustainable Agriculture Information Service, 2013, http://www.attra.ncat.org/attra-pub/download.php?id=441.

32. Ibid.

33. Kyle H. Clark and Kimberly A. Nicholas, "Introducing Urban Forestry: A Multifunctional Approach to Increase Food Security and Provide Ecosystem Services," *Landscape Ecology* 28, no. 9 (2013): 1649–69.

34. Ibid., 1665.

35. Fruit Tree Planting Foundation, "Mission," http://www.ftpf.org/mission.htm.

36. Troy D. Glover, "The Story of the Queen Anne Memorial Garden: Resisting a Dominant Cultural Narrative," *Journal of Leisure Research* 35, no. 2 (2003): 190–212; Glover, "Social Capital in the Lived Experiences of Community Gardeners," *Leisure Sciences: An Interdisciplinary Journal* 26, no. 2 (2004): 143–62; Karl Linn, "Reclaiming the Sacred Commons," *New Village* 1, no. 1 (1999): 42–49.

37. Kimberly Shinew, Troy Glover, and Diana Perry, "Leisure Spaces as Potential Sites for Interracial Interaction: Community Gardens in Urban Areas," *Journal of Leisure Research* 36, no. 3 (2004): 336–55.

38. Joan Twiss et al., "Community Gardens: Lessons Learned from California Healthy Cities and Communities," *American Journal of Public Health* 93, no. 9 (2003): 1435–38.

39. James R. Farmer et al., "Why Agree to a Conservation Easement? Understanding the Decision of Conservation Easement Granting," *Landscape and Urban Planning* 138 (2015): 11.

40. Martin Bailkey and Joe Nasr, "From Brownfields to Greenfields: Producing Food in North American Cities," *Community Food Security News*, Fall 1999/Winter 2000, Special Issue: *Growing Food in Cities: Urban Agriculture in North America* (2007): 6.

41. Jac Smit, Joe Nasr, and Annu Ratta, *Urban Agriculture: Food, Jobs, and Sustainable Cities* (New York: Urban Agriculture Network, 1996), 1.

42. Rich Pirog and Andrew Benjamin, "Checking the Food Odometer: Comparing Food Miles for Local Versus Conventional Produce Sales to Iowa Institutions," Leopold Center for Sustainable Agriculture, July 2003, http://www.leopold.iastate.edu/pubs-and-papers/2003–07-food-odometer.

43. Alison Hope Alkon, *Black, White, and Green: Farmers' Markets, Race and the Green Economy* (Athens: University of Georgia Press, 2012).

44. Farmer et al., "Tale of Four Farmers Markets."

45. Market Umbrella, "Social Capital Impact Study," 2012, http://www.crescentcityfarmersmarket.org/uploads/file/NEEDreportKR10-15-12_nola.pdf.

46. Ibid.

47. Patricia Allen, "Reweaving the Food Security Net: Mediating Entitlement and Entrepreneurship," *Agriculture and Human Values* 16, no. 2 (1999): 117–29.

48. Debi Kelly, "Agritourism: Selling the Farm Experience," *Missouri Beginning Farm* (blog), October 14, 2010, http://missouribeginningfarming.blogspot.com/2010/10/agritourism-selling-farm-experience.html.

49. Barb Bierman Batie, "Agritourism May Learn 'Safety' the Hard Way," *Midwest Producer*, http://www.midwestproducer.com/news/regional/agritourism-may-learn-safety-the-hard-way/article_b637d986-c290-11e4-bad6-e7aefc37f4cf.html.

50. Malinda Geisler, "Agritourism Profile," Agricultural Marketing Resource Center, June 2014, http://www.agmrc.org/commodities__products/agritourism/agritourism-profile.

51. Gustavo Ferreira, "An Overview of Agritourism in the United States, Virginia, and Surrounding States: An Ag Census Analysis," Virginia Tech, April 4, 2015, http://news.cals.vt.edu/fbm-update/2015/04/06/an-overview-of-agritourism-in-the-united-states-virginia-and-surrounding-states-an-ag-census-analysis.

52. Lindsey Day-Farnsworth et al., "Scaling Up to Meet Mainstream Demands and Improve Food Security," Center for Integrated Agricultural Systems, http://www.cias.wisc.edu/scaling-up-meeting-the-demand-for-local

-food; Michael Veldstra, Corrine Alexander, and Maria Marshall, "To Certify or Not to Certify? Separating the Organic Production and Certification Decisions," *Food Policy* (2013): 429–36, http://www.sciencedirect.com/science/article/pii/S0306919214000840.

53. Barham et al., *Regional Food Hub Resource Guide*, United States Department of Agriculture Agricultural Marketing Service, Washington, DC, April 2012.

54. Low et al. "Trends in US Local and Regional Food Systems," Administrative Public No. 068, United States Department of Agriculture, Economic Research Service, 2015. http://www.ers.usda.gov/media/1763057/ap068.pdf.

55. Ibid.

56. The Wild Ramp, "About Us," *The Wild Ramp,* http://wildramp.org/about-us.

57. Local Food Hub, "2014 Annual Report," http://localfoodhub.org/2014 annualreport.

58. Iowa Food Hub, "About the Iowa Food Hub," http://www.iowafoodhub.com/public/pageedit.aspx?pageid=1.

59. Amish Studies, "Amish Population Trends 1991–2010: Twenty-Year Highlights," http://www2.etown.edu/amishstudies/Population_Trends_1991_2010.asp. Accessed November 28, 2016, https://web.archive.org/web/20160415235137/http://www2.etown.edu/amishstudies/Population_Trends_1991_2010.asp

60. Stephan Tubene and James Hanson, "The Wholesale Produce Auction: An Alternative Marketing Strategy for Small Farms," *American Journal of Alternative Agriculture* 17, no. 1 (2002): 18–23.

61. Matt Ernst and Tim Woods, "Marketing at Produce Auctions," University of Kentucky Cooperative Extension Service, http://www.uky.edu/Ag/NewCrops/introsheets/auctions.pdf.

62. Tubene and Hanson, "Wholesale Produce Auction"; Ernst and Woods, "Marketing at Produce Auctions."

63. R. S. Mackintosh, "A Garden for Every Home," University of Minnesota, Agricultural Extension Division, *Special Bulletin* 11 (1917): 1–8, http://conservancy.umn.edu/bitstream/handle/11299/168339/mn_2000_eb_011.pdf?sequence=1andisAllowed=y.

64. Good Shepherd Food Bank of Maine, "Mainers Feeding Mainers," https://www.gsfb.org/how-we-help/programs/mainers-feeding-mainers.

65. Robin Hobson, personal correspondence with Jennifer Meta Robinson.

66. Mercer Island Farmers Market, "Food Bank and Shelter Donations," http://mifarmersmarket.org/about-the-market/food-bank-shelter-donations.

67. The produce at City Fresh can be sold relatively economically because it is bought in bulk from farmers growing produce in large quantities, say 15–20 acres of a single crop. Similarly, at the Davies County Produce Auction in Indiana, where many wholesalers, market stand operators, and others make purchases, "a flat (20 lbs) of small 'B' yellow tomatoes might sell for $6 and the same flat of larger, perfect tomatoes for $10 or $11. A half bushel of green beans (approximately 4½ gallons) might be snapped up for $14." Aimee Blume, "Farmers Offer Davies County Produce Items at Auction," Evansville *Courier & Press*, August 20, 2013, http://www.courierpress.com/features/farmers-offer-daviess-county-produce-items-at-auction—gallery-ep-297032687-324668321.html. (page discontinued). At these aggregation sites, corn may sell in a lot of 100 dozen ears and cantaloupe 150 at a time. These quantities are desirable for large-scale redistribution but inconvenient for personal buying and possibly ineffective for farmers who want the maximum value for their goods.

68. New Roots, "About Us," http://www.newrootsproduce.org/about-us.html.

FIVE

Growing Capacity

There is no more uphill business than farming. The most fortunate of us
persist without prospering.
—Jim Shepard, "The World to Come"

Several other significant trends in small farming will affect scaling up
the growing, selling, and, therefore, buying of local food well into the
future: retirement of older farmers, cultivation of new ones, and food
policy organizing at the community level. The growth in demand for
local food means more opportunity for growers to join markets and
CSAs and to create other distribution streams from a single farm operation. But such opportunities are only part of the equation: most market
growers maintain a second job off-farm, make little profit from their
participation in markets, and face numerous logistical and social challenges to remain in the profession. In a significant and promising development, more women now operate and staff farms, and the numbers
of growers from Hispanic, American Indian, African American, and
Asian backgrounds all increased between 2007 and 2012.[1] Farmers not
cut from the classic cloth (assumed to be white, male, and operating
within a nuclear family) often face uphill challenges to make community, finances, family, and education work for them. Fortunately, recent developments in farming education and food policy efforts put
local food in a good position to scale up capacity with a diversity of
new farmers.

Women Farmers

We know American farmers are aging. In 2012 their average age
rose to fifty-eight while their overall numbers fell.[2] A funny adage advises that old farmers never die, they just get plowed under, and indeed
a quarter of a million farmers are seventy-five or older.[3] In the North-

east, nearly 30 percent of farmers are likely to get out of farming in the next ten years, with 90 percent of those having identified no person to assume the farm, its operations, or its position as a community fixture.[4] Even though almost three hundred thousand farms launched between 2002 and 2007, they yield a net increase of only seventy-five thousand. These farms tend to be more diversified, with fewer acres, younger operators, and more off-farm jobs compared to all farms nationwide. Meanwhile, recent decades have seen midsize farms getting squeezed out. Most farms are either quite small or very large. What makes farming so hard for new people to break into and thrive? A focus on women farmers provides a glimpse into these challenges.

The number of women interested in farming, especially organic farming, coupled with their low level of financial success leaves a lot of room for improvement, not to mention the possibility of more stable lives for the family members around them. When women make occupational choices, they tend to value altruism more than men do; women prioritize diverse goals in their career decisions, including marriage and family, while men tend to focus more narrowly on employment.[5] As we can see in the brief cases that follow here, women farmers often feel they must make choices that only indirectly move them toward their long-term goal of owning a small, sustainable farm but that maximize their immediate ability to provide some of the modest elements of a good life for themselves and their families. The stories they tell about their lives emphasize their relationship to communities and families, their tenuous financial situation, and their quest for education. The circuitous paths they take to being fully vested farmers indicate substantial costs that could be turned, instead, to individual and social gains.

Women represent 30 percent of farmers and ranchers in the United States, a significant portion that has held fast since 2007 and a notable increase from 1994, when women made up only 7.6 percent of the total number of farm operators.[6] Women have maintained this higher percentage even as the overall number of farmers dropped, as reported in the most recent USDA agricultural census at this writing, in 2012. Of the 3.2 million *principal* farm operators in the United States, women make up 14 percent.[7] If all operators are counted, not just principal operators but also others who have a say in the operation of a farm, the number of women farmers increases to one million.[8] Nearly all (96 percent) secondary women farm operators contribute to farms with a male principal operator, usually the woman's husband.[9] No matter how you count them, women are working more farms and ranches, operating more land, and producing a greater value of agricultural products than they were twenty years ago. Moreover, they are disproportionately represented in organic farming, with about a quarter of organic farms run by women.[10]

However, the news is not all good. Women principal farmers control only 7 percent of US farmland and earn only 3 percent of farm sales.[11] Moreover, their farms tend to be very small, with the majority having sales of less than ten thousand dollars a year.[12] Their success rate looks much like that of farmers from most ethnic minorities, for whom the largest proportion of farms earns less than ten thousand dollars annually.[13] An exception to this trend is that farms operated by Asian growers had the lowest percentage of farms earning less than ten thousand dollars a year, at 43.4 percent, and as a group had the highest percentage of farms earning one hundred thousand dollars or more, at 26.8 percent. On the other hand, the USDA counted only 33,371 farms in 2012 with what the survey called "black" principal operators. Of those farms, 56.6 percent earned less than ten thousand dollars in annual sales while only 18.4 percent earned one hundred thousand dollars or more.[14] Among women farmers, the 21 percent who specialize in poultry, specialty crops, grains, or dairy had the most sales, controlling 72 percent of sales from all women's farms.[15] Women are of special interest for local food because they have increased their operation of small farms. In this sense, they represent potential that is yet to be tapped: they have the desire to farm but still have substantial room to grow into their potential. Who are the women of small farms? What do they need to succeed? How will they get it?

Some women growers for local food venues describe their entry into the field as a matter of luck.[16] Vegetable vendor and vineyard owner Brenda Simmons jokes, "I think I made a mistake several years back when my husband asked me to drive a tractor." She says, "I just came out of the blue" from a full-time public school teaching position into farming. She now raises six hundred acres of corn, beans, and wheat with her husband, David, plus twenty-five acres of produce and twelve acres of grapes on his family's 120-year-old farm. They also run a farm store for produce and added a "wine garden and banquet hall" that is available for events.[17] Similarly, honey specialist and teacher Chris Hunter says with affected mystification, "I just acted interested! . . . I acted interested when we were dating, and look what I got!" The business she runs with her husband, Tracy, continuing his family's 150-year history of beekeeping, sells honey, pollen, candles, lip balm, and other home-crafted products every Saturday at six farmers' markets and many fairs, festivals, and stores. From those first seemingly minor expressions of interest in their husbands' passions for agriculture, these women have become essential operators in their farm businesses. Their funny simplifications of their professional journeys indicate the indirect route that even these highly successful and long-standing market vendors took into the profession. The following three cases look into the lives of small farmers who are women and show their particular concerns with community, family, finances, and education.

Case 1: A Spiritual Path

In one pathway into farming, J. D. Grove envisions her life as a journey out of the activities and identities she thought were expected of her and into a life that she thinks of as "living as much as possible according to my beliefs." The daughter of a writer and an academic, she planned a future in New York City interning at a prominent publishing house. In those days she felt she had been "led to believe I'm weak," and her approach to life was "How can I fit myself into society and be okay with doing it?" Dropping out of school and joining a migrant farm crew "changed my sense of myself in a real permanent way." She felt strong and capable and learned to be a valuable part of a farm crew. She left, however, when the homophobia of a farm owner in Florida became threatening to both her physical safety and her sense of herself. When she expressed interest to her grandmother in building her own house, she discovered that the family owned an old farm in Indiana that no one currently lived on. Grove and a girlfriend "immediately took our packs and hitchhiked up here." What she inherited was a central Indiana farm with at least forty acres of arable land that had been leased for decades to conventional corn and soybean farmers. The two women built a primitive cabin on the land and rowed out farmers' market crops on a small part of it while the rest was leased as usual to pay the taxes. The relationship did not last, however, and Grove left the farm for Bloomington, where she found a community more to her liking than the traditional farming villages farther north. She has not lived on the farm full-time yet. It is remote from her social networks and from farmers' markets that will allow her to charge prices consistent with the costs of organic methods. But she remains committed to this vision of her life, which she describes as "more like my spiritual path." Several years ago, she bought a "fixer upper" house near Bloomington, out in the direction of the more rural farm, and created a nuclear family with a partner and their toddler son. When they were contemplating having a second baby, she realized "it will set me back two more years. . . . It's such a slow process. I'm getting older. When am I going to be established?" She regretted wasting time by going directly to college after high school, saying she "should have not tried to fit myself into society from the beginning." Recently, after the birth of their second child, her family has at long last moved onto the farm she inherited, which she calls Fullcircle Farm. And in 2016 she launched Conspire: Contemporary Craft boutique in nearby Greencastle, featuring her farm-made Teehaus Bath & Body products along with other handmade goods and a local art gallery.

Case 2: A Self-Guided Education

A woman we will call Rebecca Wright emphatically focuses on constructing a unique education to support her evolving skills in farming. A single woman with a commitment to being involved in the food industry, she began her "path," as she puts it, when she spent a summer as a volunteer on another woman's farm helping to prepare for the Saturday farmers' market. That, she said, opened "a new world for me." By the end of the season, she was also helping at the market, finding the exchanges and connections with customers rewarding. Through the market, Wright made the acquaintance of a vegetable grower and worked for him on his farm for several seasons, first as an intern and then as an apprentice—development terms that she says reflect important distinctions in the level of skill she is able to bring to tasks. Able to envision a "meaningful, entertaining, inspiring" work life for the first time, she talked her way into an apprenticeship at another farm, for room and board and a very low stipend, for yet a third season so that she could get experience on a more diversified farm. From there she moved as an hourly hand to a fourth farm, again in learning mode, where she thought she could continue her education with large livestock, which was her special interest. However once there, Wright found that her small physical size and gender as well as the production orientation of the farm—which kept workers specialized in narrow tasks—gave her little chance to develop her knowledge of how to "grow nutritious food in a smart way." Disappointed, she left that job after just a few months to take on an agriculture-related position in local government. When we talked, she was working three jobs and unable to afford a down payment for her own farm. She keeps her dream of a farming life alive with chickens and a vegetable patch in the backyard of her home in the city. She plans to move to the country as soon as that is feasible while simultaneously volunteering with local advocacy organizations on food and justice-related issues.

Case 3: The Friends and Family Plan

Tansy Norris, as we will call her, grew up in farming country in southern Indiana, where it was not unusual to see farms foreclosed on. She lives on a mixed livestock farm with her husband and child, and says of farming, "We came to this through the back door." Credentialed as a social worker and having worked in that field for several years, Norris had no formal training for farming. She decided to seek a lifestyle that would allow her family to grow and be healthy, and that was on a farm. She took a year to transition, working both her counseling job and the farm, but decided she did not want to do two jobs poorly. Her priority was to own the farm and use it to its fullest financial capacity rather than to lease land beyond financially sustainable levels. Norris says she went into country life with ambitious aspirations about the philosophically right way to grow, but she has found that what works is more important than abstract ideals: "There is no book of knowledge in this." Instead, the job is all about solving problems as they emerge. Finding reliable help to drive her chickens to a distant processing facility is an ongoing challenge. Frequently the only woman at feed stores and farming groups, she does not let gender differences stand in her way. And now her success is well-enough known that new growers often come to her for advice. Two of the most important things she tells them are "be open to other ways" and "if it's not working, stop doing it": there is more than one way to do things right. Summarizing what works for her now, Norris says that a family farm means everyone "wears a lot of hats," and they wear the hats for the jobs that they are best at, even if those don't align with traditional gender roles: "We have kind of settled in over the years for what works for us." For Norris, that means she oversees livestock, including taking the animals for processing, while her husband excels at less visceral tasks. She looks for balance and gets by on help from the "friends and family plan." The property she farms has been in her family since the 1960s, and she could not have succeeded in her farming career, she says, without her family and its farmland.

Passion and Practicality

These cases indicate the double-edged sword of passion and practicalities that many growers in the local food movement experience, regardless of their gender or ethnic background. They cannot succeed without intense commitment, yet farming inevitably presents practical and sometimes prohibitive problems. For women and other non-traditional demographics, identity can present additional hurdles. Although not all of the women interviewed saw gender as a specific impediment to pursuing farming, the mothers among them did indicate the "burden" of being the primary child-care provider and reported greater or lesser success in farming when those responsibilities were included. At least two women specifically told stories of sexual harassment during their farming experience, and another indicated that her small size limited her ability to accomplish some tasks. Norris indicated that she had perhaps not been aware enough to pick up on any skepticism about her abilities down at the local feed store, where she was always the only woman, but she said that she never felt intimidated, and that, based on her success, she can now go "toe to toe" with any man there. After all, she says, "We are all in this thing together."

The professional paths these women farmers describe is much like an agricultural corollary to the "swirling" activity observed in higher education today whereby students no longer complete a degree in four years at a single institution but extend, interrupt, and transfer their studies.[18] Similarly, many women growers have not only attended one or more colleges but also may have learned via a range of cobbled-together opportunities: noncredit courses at unaccredited education centers, chamber of commerce business development classes, agricultural conference presentations, unpaid volunteering, unpaid farm internships, participation as a WWOOFer (World Wide Opportunities on Organic Farms volunteers who work in exchange for food, accommodation, and learning opportunities), paid apprenticeships, working as hourly paid farm hands, and so on.[19] Many of them seek information from books, limited-run and self-published pamphlets from the back-to-the-land movement of the 1970s, and the internet.[20] In addition, when they can, they seek out individualized advice from more experienced growers. The three women growers in the case studies had taken college courses, graduated with undergraduate degrees, or attained professional certifications and advanced degrees, but none had taken courses in the agricultural sciences.

Coming as they do from outside of a standardized educational system, and often feeling that county extension services have little to offer them, many would-be sustainable farmers turn to farm internships for the training they are seeking, as Wright does. However, quality and content are uneven across internship opportunities, and positions themselves are usually unpaid. Although participants may well be happy with an internship or volunteer opportunity because they are gaining skills, in a worst-case scenario they can be put to hard and even dangerous tasks with little training or supervision. Indeed, few farm internship programs are run by people with training in teaching, and even skills taught well may be presented in isolated situations that make applying them as an independent farmer in another location quite difficult.

Growers, who actively work with natural processes, need a host of skills, some of them generalizable and some specific to their locale. Indeed, growers often feel they need easy and timely access to highly nuanced and contextual knowledge, "knowledge beyond what you can read in books," as Norris, a voracious reader, puts it. For information that is more locale-specific, when they can, these growers seek out individualized advice from those with more experience. Farming is all problem solving, says one person, who doubts whether the necessary mind-set of care and willing accountability can be taught. Another grower emphasizes learning on the job, saying there is much guidance in what "the plants tell you." And a heavy user of electronic resources said, "It is too complicated, requires too much knowledge to be flailing around on the internet. . . . It takes a lifetime's worth of accumulated knowledge" to be a successful farmer. In one recent example of the difference between information and knowledge, a grower spent substantial time on the internet researching the design of a hoop greenhouse. This was to be a major investment of his quite limited income, but one designed to return a longer growing season and more income. He chose the optimal design, purchased the materials, assembled the volunteer help he needed, and put up what turned out to be a structurally flawed greenhouse. Whether the problem was in the design, the instructions, or the execution was not entirely clear to him, but the result was the same: a wasted investment that will set back the modest expansion of his business at least a calendar year. Another grower said that early on she struggled to evaluate the health of her livestock when a more experienced farmer could have shown her in a moment just what to look for. The breadth of knowledge necessary is daunting. As Norris puts it, "A family farm means everyone wears a lot of hats," as farming requires skills in accounting, business planning, soil science, meteorology, small engine mechanics, entomology, and perhaps in grant writing, animal husbandry and medicine, electrical wiring, carpentry, plumbing, and more.

"Farming has changed, and farmers now have to do things they are traditionally really bad at: marketing, educating consumers, collective action, communication. . . . And it can't be a coincidence that women are traditionally good at those things," according to Cheryl Rogowski.[21] She runs the W. Rogowski Farm, which was started in the 1950s by her parents and won a MacArthur award for innovations to connect the farm with its customers and employees.[22] She deliv-

ered to the elderly, helped immigrant farmers from Mexico and Gua-
temala, did a catering business, and sells at eight weekly farmers' markets. She says, "Women farmers aren't a special-interest group. . . . Our
issues are the same as all American farmers—we all want to keep our
farms, and we have to make money from them. But women have come
up with a lot of the new ways of doing it." There are now networks of
women farmers and a national conference for women in sustainable
agriculture.

Which piece of the farm gets the frost first, which areas of the field
need more or less fertilizer, how much rainfall tends to flood the creek,
where to go for the cleanest feed or the healthiest chicks, how to get a
spot at the farmers' market, and how to negotiate the unwritten conventions of business can all be learned more readily if one knows where
to look for guidance. One market vendor remembered feeling pres-
sured to raise prices on her first day at the market, and others have experienced the cold shoulder when they ask for growing tips from more
established vendors whose offerings they seem to duplicate. Farmers
who are new to the business and the community around them may
not always know where friendly and wise advice can be found. Dis-
tinguishing certain people and places as experts and venues that are
open to mentoring relationships would facilitate timely learning. One
woman said she identified an advisor on organic methods at a farmers'
market only by the other woman's moth-eaten sweaters and longjohns
under her floral skirts. When asked, however, the woman in a sweater
acknowledged that she does not consider herself expert enough to advise anyone. Less an expression of modesty, she is partly misjudging
her own accomplishments and partly acknowledging the complexity
of giving sound advice that works in a specific context.

These circumstances indicate several recommendations to set new
farmers on a successful path, women and men alike. First, farmers need
accessible support for acquiring the diverse kinds of knowledge they
need in order to be successful. And educational opportunities need
to be available at more flexible times and places than traditionally offered by land grant universities. New farmers are probably looking less
for degrees and certifications, and often already have those in other
fields, than they are for timely, basic, or applicable knowledge. Moreover, they need to acquire information where they have land, jobs,

day care, and connections, and also when they have time, which may mean the off-season for their type of farming (winter for some, summer for others).

Second, new farmers need to know where they can find expert advice. Moreover, since a person's capabilities develop asynchronously (faster in some domains than others) and in relation to identity (more readily for some people than others), it would be helpful for new farmers to know which people would be willing to answer which kinds of questions. The whole community would benefit from clear pathways to expertise.

Third, farming as a profession needs to be moved from the margins into a respected place in society. One grower admits her clear impression that she dwells "on the fringes of society. I don't think this is valued by the larger culture yet." In the larger society, she realizes, farming is "not associated with intelligence." Such stigmas can ripple into major obstacles for those who are inspired to become farmers.

The Challenge of Land Acquisition

At six to ten thousand dollars per acre in many places, land ownership can be the major obstacle that keeps people from succeeding in the profession or from entering it at all.[23] Growers report that banks are reluctant to extend loans for the uncertain business of farming, especially for untested farmers, no-spray and specialty crop farmers, and those with little credit history. Indeed, new local food growers, almost by definition, tend not to prioritize a high income, so their financial history is likely to work against them.

As the case studies indicate, people try many alternative approaches, beyond bank loans and land contracts, to affording and acquiring farmland. Inheriting a farm is the most traditional way of acquiring land, but locally oriented farmers may find that the distance from markets and like-minded communities make living on the old family place unworkable. Moving away from urban centers and their sprawling surrounds is one way to lower the price of entry. However, local food growers need customers, and customers prize the fresh and local.[24] So even more than with commodity farmers, the land that local food growers purchase has to be within striking distance of wherever they are going to sell their products—farmers' markets, community-supported agriculture subscriptions, food hubs, restaurants, wholesale buyers, or others. Many locally oriented farmers would like their customers to visit the farm, share in its beauty, see firsthand where their food is grown, and "maybe even get their hands a little dirty." However, the farther away from an urban center a farm is located, the less likely that is to happen, says one farmer.

Sometimes various free arrangements work with amenable landowners: trading labor for land residency and taking on a dormant farm may seem very appealing, but if arrangements fall apart, the tenant may be left with few assets to show for many years of work. Many investments—like buildings, fences, orchards, soil tilth, and connections to place and community—cannot be moved, and the labor in making them can rarely be recouped.

Simple arrangements in which people pool their money and live on commonly owned property provide useful alternatives but are also often fraught with relationship problems and may dissolve completely when couples separate or friends fall out. Nevertheless, new, more carefully designed models for cooperative housing and cooperative neighborhoods, sometimes with CSAs and farms incorporated into them, continue to be developed and disseminated. And some of the longest-lasting cooperative arrangements (as long as forty or fifty years) have relied on contiguous rather than co-owned properties. That is, these properties can be purchased with pooled funds, but they are then legally divided and deeded to different owners. This arrangement offers a balance of separate and self-determining but also proximal and cooperative ownership and allows some groups to increase their landholdings by encouraging compatible people to purchase land around or near the original core properties. In this way, some groups have managed to survive long-term challenges and changes in life, including child rearing, divorce, remarriage, and death.

Recently, organizations specializing in land transfers have begun assisting with farms that move "outside" the family. According to data from the USDA's National Agricultural Statistics Service (NASS), approximately eight and a half million acres in the thirteen-state north central region will sell outside of the family.[25] Land-link programs, which attempt to find new farmers to replace those transitioning out, have cropped up in eleven of these thirteen states. Unfortunately, the success rate for good matches remains low even though land seekers outnumber retiring farmers ten to one.[26]

Land conservation trusts are one powerful possibility for helping new farmers make the land connection. Guardians of over forty-seven million acres in the United States, these nongovernmental land trusts preserve undeveloped farmland and natural areas by buying them outright, receiving "fee simple" (full) ownership via donation or purchase or by controlling the rights to development and harvest through a conservation easement on property owned by another entity.[27] Much of the acreage protected by land trusts allows for farming; however, well-meaning conservation trust officers may not realize that leasing to farmers who use conventional growing practices degrades soil, air, and water quality. Thus, without careful orientation, conservationists miss an opportunity to reach their organization's mission more effectively. Nonetheless, partnerships between land trusts and beginning farmers can offer significant benefits, giving farmers access to arable lands, often at reduced rates, as well as facilitating environmental stewardship, supporting agricultural jobs and lifestyles, and increasing the supply of local food.

As an example, the Athens Land Trust in northeast Georgia has developed an outreach program that educates new and current farmers on conservation practices, promotes farming as a career for underserved populations, and links land seekers with owners.[28] Other land trusts are not only connecting farmers with private landowners but also leasing trust property directly to them, as the Kestrel Land Trust in the Pioneer Valley of western Massachusetts does, for example.[29] Even in urban areas, private trusts and governmental units are realizing that sustainable farmers can rehabilitate the land they control in ways that benefit the surrounding community economically, socially, and environmentally. Farmer Amy Matthews runs South Circle Farm just two miles from downtown Indianapolis on reclaimed industrial land owned by a nonprofit organization.[30] Matthews oversees a very small, one-and-a-half-acre, plot of intensive and diverse food production that has a big impact. In addition to vending at farmers' markets and through their CSA, South Circle offers youth gardening programs and educational workshops on such topics as backyard chickens, organic gardening, and mushroom cultivation. Creative interventions like this, tucking a vibrant, welcoming community center into a struggling urban neighborhood, make the land connection possible for small farmers and grow local food capacity.

The Challenges of Family and Community

Buying land on its own does not mean entry into the surrounding community. Even after the land connection is made, social connections may lag; rural areas have their own social norms that have been developed over generations and may set high-stakes challenges for newcomers.[31] One grower new to an area was shocked when her rural neighbors shot her wandering dog. Another, who had been having trouble with a neighbor's dog killing his chickens, was advised by a longtime resident, "I never shot a man's dog without warning him first." A couple new to livestock received repeated calls the first few years from a none-too-happy neighbor that their thirty-plus cattle had ended up in his corn. An urban farmer had to scour the neighborhood to find her bicycle and garden cart after they had been wheeled away one night. In addition, many farmers require short-term help to put out a crop, beat a rain, or skin a greenhouse in the evening when the wind drops. The actions of surrounding landowners must not jeopardize water supply or quality, organic status, or visits by CSA shareholders. Schools, religious institutions, lifestyle tolerance, and kindness to children, too, are just some of the social elements that a farmer may find necessary to establish a satisfactory life.

Growers who are parents may find they have to drive miles, pay tuition, or turn to homeschooling if they want alternatives to the rural schools. Female and LGBTQ growers living among farming communities with more traditional gender roles may struggle to find friends, partners, and allies. Mary L. Gray, in *Out in the Country*, demonstrates that gay and lesbian cultures exist in the rural United States, despite their apparent absence, but people may gather in repurposed public and semi-public places, like Walmart, instead of more easily identifiable clubs, festivals, and bars. Thus, growers who have transplanted themselves from cities where they expect gay culture to appear in certain ways and places may not recognize where to find a like-minded community.[32] Similarly, newcomers to a rural area may feel too culturally different to fit in at traditional rural gathering places, such as churches, fire stations, or "liars benches." One new farmer who describes "a great sense of community with our neighbors" nonetheless notes that she feels that she is outside the rural mainstream: "They have their space, we have ours, yet we share resources, knowledge, and are always there for each other. We have our neighbors, but really we need more than that." Another farmer explained the cultural rift she feels from her rural neighbors in terms of child rearing:

> One of the biggest reasons I desire community is for my children. It takes a village to raise children . . . this is no joke. I also desire the social aspect of it and working together for the greater good, sharing in the work and sharing resources, but my kids need community more than anything. . . . They need other adults to guide them as they grow, other perspectives on life, other interactions with adults, and more children to play with.

She noted that although the father of her son is in the home, when child care falls through, "the burden is put mostly on women." She said, "I feel really alone in this." Some rural newcomers bring their own community with them by moving in groups to own property in common or under the auspices of one individual. But such strength in numbers may also underline differences from the surrounding community.

The Challenges of Teaching and Learning

Successful farming, Sage Goodell says, requires an "intimate relationship" with a piece of land:

> I know this land as I know a lover. . . . I know her curves, her sweet spots, I know where she is rougher and the places I am not yet comfortable going. I know how she handles extreme situations and her constant song of happiness. I know where things grow well and where they don't. I know the areas that need work. I know where the sun sets on the summer solstice. I know where the geese nest in the spring. I know where the heron fishes in the evenings. I know where the garden is too wet for spring plantings and that funny water vein that runs straight through several beds. I know those places where she needs some serious work. I know the challenges she brings me

HISTORY, PHILOSOPHY, POLITICS, ETHICS	WHOLE FARM SKILLS	PLANTS	ANIMALS	SOIL AND WATER
ANCIENT HISTORY OF CULTIVATION	GENERAL BUSINESS PLANNING	BASIC BOTANY	BEEKEEPING	COMPOSTING
MODERN HISTORY OF AGRICULTURE	YEAR 2 BUSINESS PLAN	CROP SELECTION	WHOLE FARM INTEGRATION (GRAZING ROTATION) (PLANTS/ANIMALS)	LAND TILLAGE
??? PRODUCTION	AFTER Y2 BUSINESS PLAN	SEED SOURCES	CATTLE	LAND CONSERVATION
MODERN FARMING PHILOSOPHIES	MARKETING STRATEGIES	SEED SELECTION	SHEEP	WATER CONSERVATION
FOOD AND CULTURE	BASIC AG. LAW, INSURANCE	SEED SOWING / SEED PRODUCTION TECHNIQUES / BREEDING	HOGS	IRRIGATION
CLIMATE CHANGE	GAINING CERTIFICATION(S)	TRANSPLANTING	MILK COWS	SOIL STRUCTURE(S)
LOCAL FOOD SECURITY	EQUIPMENT, DRIVING	SUCCESSIONAL PLANTING / TRANSPLANTING TO FIELD	POULTRY / MEAT & EGGS	SOIL TESTING
LOCAL POLITICS	IMPLEMENTS	DIRECT SEEDING	GOATS	SOIL IMPROVEMENT
SCALE	EQUIPMENT MAINTENANCE	CULTIVATION TECHNIQUES	RABBITS	METEOROLOGY
LITERATURE OF FARMING	CARPENTRY	FERTILIZATION - FIELD / FERTILIZATION - PLANTS	FISH	MICROBIOLOGY
FUTURE OF FARMING	WELDING / ELECTRICAL	HARVEST	HORSES	NITROGEN FIXATION
HORSE OR TRACTOR?	PLUMBING	STORAGE	ANIMAL SLAUGHTER	NUTRIENT RECYCLING
GMO DISCUSSION	PAINTING	ROTATION IN FIELD	??? SLAUGHTER	
FARM MEDIA (PUBLICATIONS, DIGITAL, BOOKS)	FARM BUILDINGS	MULCHING TECHNIQUES	??? PESTS	
LABOR	GREENHOUSES / HIGH TUNNELS / COLD FRAMES / SEASON EXTENSION / GREENHOUSE MANAGEMENT	SMALL SCALE GRAIN RAISING / COVER CROPS / SMALL FRUITS	DISEASES	
POLITICS OF FOOD PRODUCTION	FORESTRY	FRUIT TREES / FRUIT PROCESSING / MUSHROOMS	BENEFICIAL INSECTS	
WEATHER / DEFORESTATION / DESERTIFICATION	FENCING / GATES	PLANTING TREES (FOR FUEL)	PRODUCTION PLANNING	
URBAN FOOD FARMS	MAPLE SYRUP	PESTS	VALUE ADDED PRODUCTS	
FARM NEIGHBORS & NEIGHBORHOODS - POLITICS OF LAND USE	FIRST AID CERTIFICATION	DISEASES	DRAFT ANIMALS	
	HAND TOOLS	BENEFICIAL INSECTS	ANIMAL HEALTH AND WELLNESS · VETTING · HOMEOPATHY	
	POWER TOOLS	PRODUCTION PLANNING	ANIMAL FENCING	
	FIREARMS / HUNTING	SEED SAVING	TOOLS AND HANDLING TOOLS	
	RETIREMENT PLANNING	VEGETABLE PROCESSING		
	WOODLAND ECOLOGY	EDIBLE FLOWERS		
	CREW MANAGEMENT	YEAR ROUND HARVEST		
	TAXES	VALUE ADDED PRODUCTS		
	LOANS / FINANCING, GRANTS	MUSHROOMS		
	ENERGY · CONVENTIONAL · ALTERNATIVE	WEEDS		
		POST HARVEST TECHNIQUES		
		HARVEST TOOLS		
		PACKAGING		
		WILDCRAFTING		
		SEED SAVING · LOCAL SEED SAVING (MICROCLIMATES)		
		GRAIN GRINDING		
		PLANT GRAFTING		
		TREE GRAFTING		

Figure 5.1. An extensive list of knowledge domains important for farming, compiled by the curriculum committee of the proposed Indiana New Farm School. *Working draft by J. A. Hartenfeld*

and where she brings out my strengths. This is what I seek with a piece of land, what I have always desired. . . . Yes, this could be found in another piece of land, but I am five years into this relationship and it takes a lifetime to create.

Goodell describes contextual knowledge that is difficult to gain within formal educational institutions. Farming, especially when sustain-

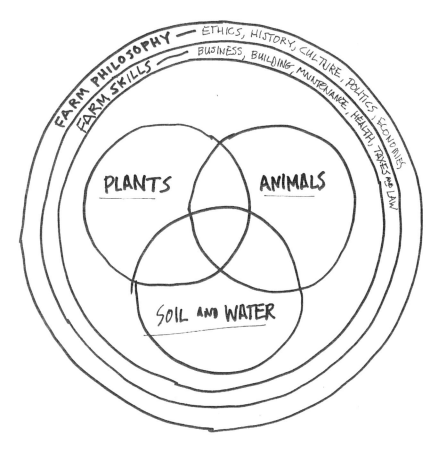

Figure 5.2. Comprehensive Venn diagram of farmer knowledge domains, designed by the curriculum committee of the proposed Indiana New Farm School. *Working draft by J. A. Hartenfeld*

able and intensive, requires this level of knowing coupled with understanding of the science of growing, business skills, mechanical acumen, and so on. Recently established farmer education programs and support systems offer new ways of acquiring these skills in ways that fit realistically into farmers' lives. In addition, they often address farming as both a skill set and an identity. They provide opportunities for generalizable skill-building, contextualized expertise, and participative learning while also supporting resources in the community. Specialty conferences have also appeared to support knowledge sharing among women, African American, Latino, and sustainable-methods farmers around the country.

Since 2008, the federal government's Beginning Farmer and Rancher Development Program has invested in new educational opportunities through competitive grants. The program supports those who have farmed or ranched for ten years or less, especially veterans and socially disadvantaged farmers, by funding workshops, educational teams, training, and technical assistance throughout the United States.[33] In 2015 the USDA reported that it had made awards for more than ninety million dollars through the program. In addition, it funds loans for ownership, operations, and value-added development. These farm schools, and others begun with private or non-federal funding, are most interesting in that they try different configurations to address the complex knowledge base that goes into farming in ways that, to a greater and lesser extent, incorporate the actual experiences, needs, and rhythms of farming life. A perhaps unexpected corollary benefit is that the training programs themselves provide a career path, and paid positions, for some small farmers.

Around the country, concern about dramatically and sustainably increasing the supply and security of farmers and locally grown food is gaining steam. Some of them seem to follow the standards proposed by Ivan Illich in *Deschooling Society*.[34] He argues that a good education system should have three purposes: (1) to provide all who want to learn with access to resources at any time in their lives; (2) to make it possible for all who want to share knowledge to find those who want to learn it from them; and (3) to create timely opportunities to discuss issues of public interest. Writing pre-internet in 1971, he advocates "learning webs," with access to educational objects and processes, exchanges that register people who are willing to share their skills, and peer matching that facilitates a student's ability to "define and achieve his own goals." In Indiana a gathering of farmers and farmworkers, would-be farmers, a grocer, the director of a nonprofit land conservancy, a historic building advocate, and staff members from local food banks and other food security nonprofit agencies met over two years to develop such a learning web—an educational program for new and transitional small sustainable farmers.[35] Their plan explicitly links the dual national problems of food security and farmer security. Their conversations eventually extended to include the county extension agent, faculty and students at the state and land-grant universities, and non-farming landowners. Their unpublished mission statement noted four main goals:

1. To teach sustainable farming skills, philosophies, and economies.
2. To counsel, network, and assist farmers (including through access to land, capital, equipment, and mentors).
3. To enhance the profile and public recognition of those who choose local, small-scale, owner-based farming that secures and enriches our community and society at large.
4. To educate the general public about sustainable agriculture.

All of these points leverage the social nature of knowledge and identity and the importance of social positioning for professional performance.[36] The first and second items acknowledge the importance of an inner circle of participation that relies on identification and connection with other farmers. The latter items, on the other hand, acknowledge the importance of an engaged community and its evaluation of farmers' work: individual customers, wholesale buyers, backyard gardeners, schoolchildren, and so on. The successful education of farmers, this mission statement suggests, requires farming skills, financial capital, and equipment as well as partnerships with other farmers and a publicly acknowledged and valued role in a community.

This Indiana group envisioned a pathway to bring beginning farmers from the periphery of professional activity to the center.[37] They imagined a program that would begin with a year of combined classroom study and hands-on experience. Topics the first year would include the basics of a successful farm venture, including planning, growing, business, management, ethics, and philosophy. In the second year, students would continue class-based study but would primarily work their own crops on land donated for such use (or their own), individually or in teams, and under the mentorship of experienced farmers. Students could choose to repeat the second year indefinitely, allowing them to revisit a complex enterprise that—by virtue of weather, bugs, seed viability, crop disease, animal whim, and so on—never repeats exactly. In the third year and beyond, these "advanced beginner" farmers would have access to mentoring, equipment, and other resources to use on their own land or on land brokered through the school. Continuing education opportunities would allow them to continue to build individual capacity and share with new and experienced growers in the community.

A multigenerational curriculum group, with farming experience ranging from zero to thirty-five years compiled a list of diverse areas of knowledge that a farmer actually needs to know about (see figure 5.1). In a later iteration, they developed a Venn diagram to describe that long list (see figure 5.2). At the center of the diagram they put natural systems: plants, animals, soil, and water. Those four are encompassed by the farm-related, practical skills necessary to interact with those systems and are elaborated with other skills that are often overlooked in the general public's understanding but essential to farm viability: facility with business, building, maintenance, health, taxes, and aspects of law. Finally, those applied skills are encompassed by a philosophy that includes ethics, history, culture, politics, and economies. The whole scheme is hand-drawn, suggesting a relationship between work and the world that involves human-scale handwork and situatedness and, in the free-drawn circles, a sense of approximation to and deviation from balance. The diagram conveys the interrelatedness of large natural systems with locally particularized ones, economies of finance with those of ecosystems and biological services, and cultural possibilities with personal proclivities.

Although its grant to the federal government program was unsuccessful, the group did move forward on an idea fondly referred to as Farmers Anonymous.[38] This peer-to-peer learning community of working farmers, would-be farmers, and interns meets informally and irregularly to problem-solve, mentor, remedy social isolation, and generally offer mutual support. The experience of those participating in this group has ranged from forty years in the profession, to a second-generation farmer, to a thirty-something woman wanting to transition from landscaping to farming, to two young women who were formerly farm laborers with ownership aspirations, and to male and female farm interns with no land, few resources, little experience, but high hopes.

The breadth of their experience helps move all comers toward a sense of professional participation and development.

Conversations at Farmers Anonymous meetings acknowledge the situated nature of agricultural knowledge. Knowledge is valid to the extent it is practical for particular contexts, and the group collectively sharpens what they have learned for transfer to new sites. The Farmers Anonymous topics, which arise mostly organically in conversation, show that these farmers are very concerned about the intersection of local trends and global influences. For example, urban sprawl, national medical policies, and global climate change come together in conversations about the local increase in the deer population and its seemingly limitless taste for foliage. Dramatic crop losses and even the elimination of some valuable crops from production prompt discussions about alternative crops and preventive measures. The local increase in the kinds and numbers of ticks along with the incursion of Lyme disease, at least partially attributable to deer, poses a special concern to outdoor workers. Farmers Anonymous provides a forum to share new preventive measures (like clothing and repellents), medical strategies (like what kind of antibiotics for how many days), and natural management practices (like close mowing, dogs, fencing, and out-of-season hunting permits). Long-term farmers in Indiana notice the warming climate, and the group actively strategizes adaptations to warming, erratic, and intense weather. In 2011 the unusually wet summer led to clouds of biting buffalo gnats that, in addition to being pests for people, were blinding chickens. However, until the Farmers Anonymous meeting, each person was problem-solving individually: they had not known that the infestation was regional. Once that was discovered, they put their heads together to devise possible solutions.

Such opportunities to problem-solve are also leavened with sociable grousing and self-deprecating humor—like the time someone was so intent on scaring away a hawk that he ran through the chicken manure in sock feet. Or the time someone caught a snapping turtle whose "hands were as big as mine." Or tales of the miraculous natural world—the hardworking dung beetle or the consumption-to-manure ratios of chickens, rabbits, horse, cow, pig, sheep, and goats (in order of best to least good, apparently). These exchanges enable people who work mostly alone and are mostly self-taught to lay out, work over, and take in not only skill-based information but also frameworks for the existential challenge of enacting who they are through how they do what they do.

Repositioning Food with Advocacy and Policy Groups

Important stakeholders in local farming that complement the capacity building of farm schools and training programs are food advocacy and policy organizations. Around the country, local, regional, and state "food policy councils" (FPCs) are advocating fair, just, and local food by expanding on and aggregating existing efforts to organize, educate, and promote farmers and quality food. According to the Johns Hopkins Center for a Livable Future (a continental network for FPCs), FPCs are part of "a long-term strategy to create systemic and meaningful improvements in the food system." These groups seek change "in public food procurement procedures, revisions in urban gardening and farming codes, and better access to healthier food."[39] Elsewhere, FPCs are advocating at the policy level (both locally and at the state level) through partnerships with food and farming advocates, city and county councils, nearby institutions, and citizens to inform such decisions as health department codes regulating egg distribution, land-use planning frameworks guiding city or county development, and food-buying practices and priorities of school systems and hospitals. According to the Center for a Livable Future, over 278 FPCs existed in North America in 2015. More than 200 of these are in the United States, with 60 found in Canada, and 6 are part of tribal nations. Representative of the diverse stakeholders in the movement, "42% of FPCs across North America are independent grassroots coalitions, 20% are housed in another nonprofit organization, 18% are embedded in government, 16% are registered 501(c)(3) nonprofit organizations," and the rest are found in universities and colleges, in extension offices, and other organizations.

While their specific goals vary, some FPCs advocate "food sovereignty"—the sharing of power among all who produce, distribute, and consume food in ways that affirm diverse identities, values, cultures, and ecologies. Their goal is to replace the priorities of the financial markets that currently drive the food industry with those of small-scale producers and consumers. In this justice-oriented framework, the goal is "just food," with nutritional, economic, social, and environmental benefits that extend beyond select populations. Food will be just when knowledge about, access to, and ability with it coalesce into a sense of shared stakes, an embrace of food as a right and resource of conceptual and material, cultural and environmental scope.

The work by FPCs can make important interventions at junctures where personal resilience, community and culture, advocacy organizations, and public policies can make or break a small farmer. Immigration policies, loan programs, food regulations, retail and wholesale outlets, and educational and cultural outreach are all within the purview of FPCs. For example, after "David Novak" emigrated from communist-bloc Eastern Europe by clandestinely traversing high-altitude mountain passages at night and hiding from border guards by day, he settled in West Virginia with few resources other than the compulsory animal science education of his youth. His successful reinvention as a popular local food farmer in the United States was made possible by training sessions he took at West Virginia University's renowned Small Farm Center. There he connected with potential customers in urban areas and learned how to develop infrastructure on the farm: building fences for laying hens, sheep, and dairy goats; planting fruit trees and berry bushes; breaking ground for vegetables and feed corn; and adding much-needed inputs to the overharvested hay fields. He was able to take advantage of a new food hub in Huntington that was founded as a result of partnerships among people from the university, a grassroots network, and a business incubator. Within this food hub Novak sells eggs, chicken, lamb, pork, fleece, vegetables, honey, fruit, herbs, and fresh-baked bread. With the passage of a raw milk bill in the state, supported by grassroots and national nonprofit groups, he now has the legal latitude to add dairy to his offerings. Six years in, his fruit crops are maturing, and Novak is poised to recoup some of his original investment and ease up on his ninety-hour weeks. But he might be in a better financial position today if farm start-up funding had been structured differently. And his doubts about the long-term sustainability of his venture might be assuaged with more social and cultural support. He experiences a persistent sense of isolation and worries that if he finds a partner who is worldly and adventurous enough to take on this risk-taking immigrant, will she be happy staying on the farm in rural West Virginia?

Thus, FPCs can provide important leadership roles as far as relocation and loan policies, food regulations, retail and wholesale outlets, and educational and cultural outreach, all of which factor into the success of small farmers. With growing numbers of immigrants, women, and other underrepresented farmers, the potential for affecting farming capacity with these issues is significant. Because one-channel subsistence farmers will face an uphill climb, FPCs can help scale up local food with policies that support an increase in acreage of existing farms and more diversified sales outlets.[40] They can design intensive support for those at-risk farmers who begin with no family land and a substantial cultural distinction from the local community. FPCs may also have a role to play in advocating a revival of the infrastructure that once supported numerous small farms, including farmer-fair policies, educated consumers, and the slaughterhouses, produce facilities, dairy processors, collective freezers, local granaries, and other community services of a decentralized food system. These efforts will affect not only the community's flow of local food but also its environmental health, as researchers have found that farmers selling direct to consumers are more likely to have a farming philosophy that exhibits greater concern for the environment.[41]

Local needs to scale up if it is to serve more than a niche crowd and reach its potential for widespread change. Many would-be farmers must work their way to competency through catch-as-catch-can programs as farm laborers, interns, and volunteers, and in community gardens and backyard experiments. New farmers are often thwarted by difficulties in acquiring the land, infrastructure, equipment, and vast and contextual knowledge needed to farm successfully. Meanwhile, longtime farmers experience increased competition from new farmers where the growth in distribution venues does not keep pace. An unsustainable number of local food farms still make under ten thousand dollars a year, and when farmers get sidetracked, slowed, or fail, society, too, loses human and financial capital. As we finish writing this chapter, a Bloomington food cooperative that buys local food announced that it was closing two of its four grocery stores, one of which was constructed with millions of dollars guaranteed by individual cooperative members. Meanwhile, a nearby orchard is considering canceling the first year of its CSA because a warm spring was followed by a late hard freeze, effectively eliminating the entire apple crop. In the time it has taken to write this book—which is, incidentally, much shorter than what it takes a standard apple tree to bear fruit or an eroded pasture to revive—mainstay community operations (both farms and distribution businesses) have closed up shop and new ones have, optimistically, put out their shingle. Local food is not only an individual's investment. As customers look to buy local food and seek to support family farms, they must also be willing to take up their half of the bargain. Knowing not just the stories but also the people behind the beautiful, delectable products of local farms should prompt society to address important gaps that exist right now in farming, gaps that potentially threaten this unique asset in the US food system.

Notes

1. USDA, "Farm Demographics—US Farmers by Gender, Age, Race, Ethnicity, and More," 2012 Census Highlights, May 2014, https://www.agcensus.usda.gov/Publications/2012/Online_Resources/Highlights/Farm_Demographics.

2. Ibid. The Agricultural Census of 2012 shows that the total number of principal operators dropped 4.3 percent from 2007.

3. Ibid.

4. Chris Coffin, "Gaining Insights, Gaining Access," Farmland.org., April 2016, https://www.farmland.org/initiatives/gaining-insights-gaining-access.

5. R. Fiorentine, "Increasing Similarity in Life Plans of Male and Female College Students? Evidence and Implications," *Sex Roles* 18 (1988): 143–58; Margaret Mooney Marini et al., "Gender and Job Values," *Sociology of Education* 69 (1996): 49–65.; Barbara A. Greene and Teresa K. Debacker, "Gender and Orientations toward the Future: Links to Motivation," *Educational Psychology Review* 16 (2004): 91–120; Jacquelynne S. Eccles, "Understanding Women's Educational and Occupational Choices: Applying the Eccles et al. Model of Achievement-Related Choices," *Psychology of Women Quarterly* 18 (1994): 585–

609. Cynthia Feliciano and Rubén G. Rumbaut, in "Gendered Paths: Educational and Occupational Expectations and Outcomes among Adult Children of Immigrants" (*Ethnic and Racial Studies* 28 [2005]: 1087–1118), present an interesting categorization of the educational and occupational outcomes of second-generation immigrants. They describe those outcomes as nonlinear, "arrived at only after individuals experience many twists and turns that are highly influenced by gender." The four categories they identify bear examination for their utility in understanding women farmers: "motivated achievers, defeatist drifters, optimistic strivers, and wishful thinkers" (1107).

6. USDA, "Women Farmers Control 7 Percent of US Farmland, Account for 3 Percent of Sales," September 2014, http://www.agcensus.usda.gov /Publications/2012/Online_Resources/Highlights/Women_Farmers /Highlights_Women_Farmers.pdf; USDA, "Census of Agriculture Shows Growing Diversity in US Farming," February 4, 2009, http://www.usda.gov /wps/portal/usda/usdahome?contentidonly=true&contentid=2009/02/0036. xml; Thomas A. Lyson, *Civic Agriculture: Reconnecting Farm, Food, and Community* (Boston: Tufts University Press, 2004), 111.

7. USDA, "Women Farmers."

8. Robert A. Hoppe and Penni Korb, "Characteristics of Women Farm Operators and Their Farms," USDA, April 2013, http://www.ers.usda.gov/media /1093198/eib111_summary.pdf.

9. Ibid.

10. USDA, "Organic Production Survey," 2008, http://www.agcensus.usda. gov/Publications/2007/Online_Highlights/Fact_Sheets/organics.pdf. Accessed November 28, 2016, https://web.archive.org/web/20160418054424 /http://www.ers.usda.gov/media/1093198/eib111_summary.pdf.

11. USDA, "Women Farmers."

12. Hoppe and Korb, "Characteristics of Women Farm Operators," 1.

13. USDA, "Farm Demographics."

14. Ibid.

15. Hoppe and Korb, "Characteristics of Women Farm Operators."

16. Consistent with the proportion of women farmers overall, Jennifer Robinson conducted about one third (sixteen) of her fifty in-depth farmer interviews between 2005 and 2015 with women.

17. Brenda Simmons, interview with Jennifer Robinson, Bloomington, Indiana, August 1, 2005, Simmons Winery, http://www.simmonswinery.com /about.html.

18. "Swirling" is said to occur when students working toward a degree in higher education enroll at two or more institutions, either simultaneously or consecutively. According to Deborah Smith Bailey, this approach allows stu-

dents to select classes from different institutions, taking advantage of unique classes, popular professors. and the flexibility of choice. The practice can save students money but potentially at the cost of coherence and time. Bailey, "'Swirling' Changes to the Traditional Student Path," *American Psychological Association Monitor* 34 (December 2003), http://www.apa.org/monitor/dec03/swirling.aspx.

19. World Wide Opportunities on Organic Farms, http://www.wwoof.org.

20. According to the USDA, 70 percent of farmers had internet access in 2015. National Agricultural Statistics Service, "Farm Computer Usage and Ownership," August 19, 2015, 5, http://usda.mannlib.cornell.edu/usda/current/FarmComp/FarmComp-08-19-2015.pdf.

21. Quoted in Julia Moskin, "Women Find Their Place in the Field," *New York Times*, June 1, 2005, D4.

22. According to its website, "The MacArthur Foundation supports creative people and effective institutions committed to building a more just, verdant, and peaceful world." See https://www.macfound.org.

23. Joseph S. Pete, "Farmland Values Notch Another Dramatic Rise," *Northwest Indiana Times*, September 12, 2013, http://www.nwitimes.com/business/local/farmland-values-notch-another-dramatic-rise/article_15b03e44-6c8b-5b65-81ff-f9ac331185b4.html.

24. James R. Farmer et al., "Agrileisure: Farmers' Markets, CSAs, and the Privilege in Eating Local," *Journal of Leisure Research* 46, no. 3 (2014): 313–28; Jennifer Meta Robinson and J. A. Hartenfeld, *The Farmers' Market Book: Growing Food, Cultivating Community* (Bloomington: Indiana University Press, 2007).

25. USDA, "Statistics by Subject," National Agriculture Statistics Service, https://www.nass.usda.gov/Statistics_by_Subject/index.php?sector=CROPS.

26. Kathryn Ruhf, "Regionalism: A New England Recipe for a Resilient Food System," *Journal of Environmental Studies and Sciences* 5 (2015): 650–60.

27. Land Trust Alliance Census, "2010 National Land Trust Census," http://www.landtrustalliance.org/land-trusts/land-trust-census.

28. Athens Land Trust, "Farmer Outreach," http://www.athenslandtrust.org/community-agriculture/farmer-outreach.

29. Kestrel Land Trust, "Conservation Is Collaboration," http://www.kestreltrust.org/learn-more---conservation-is-collaboration.php.

30. Amy Matthews, interviews with Robinson, 2010–2015; South Circle Farm, http://www.southcirclefarm.com.

31. An excellent description of how unwritten laws evolve in rural and remote places over long periods of time can be found in Robert Ellickson's *Order without Law: How Neighbors Settle Disputes* (Cambridge, MA: Harvard University Press, 1994).

32. Mary L. Gray, in *Out in the Country: Youth, Media, and Queer Visibility in Rural America* (New York: NYU Press, 2009).

33. USDA, "USDA Invests $18 Million to Train Beginning Farmers and Ranchers News," Release No. 0022.15, February 2, 2015,. The USDA maintains a list of successful grantees on its website: www.usda.gov.

34. Ivan Illich, *Deschooling Society* (New York: Harper and Row, 1971), 78, 81.

35. Jennifer Robinson attended a number of discussions about the development of an Indiana New Farm School between 2010 and 2013. The organizing committee created numerous documents, including curricula, knowledge domains, budgets, building proposals, and a mission statement. These documents remain unpublished.

36. Jean Lave and Etienne Wenger, *Situated Learning: Legitimate Peripheral Participation* (Cambridge, UK: University of Cambridge Press, 1991).

37. Ibid.

38. Jennifer Robinson wishes to thank the participants of Farmers Anonymous for allowing her to listen in on a number of meetings between 2011 and 2015.

39. Johns Hopkins University Center for a Livable Future, Food Policy Networks: Directory, http://www.foodpolicynetworks.org/directory.

40. James R. Farmer and Megan E. Betz, "Rebuilding Local Foods in Appalachia: Variables Affecting Distribution Methods of West Virginia Farms," *Journal of Rural Studies* 45 (2016): 34–42. Farmer and Betz found that more-educated farmers with smaller farms and less time on them were more likely to focus on one-channel direct marketing—for example, only through farmers' markets and CSAs. Similarly, a woman told Jennifer Robinson, "My goal with farming is to grow everything I need for my family and then just a bit more to sell to pay the bills and live a comfortable life. I don't want to get big. I love the manageable size of our garden and that we can do it with our own muscle, sweat and tears—and our tiller."

41. Ibid.

SIX

A Systems Approach to Local Food

It used to be popular to paraphrase the first two laws of ecology as "shit runs downstream, and we all live downstream." In other words, we are all connected, and we all have a stake in the actions of others. This ethic recognizes that we inevitably live in a world with others, human and not human, and we must understand the natural order and co-operate within its constraints in order to survive. Farmers' markets, CSAs, and newer trends in local food are signs of a shift in public attention to human and environmental resilience that acknowledges the interconnectedness of social and ecological systems. Local food is particularly appealing in this initiative because of its attention to relationships in a system. Selling local, it seems, is as much about learning to think in terms of systems of social and environmental factors as well as economic ones. It represents a fundamental development in how many people see the world and themselves in it, reconfiguring food from an item in a supply chain—which extracts resources like soil, air, water, and labor and moves them from one site to be used in another—to a complex package of matter and meaning tied with strands that tug on the fastenings of our world. Food is at the heart of our survival, and local food especially makes concrete the question of who survives and how. Local helps us to see the systemic nature of food and the interwoven complexities of the world within which we, mostly blithely, function every day. In this chapter we step back from the practicalities of selling locally to discuss an integrative framework that puts these many variables into a system that can help people make better-informed decisions—not just about buying and selling locally but also about environmental and human sustainability for the future. This is the turn toward local.

We propose here a new model, adapted from natural resource management, for describing the systems nature of local food. It pares away detail so that we can test our understanding and identify leverage points for new applications. Like any model, this one clarifies through "simplified abstractions."[1] Once designed, we can check it against our mental models and, in recursive process, correct our explanations for how the world works.[2] With such a model, decisions—about which farmers' market to join, how to structure CSA shares, how to increase customer numbers through a website, and so on—can be reviewed in a larger context. The more accurately our models represent the way things work, the more we can use them with intention.

Systems and Sustainability

Selling locally inevitably operates in systems of relation: actions and events affect and are affected by people, animals, materials, and processes in feedback loops. It follows that other than in the direst circumstances, and perhaps even then, feeding people requires more than getting a certain numbers of calories to them each day, because food is inseparable from a host of social, environmental, and economic interactions. Further, substances do not become food until they pass through the meaning-making machine of culture, which is also engaged with elemental and environmental systems. The systems framework we propose steps back from specifics in order to get a broader view of the actors and resources in a system. This distance allows us to identify important flows, interactions, outcomes, and points of intervention that leverage the whole system, even as elements within it change. Understanding the system and monitoring it can inform and empower policy makers, advocates, farmers, and customers who help set the conditions in which local food operates so that it includes environmental resilience, economic justice, and social and individual well-being. In this way, "community supported agriculture," the theory, can be realized in the broadest sense: agriculture that supports and, in turn, is supported by the community.

Modeling local food offers a prime opportunity for intentionally designed research for sustainability. Design-based research, also known simply as "design research," advances design, research, and practice simultaneously and is widely used in fields that integrate research and application. It differs from basic, so-called gold-standard research, which aspires to laboratory controls, blind studies, and pre-conceived operational protocols. Instead, it operates in the messy realities of the field, beginning from conjectures about what will work and drawing inspiration and discovery from the dynamic complexities of the real world. Design-based research is "pragmatic, grounded, interactive, iterative and flexible, integrative, and contextual"; it assumes that we can advance transferable ideas with input from practice, data gathered midstream, and revisions to operations based on many feedback loops available in the field context.[3] It also allows for a new kind of reasoning, which Jon Kolko calls abductive reasoning: the process of envisioning "what might be so."[4]

Local food is just such an imagining: an ongoing "experiment" in which plans unfold pragmatically, interactively, and flexibly. Designs are revised in midstream as information becomes available and corrections are called for. Decisions always drive toward "what might be so," but they are guided by complex social, economic, and environmental intersections. For example, a market vendor may anticipate that a new kind of cucumber will be a big hit with customers; she may find the seed, grow the squash successfully, and transport it to market in what ought to be lucrative quantities. But if people simply don't buy it (it's too new, too odd, tastes too different from old favorites), she may decide her limited truck space is better devoted to something more popular and end up composting the whole squash crop. Likewise, a food bank may be philosophically committed to growing the next generation of healthy eaters by involving schoolchildren in their community garden in small weeding and planting tasks. But late in the season, it may set aside its educational mission to swap in adult volunteer labor so that necessary farm work gets finished in light of an early frost warning. The immediacy of local food—short distances, identifiable people, visible impact, lived politics—helps us to think in terms of systems and make informed and intentional plans for the future.

A Systems Approach

The factors in a local food system are multivariable, nonlinear, cross-scale, and changing. They include complex interactions with interests, processes, and outcomes. This complexity urges us to move

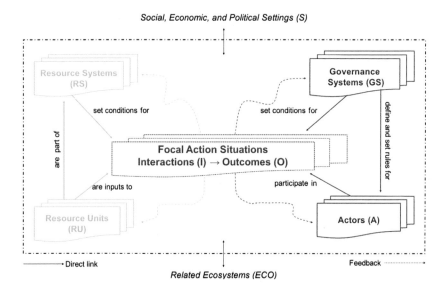

Figure 6.1. Revised social-ecological system (SES) framework with multiple first-tier components. *Michael McGinnis and Elinor Ostrom, 2014*

beyond simple descriptions in order to grapple with the complexity of food's intersecting subsystems—the local ecology; the farm; available distribution systems; rules and policies; and the people who grow, move, buy, and consume it. This complexity calls for a systems theory approach.[5] Rather than isolating variables or simplifying processes, systems thinking embraces the richness of "interlocking and interacting interests and considerations."[6] It uses an array of tools to organize findings from diverse contexts into a common framework that can be transferred to new situations. A systems approach allows us to make comparisons that project whether a local food innovation that works for one population, time, and geographical location will be successful in another.

Especially well-suited to understanding food is the social-ecological systems (SES) framework conceptualized by Nobel Laureate Elinor Ostrom. Ostrom used SES to illuminate how people collectively manage natural resources. Despite earlier theories that people using the same resource would compete with each other to its long-term detriment, her work on "common pool resources" shows that even in the absence of official policies to protect resources on which communities depend, community members do voluntarily act to further their long-term interests.[7] Garrett Hardin had theorized that unregulated pastureland would be overgrazed into economic and environmental collapse, but Ostrom identified many cases from around the world in which communities successfully self-manage common pool resources, including fisheries, pastures, woods, lakes, and groundwater basins.[8]

Ostrom's primary model for the factors impacting the commons, meaning the cultural and natural resources available to all citizens, is the SES framework. It identifies and organizes important factors in a commons system that reflects linkages, feedback loops, and other complexities that affect its operations.[9] As a model, the SES moves beyond describing any particular system "to organize findings" in ways that allow "isolated knowledge" to accumulate. Thus, we can adapt it to local food systems, which are similarly complex examples of human-ecological systems and use it to move our observations beyond particular examples to generalizable accumulations of knowledge.[10] By recursively checking theory-building with experience, and vice versa, we posit an approach that brings "Ostrom's Law" to life: "A resource arrangement that works in practice can work in theory."[11]

Ostrom and Michael McGinnis illustrate the core areas and feedback loops for analyzing any SES that includes four major subsystems (resource systems, resource units, governance, and actors (also referred to as "users" in earlier texts) that are centered on a "Focal Action Situation" (see figure 6.1).[12] This figure represents the complexity of an action situation graphically, by showing the four main subsystems. It also alludes to their relationship to external ecosystems and to social, economic, and political settings. Moreover, it suggests that secondary variables are nested within the four primary subsystems. Each of these subsystems includes certain variables, listed in detail in Ostrom's earlier work (see table 6.1). Each variable is generalized from many case studies to present a generalized factor that might pertain cattle herds as well as to alfalfa crops.[13] A local food system, for example, might include:

Table 6.1. Second-Tier Variables of a Social-Ecological System

Social, economic, and political settings (S)
S1 Economic development. S2 Demographic trends. S3 Political stability.
S4 Government resource policies. S5 Market incentives. S6 Media organization.

Resource systems (RS)	*Governance systems (GS)*
RS1 Sector (e.g., water, forests, pasture, fish)	GS1 Government organizations
RS2 Clarity of system boundaries	GS2 Nongovernment organizations
RS3 Size of resource system*	GS3 Network structure
RS4 Human-constructed facilities	GS4 Property-rights systems
RS5 Productivity of system*	GS5 Operational rules
RS6 Equilibrium properties	GS6 Collective-choice rules*
RS7 Predictability of system dynamics*	GS7 Constitutional rules
RS8 Storage characteristics	GS8 Monitoring and sanctioning
	processes
RS9 Location	

Resource units (RU)	*Users (U)*
RU1 Resource unit mobility *	U1 Number of users*
RU2 Growth or replacement rate	U2 Socioeconomic attributes of users
RU3 Interaction among resource units	U3 History of use
RU4 Economic value	U4 Location
RU5 Number of units	U5 Leadership/entrepreneurship*
RU6 Distinctive markings	U6 Norms/social capital*
RU7 Spatial & temporal distribution	U7 Knowledge of SES/mental models*
	U8 Importance of resource*
	U9 Technology used

Interactions (I) → *Outcomes (O)*	
I1 Harvesting levels of diverse users	O1 Social performance measures (e.g.,
I2 Information sharing among users	efficiency, equity, accountability,
I3 Deliberation processes	sustainability)
I4 Conflicts among users	O2 Ecological performance measures
I5 Investment activities	(e.g., overharvested, resilience,
I6 Lobbying activities	biodiversity, sustainability)
I7 Self-organizing activities	O3 Externalities to other SES's
I8 Networking activities	

Related ecosystems (ECO)
ECO1 Climate patterns. ECO2 Pollution patterns. ECO3 Flows into and out of focal SES.

*Subset of variables found to be associated with self-organization.
Note: We have retained Ostrom's original coding for the variables in this table but have eliminated them from the text for the sake of clarity.
Source: Elinor Ostrom, "A General Framework for Analyzing Sustainability of Social-Ecological Systems," *Science* 325, no. 5939 (2009): 421.

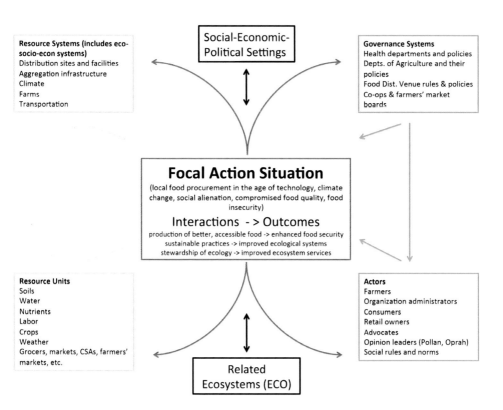

Figure 6.2. Local food systems as applied to the social-ecological systems (SES) framework. *Adapted by the authors from Michael McGinnis and Elinor Ostrom, 2014*

- a *resource system* of farms in the local foodshed of a city
- *resource units* of what is produced, what soils are available, what water supplies exist, etc.
- *actors*, such as farmers, aggregators, consumers, and restaurants
- *governance systems* of organizations and rules, such as local farmer cooperatives, a farmers' market governing board, National Organic Program guidelines, and Good Agricultural Practices (GAP) certification.

According to Ostrom, each of these subsystems can be described individually, but they also interact to produce outcomes at the SES level.

And those outcomes also affect the subsystems, their components, and other systems. In other words, a reciprocal relationship exists among elements in these subsystems: actors create governance systems and live in their context, while resource units exist within and move among resource systems. Together, they all affect the context in which action can and does occur.[14]

Small differences in how items in a system interact can mean quite different outcomes. For example, when the advisory board of a farmers' market in southern Illinois decides what "local" means there, it significantly affects not only offerings at that market but also who grows the food, what agricultural methods they use, what future fertility the soil will support, what kinds of pollution enter the air and water, the health of people in nearby communities, the vibrancy of wildlife in nearby ecosystems, the money that is spent with local businesses, the availability of heritage cuisine ingredients, types of irrigation, language training needed for public schoolchildren, cultural accommodations in nearby hospitals, jobs in organic production monitoring, and so on. Clearly, the entirety of a region's circumstances is not traceable to a single decision to make a market producer-only, in-state-only, or organic-only; however, as part of the system, it necessarily produces complex interactions and outcomes.

Using the SES to Analyze Local Food Hubs

The SES framework, as adapted to local foods, helps identify leverage points among the numerous interactions possible. Figure 6.2 teases out variables that influence the success, resilience, and robustness of the system, even though the framework we illustrate may be too abstract to recommend *particular* actions or conclusions.[15] Rather, the goal is for the framework to represent real situations in ways that provide insight and transferability. For example, an SES analysis of a successful local food system would project that positive interactions will lead to positive outcomes: the production of healthful and accessible food will result in enhanced food security; sustainable food practices will lead to improved ecological systems; ecological stewardship will lead to improved ecosystem services; accountability and the rehumanizing of food relations will remedy social alienation; and that in turn will build community and foster social justice.

But that is all very general. Working with more specificity, the SES framework allows us to pose important questions that influence the future of local food. One such question, which might aid a community as it decides where to dedicate scarce financial resources, is: when does it make sense to invest in one of the emerging trends in local food—say, aggregation through a new food hub? We know that food hubs offer greater purchasing and distribution potential. Common among their many models is aggregation: food grown by local farmers is brought together in a central place from which it can be distributed to large and small buyers. Aggregation is appealing because it presents the possibility of larger audiences for local food that small farmers cannot satisfy on their own, at least not while maintaining the social independence and the intensive ecological stewardship principles that drew many to small farming to begin with.[16] Moreover, the US and state departments of agriculture have recently emphasized hubs as the next step in the American food system—bolstering food quality and sovereignty. The increased demand means that traditional direct-to-consumer volumes are too small. Food hubs offer a way for small farms to collectively meet the greater needs, allowing the lifestyle and diversification that many farmers want while bringing small quantities together for easier access by consumers. Still, while food hubs seem to boom in some regions, in others momentum lags. How are municipalities going to decide whether their region might be a viable one for a food hub? How will they gauge whether the investment in money, time, space, human resources, and social capital necessary to develop a hub will be worth it instead of, say, adding a new farmers' market or CSA?

The SES framework helps with that decision. It identifies the variables that are critical for a food hub, which are different from those encountered with farmers' markets and CSAs. For example, while farmers' markets, CSAs, and front porch drop-off sites provide great autonomy to farmers, leaving largely to their discretion the varieties and quantities to grow, along with the timing of deliveries, the duration of the season, and the setting of prices, a food hub requires an initial cooperation among a group of farmers to create an infrastructure

Figure 6.3. Farmer Tim Alexander of Henderson, Kentucky, poses early one
September morning as he prepares for the annual freshwater shrimp harvest.
Photograph by James R. Farmer

and then ongoing coordination with that group to accumulate and distribute saleable quantities of marketable products. An articulation of
the challenge of starting a food hub, then, might be that "actors" (for
example, farmers) will choose to join a food hub, or start their own,
once its benefits outweigh those of alternatives (such as direct markets). Checked against experience, though, we can see that numerous
"second level" variables come into play, each with its own impact on
the system and the choices people make.[17] Ten of those variables are
especially significant in whether people will willingly organize themselves through collective action in a given situation, and nine of them
are especially significant for a food hub. We will talk through the importance of these nine variables first and then show how they can be
used to compare two real-life food hub situations.

1. Size of the Resource System

The resource system identified for a food hub has to be amenable to collective action. For example, an area the size of the twelve states making up the US Midwest would likely be too big in geography, scope, and actors for collective action. Similarly, a resource system that encompassed the smaller geographic area of south-central Appalachia would probably be too diverse culturally, politically, and climatologically to provide much basis for collective action around a food hub. On the other hand, a very small resource system, say only a small block of residents, might not adequately "generate substantial flows of valuable products."[18] Thus, a food hub would probably be better supported by a moderately sized resource system, say the local foodshed of a midsize city—such as Bloomington, Indiana, or Huntington, West Virginia.

2. Productivity of the Resource System

By this logic, people in a particular region, with similar characteristics and appropriate buying populations, as with Bloomington and Huntington, would be much more likely to act cooperatively to create a food hub than a larger or more heterogeneous group dispersed around the country with little to activate their collective interests. The optimal situation for collective action, according to Ostrom, balances the size and productivity of a resource system. That sweet spot exists at the intersection of two continuums: one describing availability (ranging from super saturated to extensively exhausted resources) and the other describing development (from very abundant to hardly developed resources). If adequate options for local food already exist, then a community will not need to add a hub; if too few farmers with too few products supply an area, then similarly the community will not need a hub.

3. Resource Unit Mobility

According to common natural resource models, we should see less collective action when resource units are more mobile. For example, food became more mobile in the late 1800s. Trains started carrying cattle from the fields of Iowa, Nebraska, and Kansas to the stockyards of Chicago. Apples were shipped from Washington state to Washington, DC. And milk that was pasteurized and then ultra-pasteurized had enhanced shelf life and thus greater mobility. At this scale of mobility, the USDA, representing Americans, could enforce certain standards or cut certain deals with industry, but meaningful collective choices by people were not possible. Local food, on the other hand, builds in some limits to mobility because it prioritizes freshness, proximity, and social connections. An interesting caveat, however, is that as the local movement grows, the ubiquity of the food and the mobility of the consumers may diminish the need for collectivity. In other words, when buyers can acquire "local" goods practically anywhere (farmers' markets, farm stands, CSAs, restaurants, wholesalers, grocers, co-ops, etc.), that ubiquity may actually undermine the whole idea that food can connect one to place and community.

4. The Number of Actors

With too many individuals involved, it is often a challenge to reach collective decisions. On the other hand, involving too few individuals makes delegating and completing responsibilities improbable. Because food hubs often affect a broad group of stakeholders (farmers, individual customers, institutional customers, merchants, commercial distributors, town administrators, parks personnel, urban planners, educators, food security nonprofits, neighborhood associations, land conservation groups, water managers, and so on), the leadership team needs to be kept to a workable number while farmers may need to be actively recruited to keep up supply.

5. Leadership and Entrepreneurship

Leaders always matter in establishing grassroots organizations.[19] According to Ostrom, a group is apt to be successful when its leaders have "entrepreneurial skills and are respected as local leaders as a result of prior organization."[20]

6. Norms/Social Capital

Leaders are likely to be successful when they have the skills and associations that the local society tends to respect, including sharing "moral and ethical standards regarding how to behave in groups they form."[21] While individuals involved in starting a food hub may not have prior experience in that exact task, the skills and social capital they have accrued through farming and direct marketing are likely to garner the respect and following they need to recruit other growers. On the other hand, farmers tend to be solitary workers and may have limited patience for the coalition building and evening committee meetings necessary to establish a food hub. So a hub may need a team of entrepreneurial types to carry such a complex goal to fruition.

7. Collective Choice Rules

Ostrom argues that change is most possible when people have the autonomy to develop, monitor, and enforce some or all of their own rules. For creating a food hub, this might mean that farmers are able to craft rules that will support both a well-functioning hub and their own interests. For example, farmers might decide that the optimal delivery and pickup days for a hub should complement but not compete with the local farmers' market day. That sort of decision would expand the number of days local food is accessible in a community and spread harvesting out over the course of a week. Without farmer input, however, a hub could organize for the convenience of the customers, perhaps establishing pickup hours that accommodate standard school or work schedules but conflict with Saturday markets. Successful collective choice rules should mean lower expenses—in terms of time, money, and other significant factors—for participants as they develop and manage the hub.

8. Knowledge of SES/Mental Models

A shared understanding of the elements of the social and ecological system makes a difference in how people negotiate them.[22] For example, if people share an understanding that a full, grocery store-like selection of food must be on hand before opening a food hub, then their mental model may conflict with the ecological and economic realities of farming, which require months or even years of lead time. On the other hand, if a hub does not open quickly enough, failing to match growth in demand, then actors may come to believe that a hub cannot address their needs and gravitate to alternatives, leaving a shortfall when it actually opens.

9. Importance of the Resource

Ostrom explains that many successful examples of self-organization occurred when actors were "dependent on the resource system for a substantial portion of their livelihoods or attach[ed] high value to the sustainability of the resource."[23] In the food hub scenario, greater importance (high dependence and high value) would suggest greater viability. On the other hand, if farmers or buyers need no further distribution outlets or do not value them, then that locale will be less likely to generate an initiative for a new hub.

The nine variables discussed here, among ten identified by Ostrom as *significant*, become even more useful when we add *predictability of system dynamics* and *number of units*. Together, these eleven variables help explain why local food hubs occur unevenly across the United States. Seen in realistic contexts, the variables help us discern what works and what matters in local food systems. The two following case studies bring these variables to life. Each case is inseparable from the rich detail of its context, yet when we position them in the "simplified abstraction" of the SES framework, we can compare them with fewer distractions. Thinking in terms of systems like this also allows us to consider how to transfer the lessons of Bloomington and Huntington to other contexts (action situations).

Case 1: Bloomington, Indiana

At first Bloomington seems primed for a food hub. The town is a regional economic powerhouse and thus a center for food distribution of many types (chain groceries, discount stores, restaurants, specialty food trucks, multiple farmers' markets, university cafeterias, and so on). But it is not home to a formal aggregation point for locally grown products, what we are calling a local food hub. Analysis using the SES variables that are vital to collective action suggests that despite indicators to the contrary, Bloomington is *not* as viable a location for a local food hub as it might appear.

Bloomington is home to several hopping farmers' markets, an assortment of nearby small farms, and high-profile popularity of local food throughout the community—attributes that one might expect would make it a promising location for a local food hub. The city was among the first wave of farmers' markets in the mid-1970s, which run today on Tuesdays, Wednesdays, and Saturdays. It also supports at least seventeen CSAs and a Local Growers' Guild of about one hundred members.[24] Local food can be found regularly at the local cooperative and several chain grocery stores as well as in restaurants around town.

The community has a long-standing interest in local food, supported by many farmers who have relationships with steadfast customers and sales venues. The culture of the community includes significant knowledge about local food—its value, its cultivation, its preparation—and this knowledge is passed on through such educational sites as family-farmer organizations, permaculture workshops, volunteer opportunities, media coverage, and city infrastructure. Taken together, all of these indicators seem to support a stable level of "predictability of system dynamics" and a positive scenario for the development of a food hub.

The number of potential actors in a food hub—such as farmers, consumers, restaurants, and food banks—represents a significant proportion of the area's population. The city sponsors two weekly markets during the growing season, including a Saturday market that features 119 stands contracted for the eight-month season and attracts over ten thousand customers at its height, about 12 percent of the city's eighty thousand residents.[25] Several private markets and regular truck stands also operate around town. Approximately 163 farms serve the "local" needs of the surrounding county (43 in the immediate county alone).[26] In addition, large institutions—such as restaurants, hotels, university food services, and hospitals—seek more stable supplies of food at greater quantities than are generally accommodated by current sources.

Currently, several instances of leadership and entrepreneurship for cooperative action around local food exist, including within the membership of the Local Growers' Guild, a regional family farming cooperative begun in 2004; the staff and advisory boards of the five regular farmers' markets; the organizers behind locally focused bakeries, nurseries, restaurants, and distilleries/breweries; and community members who sit on local and statewide boards setting food policy, such as the Bloomington Food Policy Council and the Indiana Locally Grown initiative. Radio programs on green and sustainable eating air weekly on the public and community stations, multiple food summits and councils meet regularly, and the city-sponsored farmers' market is the most popular event in town. The state university in town hosts an annual showcase of ways to "eat green," and a farm market sets up weekly near the Starbucks in the student union. Such intensive involvement by a large portion of the community suggests that the social norms/capital and mental models of many in the Bloomington area view local food positively and that there is capacity to expand leadership and entrepreneurship in this area. Furthermore, the popularity, expertise, and history of local food in the area suggest that this resource is considered important. In short, local food matters here, and more, via a food hub, might be even better.

Do potential leaders in Bloomington have the autonomy to develop, monitor, and enforce rules that support collective action around a hub (collective choice rules)? Existing organizations suggest they do. The Bloomington Community Market is managed by the city of Bloomington but governed by an elected advisory board that includes farmers, customers, and city employees who guide the development of rules and policies. Similarly, the Local Growers' Guild is governed by elected farmers, community members, and advocates who advise and approve the development of rules and policies. The Bloomington Winter Farmers' Market is an especially good example of autonomy and depth of leadership. A farmer with financial support from the local Slow Foods chapter founded it. Then, guided by an advisory council of producer and customer representatives, it acquired administrative support from the Local Growers' Guild, and most recently it moved under the umbrella of the Center for Sustainable Living.[27] Moreover, a Wednesday market organized by farmers and hosted on private property adjacent to the city's largest shopping mall has been in operation some twenty years. This extensive participation by individuals and collaboration among community organizations suggests that a collectively organized food hub would likewise be able to develop people-centered frameworks of governance.

In the case of Bloomington, the size of the resource system, or foodshed, provisioning the town can be described by the vast majority of farms serving its farmers' markets—most found within sixty miles of town and many much closer. Farms (or gardens) close to the center of Bloomington tend to be small, even niche or micro (specialized or very small), in both acreage and production. Such constraints mean that direct-to-consumer sales with their higher prices are the most viable option for growers. Larger farms with greater production capacity tend to be located farther away in the surrounding counties, which means they can diversify their customer base by selling in other nearby counties and multiple marketplaces.

In the greater Bloomington area, the productivity of the resource system is affected by such variables as farm size, topography, soils, and soil fertility. In terms of topography, much of the area is characterized by both unglaciated ridges and glacial valleys created by meltwaters. Unlike farther north, in what is now flatter, more fertile terrain, the Bloomington area did not receive mineral and topsoil deposits at the end of the last ice age. These ecological and environmental conditions have in large part defined the farming options possible in the area. Consistently here, farmers who serve national markets by growing conventional crops (corn, soy beans, wheat) and using conventional production and distribution methods work the prime farmland (which is minimal). In contrast, new and beginning farmers (and even those who started some thirty or forty years ago) are often limited to marginal parcels by finances or land availability. Often they set up on old farms or abandoned homesteads, perched on a ridgetop without consistent access to a good water source, in a deep holler without full sun, or on clay-heavy, thin, or Borden siltstone soils. All of this means that probably only small areas of a farm are conducive to good growing. Thus, many farms around Bloomington are suited for direct-to-consumer outlets that allow higher prices for smaller quantities.[28] From the 1920s to the 1980s, farms in this area may have grown twenty-five-acre apple orchards or ten-acre green bean fields, but today farms of that capacity are rare.[29]

Finally, much of what is being produced for local distribution in Bloomington falls into the "mobile" or shippable category: fruits, vegetables, eggs, and frozen meats (resource unit mobility). Less mobile, highly perishable products—such as dairy, fish, fresh meat, and live animal sales—are uncommon in the area. At the same time, customers themselves can also be considered very mobile, with plenty of local food outlets in the area so that they can choose when and where to shop. This extensive number of units for distribution includes the community's five farmers' markets, the local cooperative grocery, Lucky's Market (a natural foods chain), a planned 365 by Whole Foods Market store, several restaurants, CSAs, farm stands, and front-porch pre-order sites.

The limited productivity taken together with the saturation of current venues and mobility of customers suggests that, appearances to the contrary, Bloomington is *not*, in fact, a likely candidate for a new food hub.

Case 2: Huntington, West Virginia

One type of food hub that successfully supplements farmers' markets, CSAs, and other direct-to-consumer methods operates in Huntington. Selling to both retailers and individuals, the Wild Ramp market offers quality produce, dairy, eggs, and meats, as well as value-added products and artisan crafts from the immediate area, such as creative art, wearables, and personal care products. Not just a warehouse for product aggregation, the Wild Ramp adds an innovative twist to the conventional hub, blending wholesale and retail distribution. It offers group marketing, cold storage, and value-added facilities in a health department-certified kitchen and adds a retail storefront that allows farmers to charge direct-to-consumer prices. Such value-added opportunities help them recover from the lower wholesale prices of an ordinary hub: farmers selling at the Wild Ramp receive 90 percent of the value of their products instead of the 50–60 percent typical of a hub. Moreover, instead of imitating the one-size-fits-all wholesale warehouse model common in the industry by aggregating similar products from many farms, Wild Ramp allows the name of the farm to follow its produce. In this way, farmers can maintain a connection between their identity and values and the quality of their work.

Huntington is not generally known as a mecca of trendy food. In fact, in 2008 it was named the least healthy city in America by the Centers for Disease Control, in no small part due to food insecurity, poor eating habits, and epidemic-level obesity. The city's rating was reported widely enough that chef and media personality Jamie Oliver pledged that his "food revolution" would overhaul school lunches, and clergy preached the benefits of healthy eating from pulpits across the city. On the surface, Huntington seems less likely than Bloomington to sponsor a healthy-eating food hub; however, the SES framework shows that significantly different secondary variables do in fact make it a viable location. Thus, the success of the Wild Ramp is no surprise.

Huntington's resource system can be considered about the same geographic size as Bloomington's, about one hundred miles from the center. The population of potential consumers is similar, too, with about 140,000 individuals living in Monroe County, Indiana, and 100,000 living in Cabell County, West Virginia. At first glance, Huntington's mountainous topography and resulting fragmented rural road network suggest lower agricultural productivity levels like Bloomington's. But in fact the Ohio River, with its back-and-forth meanderings over millennia, has created a flat, fertile valley with excellent sites for produce farming. Not only that, but the rolling and steep hills alongside the valley offer ideal lands for grazing and orchards.

The topography of Huntington's resource system also provides predictability in system dynamics, through stable microclimates and weather patterns. Farms tucked into the Ohio River Valley have warmth from the river to help maintain moderate temperatures in the late fall. Meanwhile, orchards planted on the ridgetops receive the benefit of the cold rolling down into the valleys, which protects them from extreme temperature swings that would kill the spring blossoms of apple, pear, and peach trees or freeze fruit in a late fall cold snap.

In fact, West Virginia has the highest frequency of small farms in the United States, a vibrant small farm program through West Virginia

University, and a history of "small scale" or specialty-crop agriculture since about 1775. All of these factors contribute to substantial institutionalized knowledge of the area's social and environmental systems.

So while it is similar in appearance to southern Indiana's wooded hillsides, Huntington has the advantage of large tillable tracts that support enough agriculture for direct and indirect distribution. These productivity levels support Huntington's greater consumer potential. The city is well positioned at a lengthy driving distance from other distribution centers. Besides Charleston, West Virginia, 53 miles away and with only fifty thousand inhabitants, the nearest large cities are Lexington, Kentucky, and Columbus, Ohio, at 125 and 138 miles away, respectively. This buffer gives Huntington room to cultivate local food buyers. Compare its location to Bloomington's, which is 50 miles from the greater Indianapolis metropolitan area of six million people, putting huge food industry networks just an hour's drive away—an easy distribution distance for trucking companies. Indeed, the divided state highway between Indianapolis and Bloomington is currently being upgraded to interstate specifications, underwriting industrial shipping while disrupting local routes.

In addition, the Bloomington and Huntington scenarios diverge most importantly in resource unit mobility, leadership and entrepreneurship, number of actors, norms/social capital, importance of resource variables, collective choice rules, and number of units. Food is mostly a mobile product, given appropriate infrastructure (resource unit mobility). But the more mobile resources are, the more challenging it becomes to organize collective action. Local foods produced in and around the relatively isolated Appalachian city of Huntington have decreased mobility: West Virginia's arduous transportation networks make it difficult to get goods to market.[30] Another factor to consider is that distances between metropolitan areas decrease trucking traffic. So even though Huntington has improved its technology and infrastructure to be comparable to other cities its size (or larger), we suggest that local food produced in and around that city remains less mobile.

Moreover, the saturation of local food distribution venues (number of units) varies dramatically between Huntington and Bloomington. While Bloomington offers a plethora of options, choices are more limited in Huntington. Apart from its single farmers' market, the local meat market (which may or may not always have locally sourced meats), underground distribution networks, and a single CSA, not many other options existed in Huntington before the Wild Ramp. Thus, this food hub was able to meet a community need.

While Bloomington had long ago developed social and cultural outlets for its progressive politics, in the early 2000s Huntington had a lot of room and energy to grow. An intimate group of Huntington residents, mostly transplants and returning residents, began to adapt initiatives they were familiar with elsewhere to this new locale. They, in turn, tapped more potential "actors" from groups active in many other contemporaneous initiatives (leadership and entrepreneurship). Students at Marshall University investigated the initial capacity (number of actors; productivity of resource system) in the region to organize and supply a new hub:

> They measured access to local foods in the tri-state area and identified opportunities to increase that access. They joined forces with Unlimited Future Incorporated and Create Huntington to open up a discussion regarding the creation of a local foods market. The first meeting dedicated to the concept of a local foods market was held in January 2012. A core group of citizens quickly came together and some of those citizens visited Local Roots Market & Cafe, a local foods store located in Wooster, OH. Tri-State Local Foods, a non-profit organization, was formed and the search for a location began.[31]

Today, the majority of farmers or artisans (about eighty-nine) supplying Huntington's Wild Ramp hub are located within 50 miles of the central city, with eleven others within 100 miles. Just a handful (about five) are located 100–150 miles away, with more farms breaking ground annually.[32] Currently, over one hundred farms sell their farm products through the Wild Ramp, which is staffed by more than thirty regular monthly volunteers and two paid employees.

Unlike in Bloomington, Huntington's norms and social capital do not prominently feature healthy and environmentally sound food choices. Local is pervasive enough in the larger Bloomington culture that highly regarded restaurants are founded on the principles of "local, seasonal and organic ingredients" that create a "unique Indiana cuisine" and feature "dinner menus and daily specials that change with the availability of local ingredients and the bounty of both Southern Indiana and the world."[33] In Huntington, on the other hand, local was mostly an underground movement, with clandestine egg drops on porches and raw milk shares crossing the Ohio River hidden away in private cars like sought-after contraband. However, the Wild Ramp now provides a public face for the local movement. It gathers all of these individuals and more, over thirty volunteers per month, to sort farmer drop-offs, stock shelves, clean prep space, work cash registers, and much more. No longer under the radar, local is becoming a norm through the Wild Ramp.

The norms in Huntington that support the success of the Wild Ramp include community solidarity and resilience. Marshall University, a local university of fourteen thousand students, draws 80 percent of the student body from within ninety miles of Huntington. The community was galvanized when a plane crash in 1970 took the lives of Marshall University's football team and several community members. All of the seventy-five people on board the plane were killed, including thirty-seven members of the Thundering Herd, twenty-five boosters, eight coaches, and five flight crewmembers. In short, everyone from Huntington who was alive in the 1970s knew someone on that plane. The scale of the tragedy meant people relied on each other for support and learned the value of community. The intensely regional pull of the university and the tragedy-inspired solidarity means that a cap-and-gown divide seems absent here, and the community's resilience seems palpable. People know they are connected to one another.

Local food demonstrates these connections and thus becomes elevated in importance. The national scrutiny of Huntington's obesity problem, the isolating nature of the rugged topography, the long history of small farms, all contribute to local food as an important articulation of the area's culture. This dynamic appears to culminate with the Wild Ramp—the local nonprofit that has become a beloved demonstration of pro-environment, self-reliant, good-food solidarity. Its grassroots origins allow key stakeholders—food activists, consumers, and farmers—the autonomy to develop collective choice rules that reflect their culture and respect their community members.

The SES framework illuminates critical variables that affect collective action. Taken together, they can explain the viability of a food hub in Huntington, which has one, and the failure of plans to create one in Bloomington. It is possible to discern that Bloomington, with its high visibility and myriad outlets for local food (even if sometimes availability is not sufficient), already provides an informal, distributed, agile, hub-like situation that supplants the need for something more formal, singular, and slow that caters to retail distribution—like the Wild Ramp. In fact, the ubiquity of local food in Bloomington, from truly local sources to superficial corporate labeling, suggests that "local" itself may be in danger of jumping the shark—it may be so prevalent that it no longer serves to tie people to place and community in meaningful ways. SES shows that Huntington, on the other hand, may never see the number of CSAs or farmers' market attendees that Bloomington does. But it has the right mix of abundance and scarcity, resources and capacities, to make a local food hub work.

Both towns foster robust local food systems that look quite different. It seems, as is fitting, that what works and what matters in local food is context-sensitive, involving many mechanisms and unique intersections. Of course, because food systems are so complex, we must exercise care in extending the Bloomington and Huntington lessons to new places. Still, the SES framework can help decipher these kinds of dense systems, helping us understand why similar locales might, in practice, operate quite differently. Beginning to think in terms of systems like this represents a major shift from the simple production-line thinking that remains an influential remnant of the industrial age. As the world begins to grapple with the myriad ramifications of climate change, we see how important it is to be able to visualize the far-reaching implications of even simple decisions so that we can intervene early. If we realize that we are all both downstream and upstream from somewhere else, then we can understand anew that our decisions carry a weight of responsibility. Using SES to match theory and practice promises, especially comparatively, can help us make informed decisions about food for the future.

Notes

1. Amanda Sorensen et al., "Model-Based Reasoning to Foster Environmental and Socio-scientific Literacy in Higher Education," *Journal of Environmental Studies and Sciences* 6, no. 2 (2015): 287–94.

2. Ibid.

3. Feng Wang and Michael Hannafin, "Design-Based Research and Technology-Enhanced Learning Environments," *Educational Technology Research and Development* 53, no. 4 (2005): 7.

4. Jon Kolko, "Abductive Thinking and Sensemaking: The Drivers of Design Synthesis," *Design Issues* 26, no. 1 (2010): 15–28.

5. Elinor Ostrom, "Sustainable Social-Ecological Systems: An Impossibility?," paper presented at the meeting of the American Association for the Advancement of Science, San Francisco, February 15–19, 2007, http://www.mcleveland.org/Class_reading/Ostrom_Sustainable_Socio-Economic_Systems.pdf.

6. *Pushpanathan v. Canada* (Minister of Citizenship and Immigration), [1998] 1 S.C.R. 982, para. 36; Elinor Ostrom, "A General Framework for Analyzing Sustainability of Social-Ecological Systems," *Science* 325, no. 5939 (2009): 419.

7. Ostrom, "General Framework," 419.

8. Elinor Ostrom, *Governing the Commons: The Evolution of Institutions for Collective Action* (Cambridge, UK: Cambridge University Press, 1990); Garrett Hardin, "The Tragedy of the Commons," *Science* 162, no. 3859 (1968): 1243–48.

9. Ostrom, "General Framework."

10. Xavier Basurto and Elinor Ostrom, "Beyond the Tragedy of the Commons," *Economia delle fonti di energia e dell'ambiente* 52, no. 1 (2009): 35–60; Ostrom, "General Framework."

11. Lee Anne Fennell, "Ostrom's Law: Property Rights in the Commons," *International Journal of the Commons* 5, no. 1 (2011): 9–27.

12. Michael McGinnis and Elinor Ostrom, "Social-Ecological System Framework: Initial Changes and Continuing Challenges," *Ecology and Society* 19, no. 2 (2014): 30.

13. Ostrom, "General Framework." Note that the secondary-level variables in table 6.1 are not listed in order of importance, as not all variables have equal weight in or even pertain to every SES situation.

14. Ibid, 420.

15. For instance, in the Actors (A) subsystem, secondary-level variables include farmers, organization administrators, consumers, retail owners (restaurants, small grocers, etc.), and local food advocates. Governance Systems (GS), which set rules, policies, and guidelines for the actors, pertain not only to offi-

cial government but also to other systems in which rules and policies are constructed. Governance Systems, then, may be as formal as Good Agricultural Practices (GAP) certification or National Organic Program (NOP) policies, as participant-defined as farmers' market boards, or as implicit as the social norms that bring women disproportionately into the ranks of food security volunteers. The Resource Systems subsystem includes entities or cycles affecting local foods in a given area, such as infrastructure for moving food, refrigerating it, and shipping it. But it also includes items that are vastly complex in their own right, such as climate and the viability of farming. Finally, those resource systems are comprised by variables at the level of Resource Units, such as number of cattle, individual trees, yield of tomatoes, and rainfall.

16. This is not to say that only small and micro-farmers want to be or can be ecological stewards or environmentally sustainable; rather, small farmers are often drawn to that scale of agriculture that allows for hands-on, labor-intensive methods. For example, some small farmers we have interviewed say that they prefer plowing with animals or walk-behind tractors because they feel a connection to the soil and surroundings that large-scale methods do not allow. They feel that to trade in intensive methods for greater income would compromise their social independence and ecological stewardship. Jennifer Meta Robinson and J. A. Hartenfeld, *The Farmers' Market Book: Growing Food, Cultivating Community* (Bloomington: Indiana University Press, 2007); Jennifer Meta Robinson, "Making the Land Connection: Local Food Farms and Sustainability of Place," in *The Greening of Everyday Life: Challenging Practices, Imaging Possibilities*, edited by Jens Kersten and John M. Meyer, 198–210 (Oxford: Oxford University Press, 2016).

17. A thorough description of all second-level variables can be found in Ostrom, "General Framework."

18. Ibid., 420.

19. Ruth Meinzen-Dick, "Beyond Panaceas in Water Institutions," *Proceedings of the National Academy of Sciences* 104, no. 39 (2007).

20. Ostrom, "General Framework," 421.

21. Ibid.

22. Ibid.

23. Ibid.

24. Local Growers Guild, http://www.localgrowers.org.

25. City of Bloomington, Farm Market Directory, http://bloomington.in .gov/documents/viewDocument.php?document_id=8920.

26. Angela Babb et al., "Accessing Local Foods: The Role of Financial Incentives at Farmers' Markets," *Journal of Agriculture and Human Values* (In Review).

27. Bloomington Winter Farmers' Market, "About," http://www
.bloomingtonwinterfarmersmarket.com/about.

28. Babb et al., "Accessing Local Foods."

29. Everett Kerr, personal correspondence with James Farmer, August 22, 2015.

30. Ronald Lewis, *Transforming the Appalachian Countryside* (Morgantown: West Virginia University Press, 1998).

31. Christa Galvin, Kelly Cox, and Lauren Kemp were three students at Marshall University. See The Wild Ramp, "About Us," http://wildramp.org /about-us.

32. The Wild Ramp, "Producer Information," http://wildramp.org /producers/meet-the-producers. Accessed November 28, 2016, https://web .archive.org/web/20151128122508/http://wildramp.org/producers/meet-the -producers/.

33. Restaurant Tallent, "About Restaurant Tallent," http://restauranttallent .com/about-restaurant-tallent.php (site discontinued); Farm Bloomington, http://www.farm-bloomington.com.

Conclusion

Last Saturday was one of those days when I walked around Market and thought, "it doesn't get much better than this." The weather was gorgeous, there was music all around, people were enjoying the company of friends and neighbors, the prepared food vending area along the B-Line Trail was hopping, kids played in the fountain, and farmers' tables were full with the fruits of the labors of the year. Thank you for helping create this beautiful, welcoming, healthy, and sustainable place for the community to gather and grow strong together. It is really special.
 —Marcia Veldman, Bloomington market manager, in *The Market Beet*

Americans, in general, increasingly live as though we are detached from our intimate interconnections with the natural environment. We live a myth of human independence, aided by potent agricultural, technological, and industrial revolutions that overwhelm the regenerative processes available in healthy ecosystems.[1] Over one-third of the population of the United States does not believe in global climate change, and about half of believers do not attribute it to human activity.[2] Industrial food and agriculture provide bounty, but as employed currently, they require distance from meaningful contexts, lack resilient regeneration, and lag in ethical community relations. While plentiful and inexpensive food exists in the United States, "much of it is unhealthy, and the system is not sustainable," according to the American Public Health Association.[3] In an age of anxious disconnection from and active dissolution of the liveliness of the earth, "local" provides a means of reconnection and restoration.

Food is just one system in which we can exercise our ability to see the world more holistically and more intimately. Through food, and most vividly through local food, we can learn to see the relations "between parts and parts, and parts and wholes" in an interrelated and interdependent world, and we can work to reconnect all three of the sectors commonly identified with environmental sustainability: the so-

Figure C.1. Farmer J. A. Hartenfeld prepares to load mixed lettuces for the weekly farmers' market. *Photograph by Jennifer Meta Robinson*

cial, the environmental, and the economic.[4] Local food is small enough to grasp but big enough to matter. Through it we can think big, start small, and act now. We can identify systems that work, or almost work, analyze them through cases and model making, and thereby improve and extend them. Unless or until science fully synthesizes food in a lab, we will need to cultivate a sturdy, diversified system that includes decentralized expertise in growing, preparing, and celebrating food.

Fortunately, local food operations around the country present a range of possibilities for getting things right. How local food looks and what makes it successful are context-specific yet not entirely unique. When Bloomington farmers' market manager Marcia Veldman describes a good day for local food, many would recognize her experience: people busily collaborate to create community against the elemental backdrop of weather, seasons, and landscape. Expressive flourishes show in music, conversation, play, and walk-around food, which unfold on a stage of collective care that includes a fountain where children play and a railway track converted to a recreation path. The labors of farmers and others supply the occasion and energy for the event. An infrastructure aiming for inclusion—mechanisms to process food vouchers, free admission, diverse participation options, and municipal investment—extends the welcome. This is local food at its best. Done right, local food can help stabilize local economies both urban and rural, increase access to healthy foods, lessen environmental consequences, draw people into association with one another, and provide them with the raw materials for personal and cultural expression.

In a sense, this book is about a world in which we are not alone. Food depends on relationships and enables them. Like other technologies of human invention, the way we eat makes meaning: it orders the world in particular ways, and we experience ourselves through that world. Sometimes it helps us live harmoniously with others, and sometimes it helps us express our distinction and even opposition to them. Local at its best is not only about being together in the same space but also about *how* we are together. Food is fodder for making identities, places, and futures: a means of knowing where, when, and with whom we are in the world and what we will make of it all. Local at its best aspires to a restorative alignment that connects people to people, people to place, and place to our collective purposes: it does not recapitulate a romantic, pre-technological past but invents a contemporary way of being together that mends the distance and disturbances introduced by modern technology. At its best, local connects us to our surroundings and rebuilds community in our daily lives. It restores value to people and their work. It rehumanizes social life.

The challenge in turning to local is to remain engaged with the world. We may like the reduced food miles, lessened pollution loads, good taste, nutritional vibrancy, and low cost that recommend local goods. Still, local does not necessarily mean inward-looking isolationism. Instead, as we have seen, it acknowledges a dynamic, interactive world replete with necessary entanglements with others. Local puts us back into context, where we can gain a holistic sense of ourselves and the world. Local's greatest success will lie in using systems thinking to think big—indeed, to contribute all it can to human well-being and environmental sustainability around the world.

Local food has not yet achieved its lofty ambitions. In many ways it is still an incomplete project, still in beginning stages. To serve more than a niche crowd and realize its potential for feeding large numbers and affecting widespread institutional change, production must increase.[5] Many small farms struggle to survive, trying an all-of-the-above approach with direct-to-consumer sales, niche products, and off-farm jobs. Yet those who sell in quantity to food hubs, grocers, and restaurants also have to manage the lower price points that come with wholesale distribution. Even as we write, farms are retooling their business plans to take another shot at viability. And some are closing.

Still, for many people, local works and local matters. New, independent ventures launch almost daily. It may look a little crazy from the outside. As farmer-philosopher Joel Salatin says: "Freedom and innovation require protecting the lunatic fringe. We know that innovation comes from those who dare to question the orthodoxy of the status quo. Strong societies embrace wackos, knowing that the fringe doesn't jeopardize overall stability. And that's just what we food-growing, pastured-animal-raising folks are in today's society."[6] The farmers' markets, CSAs, and small farms we have provide a foundation for us to "make hay while the sun shines," to use an old agricultural adage. And as with hay, harvesting the potential of local food will need to be methodical: a process of labor, timing, curing, contemplation, and stamina that works with natural systems and seasons, equipment and invention, animals and economies, and people and their capabilities. Wendell Berry once observed, "Farming presents a paramount experience; it needs paramount intelligence."[7] And as long ago as 1912, a farming textbook by Edwin Jackson Kyle, a professor of horticulture and dean of the Texas A&M School of Agriculture, and Alexander Caswell Ellis, a professor of the philosophy of education at A&M, observed that we must revise the messages society sends about farming to "stop leading the farmer's children directly away from the country and into the town." Rather, they say, educators "should encourage the natural interest in which both country boys and girls, and town boys and girls, have in growing plants and animals; should show them how agriculture is receiving the best thought of many of the most intelligent men and women in the world; how it offers to them not merely a happy and useful life but as great a field for the exercise of intelligence and character and the application of scientific methods as do commerce, law, medicine, or any other field of effort."[8]

Our collective responsibility for the agricultural act that is eating means we all must have paramount intelligence to feed the world adequately, well, and justly. The local food movement is at a stage of development early enough to have the momentum of newness and invention but mature enough to indicate persistent problems. What we do in these sunny days of local food to expand its base and build the knowledge we need will allow the system as a whole to become more robust. Local growers and advocates who experiment with alternatives are building relationships and fostering systems that they hope will support a sustainable, secure, nimble, and thriving future. Since we all are implicated in the agricultural act of eating, we need to renew the social compact between we who eat and the tiny minority of people we rely on to grow our food, a compact that foregrounds mutual responsibility. All of us have a stake in our mutual experiments in food movements and the future to which we will belong. In local, micro-level behaviors can help solve macro-level problems.

Notes

1. Heather Reynolds, Eduardo Brondízio, and Jennifer Meta Robinson, eds., *Teaching Environmental Literacy: Across the Curriculum and across Campus* (Bloomington: Indiana University Press, 2010), 2.

2. Anthony Leiserowitz et al., "Climate Change in the American Mind: Americans' Global Warming Beliefs and Attitudes in April, 2013," Yale University and George Mason University (New Haven, CT: Yale Project on Climate Change Communication, 2013), 3.

3. American Public Health Association, *Toward a Healthy, Sustainable Food System*, Policy number 200712, 2007, https://www.apha.org/policies-and-advocacy/public-health-policy-statements/policy-database/2014/07/29/12/34/toward-a-healthy-sustainable-food-system.

4. Marvin Harris, "Anthropology Needs Holism; Holism Needs Anthropology," in *The Teaching of Anthropology: Problems, Issues, and Decisions*, edited by Conrad Phillip Kottak et al., 22–28 (Mountain View: Mayfield Publishing, 1997), 23.

5. James R. Farmer et al., "Agrileisure: Farmers' Markets, CSAs, and the Privilege in Eating Local," *Journal of Leisure Research* 46, no. 3 (2014): 313–28; James R. Farmer and Megan E. Betz, "Rebuilding Local Foods in Appalachia: Variables Affecting Distribution Methods of West Virginia Farms," *Journal of Rural Studies* 45 (2016): 34–42.

6. Joel Salatin, "How to Lobby for Saner Food Policies," *Mother Earth News*, June/July 2015, 59.

7. Wendell Berry, remarks at meeting with farmers and community food security partners, Bloomington, Indiana, November 12, 2010.

8. Edwin Jackson Kyle and Alexander Caswell Ellis, *Fundamentals of Farming and Farm Life*, rev. ed. (New York: Charles Scribner's Sons, 1922), xi.

BIBLIOGRAPHY

Adam, Katherine L. "Community Gardening." ATTRA–National Sustainable Agriculture Information Service, 2011. www.attra.ncat.org/attra-pub /download.php?id=351.

Alkon, Alison Hope. *Black, White, and Green: Farmers' Markets, Race and the Green Economy.* Athens: University of Georgia Press, 2012.

Allen, Gary. *Sausage: A Global History.* London: Reaktion, 2015.

Allen, Patricia. "Reweaving the Food Security Net: Mediating Entitlement and Entrepreneurship." *Agriculture and Human Values* 16, no. 2 (1999): 117–29.

American Community Gardening Association. "Frequently Asked Questions." https://communitygarden.org/resources/faq.

American Public Health Association. *Toward a Healthy, Sustainable Food System.* Policy number 200712. 2007. https://www.apha.org/policies-and-advo-cacy/public-health-policy-statements/policy-database/2014/07/29/12/34 /toward-a-healthy-sustainable-food-system.

Ames, Guy K. "Community Orchards." ATTRA–National Sustainable Agriculture Information Service, 2013. http://www.attra.ncat.org/attra-pub /download.php?id=441.

Amish Studies. "Amish Population Trends 1991–2010: Twenty-Year Highlights." http://www2.etown.edu/amishstudies/Population_Trends_1991 _2010.asp. Accessed November 28, 2016, https://web.archive.org/web /20160415235137/http://www2.etown.edu/amishstudies/Population _Trends_1991_2010.asp.

Amsden, Benjamin, and Jesse McEntee. "Agrileisure: Re-imagining the Relationship between Agriculture, Leisure, and Social Change." *Leisure/Loisir* 35, no. 1 (2011): 37–38.

Athens Land Trust. "Farmer Outreach." http://www.athenslandtrust.org /community-agriculture/farmer-outreach.

Babb, Angela, James Farmer, Sara Minard, and Marcia Veldman. "Accessing Local Foods: The Role of Financial Incentives at Farmers' Markets." *Journal of Agriculture and Human Values* (In Review).

Bailey, Deborah Smith. "'Swirling' Changes to the Traditional Student Path." *American Psychological Association Monitor* 34 (December 2003). http:// www.apa.org/monitor/dec03/swirling.aspx.

Bailkey, Martin, and Joe Nasr. "From Brownfields to Greenfields: Producing Food in North American Cities." *Community Food Security News* (Fall 1999/ Winter 2000). Special Issue: *Growing Food in Cities: Urban Agriculture in North America* (2007): 6.

Baltimore Office of Sustainability. "Homegrown Baltimore: Grow Local." http://www.baltimoresustainability.org/projects/baltimore-food-policy-initiative/homegrown-baltimore/.

Barham, James, Debra Tropp, Kathleen Enterline, Jeff Farbman, John Fisk, and Stacia Kiraly. *Regional Food Hub Resource Guide*. USDA Agricultural Marketing Service. Washington, DC. April 2012.

Basurto, Xavier, and Elinor Ostrom. "Beyond the Tragedy of the Commons." *Economia delle fonti di energia e dell'ambiente* 52, no. 1 (2009): 35–60.

Batie, Barb Bierman. "Agritourism May Learn 'Safety' the Hard Way." *Midwest Producer.* http://www.midwestproducer.com/news/regional/agritourism -may-learn-safety-the-hard-way/article_b637d986-c290-11e4-bad6 -e7aefc37f4cf.html.

Bauman, Richard, and Charles Briggs. "Poetics and Performance as Critical Perspectives on Language and Social Life." *Annual Review of Anthropology* 19 (1990): 59–88.

Belasco, Eric J., Suzette Galinato, Tom Marsh, Carol Miles, and Russell Wallace. "High Tunnels Are My Crop Insurance: An Assessment of Risk Management Tools for Small-Scale Specialty Crop Producers." *Agricultural and Resource Economics Review* 42, no. 2 (2013): 403–418.

Berry, Wendell. "The Pleasures of Eating." In *Cooking, Eating, Thinking: Transformative Philosophies of Food*, edited by Deane W. Curtin and Lisa M. Heldke, 374–79. Bloomington: Indiana University Press, 1992.

———. Remarks at meeting with farmers and community food security partners, Bloomington, Indiana, November 12, 2010.

———. *What Are People For? Essays by Wendell Berry*. Berkeley, CA: Counterpoint, 2010.

Bessière, Jacinthe. "Local Development and Heritage: Traditional Food and Cuisine as Tourist Attractions in Rural Areas." *Sociologia Ruralis* 38, no. 1 (1998): 21–34.

Bezekhaya, Abalimi. "What We Do." People's Garden Center. http://abalimi .org.za/about-abalimi/what-we-do.

Biodynamic Association. "Community Supported Agriculture: An Introduction to CSA." https://www.biodynamics.com/content/community -supported-agriculture-introduction-csa.

Block, Daniel, and Howard Rosing. *Chicago: A Food Biography*. Lanham, MD: Rowman and Littlefield, 2015.

Bloomington, City of. "About Linnea's Greenhouse." http://bloomington.in
.gov/documents/viewDocument.php?document_id=7419.

———. "About WE Farm: The Wayne-Egenolf Farm." https://bloomington.in
.gov/documents/viewDocument.php?document_id=7437.

———. Farm Market Directory. http://bloomington.in.gov/documents
/viewDocument.php?document_id=8920.

Bloomington Winter Farmers' Market. "About." http://www.bloomington
winterfarmersmarket.com/about.

Blume, Amiee. "Farmers Offer Daviess County Produce Items at Auction."
Evansville *Courier & Press*. August 20, 2013. http://www.courierpress.
com/features/farmers-offer-daviess-county-produce-items-at-auction
—gallery-ep-297032687-324668321.html.

Bowen, Sarah. *Divided Spirits: Tequila, Mezcal, and the Politics of Production*.
Berkeley: University of California Press, 2015.

Bowens, Natasha. "CSA Is Rooted in Black History." *Mother Earth News*. http://
www.motherearthnews.com/organic-gardening/csas-rooted-in-black
-history-zbcz1502.aspx.

Brown, Cheryl, and Stacy Miller. "The Impacts of Local Markets: A Review
of Research on Farmers Markets and Community Supported Agriculture
(CSA)." *American Journal of Agricultural Economics* 90, no. 5 (2008): 1298–1302.

Budianksy, Stephen. "Math Lessons for Locavores." *New York Times*. August 19,
2010. http://www.nytimes.com/2010/08/20/opinion/20budiansky.html.

Bureau of Labor Statistics. "Employment Projections." http://www.bls.gov
/emp/ep_chart_001.htm.

Byker, Carmen, Nick Rose, and Elana Serrano. "The Benefits, Challenges, and
Strategies of Adults Following a Local Food Diet." *Journal of Agriculture,
Food Systems, and Community Development* 1, no. 1 (2010): 125–37.

Carpenter, Mary, and Quentin Carpenter. *The Dane County Farmers' Market: A
Personal History*. Madison: University of Wisconsin Press, 2003.

Carpenter, Novella. *Farm City: The Education of an Urban Farmer*. New York:
Penguin, 2010.

Carro-Figueroa, Vivian, and Amy Guptill. "Emerging Farmers' Markets and
the Globalization of Food Retailing: A Perspective from Puerto Rico." In
Remaking the North American Food System: Strategies for Sustainability, edited
by C. Clare Hinrichs and Thomas A. Lyson, 260–76. Lincoln: University of
Nebraska Press, 2007.

Cascade Harvest Coalition. "Marketing Research and Strategy for Growing
Sales Opportunities at Puget Sound Farmers Markets." *Cascade Harvest
Coalition*. 2015. http://www.cascadeharvest.org/programs/farmers
-markets.

Center for Rural Pennsylvania. *Starting and Strengthening Farmers' Markets in Pennsylvania*, 2nd ed. Harrisburg: Center for Rural Pennsylvania, 2002.

Charles, Dan. "On the Farmers Market Frontier, It's Not Just about Profit." *NPR*, August 30, 2012. http://www.npr.org/blogs/thesalt/2012/08/30/160303008/on-the-farmers-market-frontier-its-not-just-about-profit.

Chile Woman, The. http://www.thechilewoman.com.

Clark, Dylan. "The Raw and the Rotten: Punk Cuisine." *Ethnology* 43, no. 1 (2004): 19–31.

Clark, Kyle H., and Kimberly A. Nicholas. "Introducing Urban Forestry: A Multifunctional Approach to Increase Food Security and Provide Ecosystem Services." *Landscape Ecology* 28, no. 9 (2013): 1649–69.

Coccaro, Kasie. "The White House Kitchen Garden Summer Harvest." *Let's Move* (blog). May 28, 2013. http://www.letsmove.gov/blog/2013/05/28/whitehousekitchengardensummerharvest.

Coffin, Chris. "Gaining Insights, Gaining Access." Farmland.org. April 2016. https://www.farmland.org/initiatives/gaining-insights-gaining-access.

Community Food Security Coalition. "What Is Community Food Security Coalition?" http://foodsecurity.org/about-us.

Cone, Cynthia A., and Andrea Myhre. "Community-Supported Agriculture: A Sustainable Alternative to Industrial Agriculture?" *Human Organization* 59 (2000): 187–97.

Conner, David. "Beyond Organic: Information Provision for Sustainable Agriculture in a Changing Market." *Journal of Food Distribution Research* 35, no. 1 (2004): 34–39.

———. "Expressing Values in Agricultural Markets: An Economic Policy Perspective." *Agriculture and Human Values* 21 (2004): 27–35.

———, Kathryn Colasanti, R. Brent Ross, and Susan Smalley. "Locally Grown Foods and Farmers Markets: Consumer Attitudes and Behaviors." *Sustainability* 2, no. 3 (2010): 742–56.

———, Adam Montri, Dru Montri, and Michael Hamm. "Consumer Demand for Local Produce at Extended Season Farmers' Markets: Guiding Farmer Marketing Strategies." *Renewable Agriculture and Food Systems* 24, no. 4 (2009): 251–59.

Consumer Protection Safety Division. United States Government. "Your Online Resource for Recalls." http://www.recalls.gov/food.html.

Cook, Daniel. "Problematizing Consumption, Community, and Leisure: Some Thoughts on Moving beyond Essentialist Thinking." *Leisure/loisir* 30 (2016): 455–66.

Corum, Vance, Marcie Rosenzweig, and Eric Gibson. *The New Farmers' Market: Farm Fresh Ideas for Producers, Managers and Communities*. Auburn, CA: New World Publishing, 2001.

Cox, Rosie, Lewis Holloway, Laura Venn, Liz Dowler, Jane Rickets Hein, Moya Kneafsey, and Helen Tuomainen. "Common Ground? Motivations for Participation in a Community-Supported Agriculture Scheme." *Local Environment* 13, no. 3 (2008): 203–18.

Crawford, Barbara, and Rebecca C. Jordan. "Inquiry, Models, and Complex Reasoning to Transform Learning in Environmental Education." In *Transdisciplinary Research in Environmental Education*, edited by Marianne E. Krasny and Justin Dillon. Ithaca, NY: Cornell University Press, 2013.

Cummings, Harry, Gailin Kora, and Don Murray. "Farmers' Markets in Ontario and Their Economic Impact 1998." *AgriNews Interactive*. http://www.agrinewsinteractive.com/features/farmersmarkets/farmersmarkets.html.

"D-Town Farm." http://www.d-townfarm.com/d-town-farmorg.html.

Day-Farnsworth, Lindsey, Bren McCown, Michelle Miller, Anne Pfeifer. "Scaling Up: Meeting the Demand for Local Food." Center for Integrated Agricultural Systems. http://www.cias.wisc.edu/scaling-up-meeting-the-demand-for-local-food.

DeLind, Laura B. "Of Bodies, Place, and Culture: Re-situating Local Food." *Journal of Agricultural and Environmental Ethics* 19, no. 2 (2006): 121–46.

———. "Market Niches, 'Cul de sacs,' and Social Context: Alternative Systems of Food Production." *Culture and Agriculture* 13, no. 47 (1993): 7–12.

Deutsch, Tracey. *Building a Housewife's Paradise: Gender, Politics, and American Grocery Stores in the Twentieth Century*. Chapel Hill: University of North Carolina Press, 2010.

D'Innocenzio, Anne. "Walmart to Purchase Produce Directly from Local Growers." *Huffington Post*. June 3, 2013. http://www.huffingtonpost.com/2013/06/03/walmart-produce-fruit-vegetables_n_3378575.html.

Donnermeyer, Joseph F. "Doubling Time and Population Increase of the Amish." *Journal of Amish and Plain Anabaptist Studies* 3, no. 1 (2015): 94–109.

Drake, Luke, and Laura J. Lawson. "Results of a US and Canada Community Garden Survey: Shared Challenges in Garden Management amid Diverse Geographical and Organizational Contexts." *Agriculture and Human Values* 32, no. 2 (2015): 241–54.

Eccles, Jacquelynne S. "Understanding Women's Educational and Occupational Choices: Applying the Eccles et al. Model of Achievement-Related Choices." *Psychology of Women Quarterly* 18 (1994): 585–609.

Ellickson, Robert. *Order without Law: How Neighbors Settle Disputes*. Cambridge, MA: Harvard University Press, 1994.

Ernst, Matt, and Tim Woods. "Marketing at Produce Auctions." University of Kentucky Cooperative Extension Service. http://www.uky.edu/Ag/NewCrops/introsheets/auctions.pdf.

Evening Song Farm Facebook Page. https://www.facebook.com/pages/Evening-Song-Farm/134669806604503.

Evenstar Farm. "What Is a CSA?" http://www.evenstarfarm.net/whatIs.html.

Farm-to-Consumer Legal Defense Fund. "Raw Milk Nation." http://www.farmtoconsumer.org/raw-milk-nation-interactive-map.

Farm Bloomington. http://www.farm-bloomington.com.

Farmer, James R. "Supporting Specialty Crops and Local Food Systems in Indiana." Specialty Crops Block Grant final report. Indiana State Department of Agriculture. 2009.

———, and Megan E. Betz. "Rebuilding Local Foods in Appalachia: Variables Affecting Distribution Methods of West Virginia Farms." *Journal of Rural Studies* 45 (2016): 34–42.

———, H. Charles Chancellor, Andrew Gooding, Devorah Shubowitz, and Adrienne Bryant. "A Tale of Four Farmers Markets: Recreation and Leisure as a Catalyst for Sustainability." *Journal of Park and Recreation Administration* 29, no. 3 (2011): 11–23.

———, H. Charles Chancellor, Jennifer M. Robinson, Stephanie West, and Melissa Weddell. "Agrileisure: Farmers' Markets, CSAs, and the Privilege in Eating Local." *Journal of Leisure Research* 46, no. 3 (2014): 313–28.

———, Vicky J. Meretsky, Doug H. Knapp, Charles Chancellor, and Burnell C. Fischer. "Why Agree to a Conservation Easement? Understanding the Decision of Conservation Easement Granting." *Landscape and Urban Planning* 138 (2015): 11–19.

———, Sara Minard, and Cliff Edens. "Use of Local Foods to Bolster Food Security of People Living in Low and Mixed-Income Neighborhoods." *Journal of Agriculture, Food Systems, and Community Development* (forthcoming).

———, Cassie Peters, Evan Hanson, and E. Meghan Betcher. *Overcoming the Market Barriers to Organic Production in West Virginia.* Morgantown, WV: Downstream Strategies, 2013.

Farmers Market Coalition. "Advocacy." http://farmersmarketcoalition.org/advocacy/snap.

Farrer, James, ed. *The Globalization of Asian Cuisines.* New York: Palgrave Macmillan, 2015.

Feliciano, Cynthia, and Rubén G. Rumbaut. "Gendered Paths: Educational and Occupational Expectations and Outcomes among Adult Children of Immigrants." *Ethnic and Racial Studies* 28 (2005): 1087–1118.

Fennell, Lee Anne. "Ostrom's Law: Property Rights in the Commons." *International Journal of the Commons* 5, no. 1 (2011): 9–27.

Ferreira, Gustavo. "An Overview of Agritourism in the United States, Virginia, and Surrounding States: An Ag Census Analysis." Virginia Tech Univer-

sity. April 4, 2015. http://news.cals.vt.edu/fbm-update/2015/04/06
/an-overview-of-agritourism-in-the-united-states-virginia-and
-surrounding-states-an-ag-census-analysis.

Fiorentine, R. "Increasing Similarity in Life Plans of Male and Female College
Students? Evidence and Implications." *Sex Roles* 18 (1988): 143–58.

Forbes, Cristin B., and Alison I I. Harmon. "Buying into Community Supported Agriculture: Strategies for Overcoming Income Barriers." *Journal of
Hunger and Environmental Nutrition* 2, no. 2–3 (2008): 65–79.

FRESHFARM Markets. "Join FRESHFARM Markets." http://freshfarm
markets.org/farmers_markets/sell_at_our_markets.php.

Fruit Tree Planting Foundation. "Mission." http://www.ftpf.org/mission.htm.

Gallardo, Karina, Aaron Olanie, Rita Ordonez, and Marcia Ostrom. "The
Use of Electronic Payment Machines at Farmers Markets: Results from a
Choice Experiment Study." *International Food and Agribusiness Management
Review* 18 (2015): 79–104.

Geisler, Malinda. "Agritourism Profile." Agricultural Marketing Resource
Center. June 2014. http://www.agmrc.org/commodities__products
/agritourism/agritourism-profile.

Gerbasi, Gina T. "Athens Farmers' Market: Evolving Dynamics and Hidden
Benefits to a Southeast Ohio Rural Community." *Focus on Geography* 49,
no. 2 (2006): 1–6.

Gillespie, Gilbert, Duncan Hilchey, Clare Hinrichs, and Gail Feenstra. "Farmers' Markets as Keystones in Rebuilding Local and Regional Food Systems." In *Remaking the North American Food System: Strategies for Sustainability*, edited by C. Clare Hinrichs and Thomas A. Lyson, 65–83. Lincoln:
University of Nebraska Press, 2007.

Glover, Troy D. "Social Capital in the Lived Experiences of Community Gardeners." *Leisure Sciences: An Interdisciplinary Journal* 26, no. 2 (2004): 143–62.

———. "The Story of the Queen Anne Memorial Garden: Resisting a Dominant Cultural Narrative." *Journal of Leisure Research* 35, no. 2 (2003): 190–
212.

Godbey, Geoffrey. *Leisure in Your Life: An Exploration.* 2nd ed. State College, PA:
Venture, 1985.

Gonzalez, Sarah. "Farmers' Markets Grow by 17 Percent in US." *Agri-pulse.* August 4, 2011. http://www.agri-pulse.com/Merrigan_Farmers_Markets
_8052011.asp.

Good Shepherd Food Bank of Maine. "Mainers Feeding Mainers." https://
www.gsfb.org/how-we-help/programs/mainers-feeding-mainers.

Gray, Mary L. *Out in the Country: Youth, Media, and Queer Visibility in Rural
America.* New York: NYU Press, 2009.

Greene, Barbara A., and Teresa K. Debacker. "Gender and Orientations toward the Future: Links to Motivation." *Educational Psychology Review* 16 (2004): 91–120.

Greenmarket GrowNYC. http://www.grownyc.org/files/gmkt/questionnaire /farmer.pdf.

Grewal, Sharanbir S., and Parwinder S. Grewal. "Can Cities Become Self-Reliant in Food?" *Cities* 29, no. 1 (2012): 1–11.

Groh, Trauger, and Steven McFadden. *Farms of Tomorrow Revisited: Community Supported Farms–Farm Supported Communities.* Kimberton, PA: Biodynamic Farming and Gardening Association, 1998.

Groundwork Farms. "Prices and Shares." http://www.groundworkfarms.com /prices-and-share-descriptions.

Growing for Market. www.growingformarket.com.

Growing Power. http://www.growingpower.org.

Guthman, Julie. "'If They Only Knew': Color Blindness and Universalism in California Alternative Food." *Professional Geographer* 60, no. 3 (2008): 387–97.

———. *Weighing In: Obesity, Food Justice, and the Limits of Capitalism.* Berkeley: University of California Press, 2011.

Hamilton, Neil D. *Farmers' Markets Rules, Regulations, and Opportunities.* Fayetteville, AR: National Center for Agricultural Law Research and Information, 2002.

Hardin, Garrett. "The Tragedy of the Commons." *Science* 162, no. 3859 (1968): 1243–48.

Harris, Marvin. "Anthropology Needs Holism; Holism Needs Anthropology." In *The Teaching of Anthropology: Problems, Issues, and Decisions,* edited by Conrad Phillip Kottak, Jane J. White, Richard H. Furlow, and Patricia C. Rice, 22–28. Mountain View, WV: Mayfield Publishing, 1997.

Hede, Anne-Marie, and Robyn Stokes. "Network Analysis of Tourism Events: An Approach to Improve Marketing Practices for Sustainable Tourism." *Journal of Travel and Tourism Marketing* 26, no. 7 (2009): 656–69.

Hendrickson, Mary, and William Heffernan. "Opening Spaces through Relocalization: Locating Potential Resistance in the Weaknesses of the Global Food System." *Sociologica Ruralis* 42 (2002): 347–69.

Herrera, Remy, and Kin Chi Lau, eds. *The Struggle for Food Sovereignty: Alternative Development and the Renewal of Peasant Societies Today.* London: Pluto Press, 2015.

Hesterman, Oran B. *Fair Food: Growing a Healthy, Sustainable Food System for All.* New York: Public Affairs, 2011.

Hinrichs, Clare C. "Embeddedness and Local Food Systems: Notes on Two Types of Direct Agricultural Markets." *Journal of Rural Studies* 16 (2000): 295–303.

———, and Kathy S. Kremer. "Social Inclusion in a Midwest Local Food System Project." *Journal of Poverty* 6, no. 1 (2002): 65–90.

Hoppe, Robert A., and Penni Korb. "Characteristics of Women Farm Operators and Their Farms." USDA. April 2013. http://www.ers.usda.gov/media /1093198/eib111_summary.pdf.

Hughes, Megan Elizabeth, and Richard H. Mattson. "Farmers' Markets in Kansas: A Profile of Vendors and Market Organization." *Report of Progress* 658. Agricultural Experiment Station, Kansas State University, 1992.

Hunger Action Network of New York State. "Community Food." http://www .hungeractionnys.org/commfood_csa.htm.

Illich, Ivan. *Deschooling Society*. New York: Harper and Row, 1971.

Indian Line Farm. "Community Supported Agriculture at Indian Line Farm." http://www.indianlinefarm.com/csa.html.

Indiana University Office of Sustainability. "Sustainability Defined." http:// sustain.indiana.edu/overview/sustainability.php.

Iowa Food Hub. "About the Iowa Food Hub." http://www.iowafoodhub.com /public/pageedit.aspx?pageid=1.

Johns Hopkins University Center for a Livable Future. Food Policy Networks: Directory. http://www.foodpolicynetworks.org/directory.

Johnson, Amanda J. "'It's more than a shopping trip': Leisure and Consumption in a Farmers' Market." *Annals of Leisure Research* 16 (2013): 4, 315–31.

Johnson, Renée, Randy Alison Aussenberg, and Tadlock Cowan. *The Role of Local Food Systems in US Farm Policy*. Congressional Research Service, March 12, 2013. http://www.fas.org/sgp/crs/misc/R42155.pdf.

Jones, Sam. "More Than 1,000 New Farmers Markets Recorded across Country as USDA Directory Reveals 17 Percent Growth." USDA. August 5, 2011. http://www.usda.gov/wps/portal/usda/usdahome?contentid=2011/08 /0338.xml.

Jordan, Jennifer A. "The Heirloom Tomato as Cultural Object: Investigating Taste and Space." *Sociologia Ruralis* 47, no. 1 (2007): 20–41.

Kaiser, Karen. "Protecting Respondent Confidentiality in Qualitative Research." *Qualitative Health Research* 19, no. 11 (2009): 1632–41.

Kelly, Debi. "Agritourism: Selling the Farm Experience." *Missouri Beginning Farm* (blog). October 14, 2010. http://missouribeginningfarming.blogspot .com/2010/10/agritourism-selling-farm-experience.html.

Kemmis, Daniel. *The Good City and the Good Life*. Boston: Houghton Mifflin, 1995.

Kennebec Estuary Land Trust. "Local Farms–Local Food." http://
    kennebecestuary.org/resources/local-farms-local-food.
Kerr Center for Sustainable Agriculture. "Farmers' Market CUSTOMER SUR-
    VEY (9/29/01)," http://www.kerrcenter.com/farmers_market/Customer
    _Survey.pdf.
Kestrel Land Trust. "Conservation Is Collaboration." http://www.kestreltrust
    .org/learn-more—-conservation-is-collaboration.php.
King, Robert, Miguel Gomez, and Gigi DiGiacomo. "Can Local Food Go
    Mainstream?" Choices Magazine. http://www.choicesmagazine.org
    /magazine/article.php?article=111.
Kingsolver, Barbara. Animal, Vegetable, Miracle. New York: HarperCollins, 2007.
Koch, Kaitlin. "How to Purchase Local Michigan Food Year-Round." Michigan
    State University Extension. January 26, 2015. http://msue.anr.msu.edu
    /news/how_to_purchase_local_michigan_food_year_round.
Kolko, Jon. "Abductive Thinking and Sensemaking: The Drivers of Design
    Synthesis." Design Issues 26, no. 1 (2010): 15–28.
Kremer, Peleg, and Tracy DeLiberty. "Local Food Practices and Growing Po-
    tential: Mapping the Case of Philadelphia." Applied Geography 31 (2011):
    1252–61.
Kyle, Edwin Jackson, and Alexander Caswell Ellis. Fundamentals of Farming and
    Farm Life. Rev. Ed. New York: Charles Scribner's Sons, 1922.
La Trobe, Helen. "Famers' Markets: Consuming Local Rural Produce." Interna-
    tional Journal of Consumer Studies 25, no. 3 (2001): 181–92.
Land Trust Alliance Census. "2010 National Land Trust Census." http://www
    .landtrustalliance.org/land-trusts/land-trust-census.
Lang, K. Brandon. "Expanding Our Understanding of Community Supported
    Agriculture (CSA): An Examination of Member Satisfaction." Journal of
    Sustainable Agriculture 26, no. 2 (2005): 61–79.
Lave, Jean, and Etienne Wenger. Situated Learning: Legitimate Peripheral Partici-
    pation. Cambridge, UK: University of Cambridge Press, 1991.
Lawson, Laura J. "History and Development of Community Gardens: A Brief
    History of Urban Garden Programs in the United States." October 2009.
    http://ljlawson.rutgers.edu/assets/pdf/UGPlecture.pdf.
Leiserowitz, Anthony, Edward W. Maibach, Connie Roser-Renouf, Geoff Fein-
    berg, and Peter Howe. "Climate Change in the American Mind: Ameri-
    cans' Global Warming Beliefs and Attitudes in April 2013." Yale Project on
    Climate Change Communication/George Mason University Center for
    Climate Change Communication. http://environment.yale.edu/climate
    -communication-OFF/files/Climate-Beliefs-April-2013.pdf.

Lewis, Ronald. *Transforming the Appalachian Countryside*. Morgantown: West Virginia University Press, 1998.

Linn, Karl. "Reclaiming the Sacred Commons." *New Village* 1, no. 1 (1999): 42–49.

Local Food Hub. "2014 Annual Report." http://localfoodhub.org/2014annual report

Local Growers Guild. http://www.localgrowers.org.

Local Harvest. "Community Supported Agriculture." http://www.local harvest.org/csa.

Lohr, Luanne, Adam Diamond, Chris Dicken, and David Marquardt. "Mapping Competition Zones for Vendors and Customers in US Farmers Markets." Agricultural Marketing Service. September 2011.https://www.ams .usda.gov/sites/default/files/media/Mapping%20Competition%20Zones %20for%20Vendors%20and%20Customers%20in%20U.S.%20Farmers %20Markets.pdf.

Low, Sarah A., Aaron Adalja, Elizabeth Beaulieu, Nigel Key, Stephen Martinez, Alex Melton, Agnes Perez, Katherine Ralston, Hayden Stewart, Shellye Suttles, Stephen Vogel, and Becca B. R. Jablonski. "Trends in US Local and Regional Food Systems." Administrative Public No. 068, USDA Economic Research Service, 2015. http://www.ers.usda.gov/media/1763057/ap068 .pdf.

Lyson, Thomas A. *Civic Agriculture: Reconnecting Farm, Food, and Community*. Boston: Tufts University Press, 2004.

MacArthur Foundation, "About Us." www.macfound.org.

Macher, Ron, and Howard W. Kerr Jr. *Making Your Small Farm Profitable*. North Adams, MA: Storey Books, 1999.

Macias, Thomas. "Working toward a Just, Equitable, and Local Food System: The Social Impact of Community-Based Agriculture." *Social Science Quarterly* 89, no. 5 (2008): 1086–1101.

Mackintosh, R. S. "A Garden for Every Home." University of Minnesota, Agricultural Extension Division. *Special Bulletin* 11 (1917): 1–8. http:// conservancy.umn.edu/bitstream/handle/11299/168339/mn_2000_eb_011 .pdf?sequence=1andisAllowed=y.

Maple Valley Farm. November 2, 2016. http://maplevalley.howardfamily enterprise.com/index.php.

Marini, Margaret Mooney, Pi-Ling Fan, Erica Finley, and Ann M. Beutel. "Gender and Job Values." *Sociology of Education* 69 (1996): 49–65.

Market Umbrella. "Social Capital Impact Study." 2012. http://www.crescent cityfarmersmarket.org/uploads/file/NEEDreportKR10-15-12_nola.pdf.

Martinez, Steve, Michael S. Hand, Michelle Da Pra, Susan Pollack, Katherine Ralston, Travis Smith, Stephen Vogel, Shellye Clark, Luanne Lohr, Sarah A. Low, and Constance Newman. "Local Food Systems: Concepts, Impacts, and Issues." USDA Economic Research Service, Report 97. May 2010. http://www.ers.usda.gov/media/122868/err97_1_.pdf.

Matson, James, Martha Sullins, and Chris Cook. "The Role of Food Hubs in Local Food Marketing." USDA Rural Development Service Report 73. January 2013. http://www.rd.usda.gov/files/sr73.pdf.

Mattozzi, Antonio. *Inventing the Pizzeria: A History of Pizza Making in Naples.* Edited and translated by Zachary Nowak. London: Bloomsbury Academic, 2015.

McFadden, Steven. *The Call of the Land: An Agrarian Primer for the 21st Century.* 2nd ed. Bedford, MA: Norlights Press, 2011.

———. "Community Farms in the 21st Century: Poised for Another Wave of Growth?" Rodale Institute. http://newfarm.rodaleinstitute.org/features /0104/csa-history/part1.shtml.

———. "The History of Community Supported Agriculture, Part I." Rodale Institute. http://rodaleinstitute.org/the-history-of-community-supported -agriculture-part-i.

McGinnis, Michael, and Elinor Ostrom. "Social-Ecological System Framework: Initial Changes and Continuing Challenges." *Ecology and Society* 19, no. 2 (2014): 30.

McGrath, Mary Ann, John F. Sherry, and Deborah D. Heisley. "An Ethnographic Study of an Urban Periodic Marketplace: Lessons from the Midville Farmers' Market." *Journal of Retailing* 69, no. 3 (1993): 280–319.

Meinzen-Dick, Ruth. "Beyond Panaceas in Water Institutions." *Proceedings of the National Academy of Sciences* 104, no. 39 (2007): 15200–205.

Mercer Island Farmers Market. "Food Bank and Shelter Donations." http:// mifarmersmarket.org/about-the-market/food-bank-shelter-donations.

Michigan Urban Farming Initiative. "Home." http://www.miufi.org.

MicroFarmLiving. "How to Earn a Green Living on a Micro Farm." 2016. http://microfarmliving.com.

Morrison, Sean. "Growth in Farmers' Markets Continues into Winter Months." *Indianapolis Business Journal.* February 19, 2011. http://www.ibj.com /articles/25401-growth-in-farmers-markets-continues-into-winter-months.

Moskin, Julia. "Women Find Their Place in the Field." *New York Times.* June 1, 2005. D4.

National Agricultural Statistics Survey (NASS). "Iowa Farmers' Market Customer Survey." November 30, 2009. http://www.nass.usda.gov/Statistics

_by_State/Iowa/Publications/Other_Surveys/2009CustomerSummary
.pdf.

National Good Food Network. "Food Hub Center." http://www.ngfn.org
/resources/food-hubs.

National Restaurant Association. "What's Hot in 2015? Discover New Menu
Trends." December 3, 2014. http://www.restaurant.org/News-Research
/News/What-s-Hot-in-2015-culinary-forecast-predicts-top.

Neal, Arthur. "Innovation Helps Fuel Growth for Winter Farmers Markets."
United States Department of Agriculture Blog. December 5, 2012. http://blogs
.usda.gov/2012/12/05/innovation-helps-fuel-growth-for-winter-farmers
-markets.

New Roots. "About Us." http://www.newrootsproduce.org/about-us.html.

Norberg-Hodge, Helena, Todd Merrifield, and Steven Gorelick. *Bringing the
Food Economy Home: Local Alternatives to Global Agribusiness.* London: Zed
Books, 2002.

North Carolina Cooperative Extension. "Community Supported Agriculture
(CSA) Resource Guide for Farmers." http://growingsmallfarms.ces.ncsu
.edu/growingsmallfarms-csaguide.

Ostrom, Elinor. "A General Framework for Analyzing Sustainability of Social-
Ecological Systems." *Science* 325, no. 5939 (2009): 419–22.

———. *Governing the Commons: The Evolution of Institutions for Collective Action.*
Cambridge, UK: Cambridge University Press, 1990.

———. "Sustainable Social-Ecological Systems: An Impossibility?" Paper pre-
sented at the meeting of the American Association for the Advancement of
Science, San Francisco, February 15–19, 2007. http://www.mcleveland.org
/Class_reading/Ostrom_Sustainable_Socio-Economic_Systems.pdf.

"Our Programs." *Mid-Ohio Foodbank.* https://www.midohiofoodbank.org
/programs-services/our-programs/UFCO.

Parsons, Julie M. *Gender, Class and Food: Families, Bodies, and Health.* New York:
Palgrave Macmillan, 2015.

Parsons, Russ. "The Idea That Shook the World." *Los Angeles Times.* May 24,
2006. http://articles.latimes.com/2006/may/24/food/fo-farmer24.

"People's Potato Community Garden, The." *The People's Potato.* http://www
.peoplespotato.com/community-garden.html.

Perry, Jill, and Scott Franzblau. *Local Harvest: A Multiform CSA Handbook.* Signature Book Printing, 2010. http://www.sare.org/Learning-Center/SARE
-Project-Products/Northeast-SARE-Project-Products/Local-Harvest.

Pete, Joseph S. "Farmland Values Notch Another Dramatic Rise." *Northwest Indiana Times.* September 12, 2013. http://www.nwitimes.com/business

/local/farmland-values-notch-another-dramatic-rise/article_15b03e44
-6c8b-5b65-81ff-f9ac331185b4.html.

Pirog, Rich, and Andrew Benjamin. "Checking the Food Odometer: Comparing Food Miles for Local versus Conventional Produce Sales to Iowa Institutions." Leopold Center for Sustainable Agriculture. July 2003. http://
www.leopold.iastate.edu/pubs-and-papers/2003-07-food-odometer.

Potts, Robert, Eric Gustafson, Susan L. Stewart, Frank R. Thompson, Kathleen
Bergen, Daniel G. Brown, Roger Hammer, Volker Radeloff, David Bengs-
ton, John Sauer, and Brian Sturtevant. "The Changing Midwest Assessment: Land Cover, Natural Resources, and People." Gen. Tech. Rep. NC-
250. St. Paul, MN:USDA Forest Service, North Central Research Station.
2004. http://www.nrs.fs.fed.us/pubs/3346.

Press, Melea, and Eric Arnould. "How Does Organizational Identification
Form? A Consumer Behavior Perspective." *Journal of Consumer Research* 38
(2011): 650–66.

Pushpanathan v. Canada (Minister of Citizenship and Immigration). [1998] 1
S.C.R. 982, para. 36.

Ragland, Edward, and Debra Tropp. *USDA National Farmers Market Manager
Survey, 2006.* USDA Agricultural Marketing Service. May 2009. http://
dx.doi.org/10.9752/MS037.05-2009.

Restaurant Tallent. "About Restaurant Tallent." http://restauranttallent.com
/about-restaurant-tallent.php. (site discontinued).

Reynolds, Heather, Eduardo Brondizio, and Jennifer Meta Robinson, eds.
Teaching Environmental Literacy: Across the Curriculum and across Campus.
Bloomington: Indiana University Press, 2010.

"Richmond Indiana Farmers Market." http://www.richmondinfarmersmarket
.com.

Robinson, Jennifer Meta. "Making the Land Connection: Local Food Farms
and Sustainability of Place." In *The Greening of Everyday Life: Challenging
Practices, Imaging Possibilities*, edited by Jens Kersten and John M. Meyer,
198–210. Oxford: Oxford University Press, 2016.

———, and J. A. Hartenfeld. *The Farmers' Market Book: Growing Food, Cultivating
Community.* Bloomington: Indiana University Press, 2007.

Roth, Cathy, and Elizabeth Keen. *CSA: Organizing a Successful CSA.* 1999.
https://www.uvm.edu/~susagctr/resources/CSA.pdf.

Ruhf, Kathryn. "Regionalism: A New England Recipe for a Resilient Food
System." *Journal of Environmental Studies and Sciences* 5 (2015): 650–60.

———, and John Mitchell. "Programming and Support for Beginning Farmers." Proceedings from the 4th National Small Farm Conference, USDA,
2005, 249–52.

Salatin, Joel. "How to Lobby for Saner Food Policies." *Mother Earth News.* June/ July 2015, 59–63.

Saldanha, Arun. "Reontologising Race: The Machinic Geography of Pheno-type." *Environment and Planning D: Society and Space* 24, no. 1 (2006): 9–24.

Sanders, Scott, *A Conservationist Manifesto.* Bloomington: Indiana University Press, 2009.

Schein, Richard H. "Race and Landscape in the United States." In *Landscape and Race in the United States*, edited by Richard H. Schein, 1–21. New York: Routledge, 2006.

Schmit, Todd M., et al. "Assessing the Economic Impacts of Regional Food Hubs: The Case of Regional Access." Northeast SARE. 2013. http://www .nesare.org/Dig-Deeper/Useful-resources/SARE-Project-Products /Northeast-SARE-Project-Products/Assessing-the-Economic-Impacts-of -Regional-Food-Hubs-the-Case-of-Regional-Access.

Sexton, Steven. "The Inefficiency of Local Food." *Freakonomics.* November 14, 2011. http://freakonomics.com/2011/11/14/the-inefficiency-of-local-food.

Seyfang, Gill. "Ecological Citizenship and Sustainable Consumption: Exam-ining Local Organic Food Networks." *Journal of Rural Studies* 22, no. 4 (2006): 383–95.

Shinew, Kimberly, Troy Glover, and Diana Perry. "Leisure Spaces as Poten-tial Sites for Interracial Interaction: Community Gardens in Urban Areas." *Journal of Leisure Research* 36, no. 3 (2004): 336–55.

Sidney, Glenn, and John Ford. "Farmstand." https://www.farmstandapp.com.

Simmons Winery. http://www.simmonswinery.com/about.html.

Smit, Jac, Joe Nasr, and Annu Ratta. *Urban Agriculture: Food, Jobs, and Sustain-able Cities.* New York: Urban Agriculture Network, 1996.

Sorensen, Amanda E., Rachel Shwom, Rebecca C. Jordan, Diane Ebert-May, Cindy Isenhour, Aaron M. McCright, and Jennifer Meta Robinson. "Model-Based Reasoning to Foster Environmental and Socio-scientific Lit-eracy in Higher Education." *Journal of Environmental Studies and Sciences* 6, no. 2 (2015): 287–94.

South Circle Farm. http://www.southcirclefarm.com.

Spitzer, Theodore Morrow, and Hilary Baum. *Public Markets and Community Re-vitalization.* Washington: ULI–The Urban Land Institute and Project for Public Spaces, 1995.

Starmer, Elanor. "High Tunnel Initiative Brings Local Foods to Detroit." *United States Department of Agriculture Blog.* February 20, 2014. http://blogs.usda .gov/2014/02/20/high-tunnel-initiative-brings-local-foods-to-detroit /#more-50193.

Stebbins, Robert. *A Perspective for Our Time: Serious Leisure*. New Brunswick, NJ: Transaction Publishers, 2008.

Stephenson, Gary. *Farmers' Markets: Success, Failure, and Management Ecology*. Amherst, NY: Cambria Press, 2008.

———, Larry Lev, and Linda Brewer. "Understanding the Link between Farmers' Market Size and Management Organization." *Special Report Number 1082-E*. Oregon State University Extension Service, December 2007. http://dnr.alaska.gov/ag/FMM/013APPJMarketSizeMgmtOrganization.pdf.

———. "When Things Don't Work: Some Insights into Why Farmers' Markets Close." *Special Report Number 1073-E*. December 2006. http://smallfarms.oregonstate.edu/sites/default/files/small-farms-tech-report/eesc_1073.pdf.

Stranger's Hill Organics. http://www.strangershillorganics.com.

Thomas, Mary E. "'I Think It's Just Natural': The Spatiality of Racial Segregation at a US High School." *Environment and Planning* A 37, no. 7 (2005): 1233–48.

Thompson, Claire. "Food Hubs: How Small Farmers Get to Market." *Grist*. March 7, 2012. http://grist.org/locavore/food-hubs-how-small-farmers-get-to-market.

———. "Say It Ain't Soil: What's the True Value of Organic Farmland?" *Grist*. June 15, 2012. http://grist.org/sustainablefarming/say-it-aint-soil-how-much-is-organic-farmland-worth.

Torres, Hilary, Rich Pirog, and Judith Barry. "Before We Seek Change, Is There a Demand for Local Meats?" MSU Center for Regional Food Systems (2014). http://foodsystems.msu.edu/uploads/files/Demand_for_Local_Meat_Review.pdf.

Trust for Public Land. "Community Gardens." http://www.tpl.org/our-work/parks-for-people/community-gardens.

Tubene, Stephan, and James Hanson. "The Wholesale Produce Auction: An Alternative Marketing Strategy for Small Farms." *American Journal of Alternative Agriculture* 17, no. 1 (2002): 18–23.

"Turner Garden." *Urban Agriculture Australia*. http://www.urbanagriculture.org.au/turner-garden.

Twiss, Joan, Joy Dickinson, Shirley Duma, Tanya Kleinman, Heather Paulsen, and Liz Rilveria. "Community Gardens: Lessons Learned from California Healthy Cities and Communities." *American Journal of Public Health* 93, no. 9 (2003): 1435–38.

United Nations. "UN Projects World Population to Reach 8.5 Billion by 2030, Driven by Growth in Developing Countries." *Sustainable Development* (blog). July 29, 2015.

———. Department of Economic and Social Affairs. *World Urbanization Prospects: The 2014 Revision.* New York: United Nations, 2014. https://esa.un.org /unpd/wup/Publications/Files/WUP2014-Highlights.pdf.

United States Census Bureau. "America's Families and Living Arrangements: 2011." http://www.census.gov/population/www/socdemo/hh-fam/cps 2011.html.

———. "State and County QuickFacts." January 7, 2014. http://quickfacts .census.gov/qfd/states/00000.html.

United States Department of Agriculture (USDA). *Census of Agriculture.* 2007. http://www.agcensus.usda.gov/index.php.

———. "Census of Agriculture Shows Growing Diversity in US Farming." February 4, 2009. http://www.usda.gov/wps/portal/usda/usdahome ?contentidonly=true&contentid=2009/02/0036.xml.

———. Commodity Areas: Definition of Specialty Crops. 2013. http://www .ams.usda.gov/AMSv1.0/scbgpdefinitions.

———. "Community Supported Agriculture." USDA National Agricultural Library. December 12, 2014. http://www.nal.usda.gov/afsic/pubs/csa/csa .shtml.

———. "Farm Computer Usage and Ownership." National Agricultural Statistics Service. August 19, 2015. http://usda.mannlib.cornell.edu/usda/ current/FarmComp/FarmComp-08-19-2015.pdf.

———. "Farm Demographics–US Farmers by Gender, Age, Race, Ethnicity, and More." 2012 Census Highlights. May 2014. https://www.agcensus .usda.gov/Publications/2012/Online_Resources/Highlights/Farm _Demographics.

———. "Farmers Markets and Direct-to-Consumer Marketing." http://www .ams.usda.gov/services/local-regional/farmers-markets-and-direct -consumer-marketing.

———. "Local Food Research and Development." http://www.ams.usda.gov /AMSv1.0/FoodHubs.

———. "Organic Market Overview." June 19, 2012. http://www.ers.usda.gov /topics/natural-resources-environment/organic-agriculture/organic -market-overview.aspx#.UdCGvzvVCSp.

———. "Organic Production Survey." 2008. http://www.agcensus.usda.gov /Publications/2007/Online_Highlights/Fact_Sheets/organics.pdf.

———. "SNAP Applicants and Recipients." http://www.fns.usda.gov/snap.

———. "Statistics by Subject." National Agriculture Statistics Service. https:// www.nass.usda.gov/Statistics_by_Subject/index.php?sector=CROPS.

———. "USDA Invests $18 Million to Train Beginning Farmers and Ranchers News." Release No. 0022.15. February 2, 2015. http://www.usda.gov/wps

/portal/usda/usdahome?contentidonly=true&contentid=2015/02/0022
.xml.

———. "Women Farmers Control 7 Percent of US Farmland, Account for 3
Percent of Sales." September 2014. http://www.agcensus.usda.gov
/Publications/2012/Online_Resources/Highlights/Women_Farmers
/Highlights_Women_Farmers.pdf.

University of Richmond. "Bountiful Benefit: New Benefit Allows Employees to
Purchase Local Produce through Payroll Deductions." June 3, 2010. http://
news.richmond.edu/features/article/-/1631/new-benefit-allows-employees
-to-purchase-local-produce-through-payroll-deductions.html.

———. "Employee Wellness." http://employeewellness.richmond.edu.

"Urban Agriculture." *Alternatives*. http://www.rooftopgardens.alternatives.ca
/about/urban-agriculture.

Van Grove, Jennifer. "How to Accept Credit Card Payments on Mobile Devices." *Mashable*. October 14, 2010. http://mashable.com/2010/10/14
/accepting-mobile-payments.

Veldman, Marcia. *The Market Beet: The Newsletter of the Bloomington Community
Farmers' Market*. August 29, 2015.

Veldstra, Michael, Corrine Alexander, and Maria Marshall. "To Certify or Not
to Certify? Separating the Organic Production and Certification Decisions." *Food Policy* (2013): 429–36. http://www.sciencedirect.com/science
/article/pii/S0306919214000840.

Wasserman, Wendy, Debra Tropp, Velma Lakins, Carolyn Foley, Marga
DeNinno, Jezra Thompson, Nora Owens, and Kelly Williams. *Supplemental Nutrition Assistance Program (SNAP) at Farmers Markets: A How- to Handbook*. US Department of Agriculture Agricultural Marketing Service. June
2010.

Wang, Feng, and Michael Hannafin. "Design-Based Research and Technology-
Enhanced Learning Environments." *Educational Technology Research and
Development* 53, no. 4 (2005): 5–23.

WE Farm. "Last 'Market' Call!!" http://us3.campaign-archive2.com/?u=5675
cf88530d6d486fca298bd&id=ec610f7b42.

———. "Meat Sales and Family." http://us3.campaign-archive2.com/?u=5675
cf88530d6d486fca298bd&id=8394e67820.

Weddle, Melissa, Stephanie West, James Farmer, and Charles Chancellor.
"Farmers' Market Consumers in NC and IN: 600 Miles but Little Difference in Who Is Shopping." Paper presented at Leisure Research Symposium, Charlotte, North Carolina, October 14–16, 2014.

"What's Hot in 2015? Discover New Menu Trends." National Restaurant Association. http://www.restaurant.org/News-Research/News/What-s-Hot-in
-2015-culinary-forecast-predicts-top.

Wikipedia. "Community-Supported Agriculture." http://en.wikipedia.org
    /wiki/Community-supported_agriculture.

Wild Ramp, The. "About Us." http://wildramp.org/about-us. Accessed No-
    vember 28, 2016, https://web.archive.org/web/20151128122508/http://
    wildramp.org/producers/meet-the-producers/.

———. "Producer Information." http://wildramp.org/producers/meet-the
    -producers.

Willamette Farm and Food Coalition. "Finding Local Food: Community Sup-
    ported Agriculture (CSA) Programs." http://www.lanefood.org/csa
    -programs.php.

Wilson, Timothy, and David Gilbert. "Affective Forecasting." *Advances in Ex-
    perimental Social Psychology* 35 (2003): 345–411.

Winer, Rose. "5 Best Apps to Guide You to Local Seasonal Produce." *Zester
    Daily.* June 25, 2014. http://zesterdaily.com/agriculture/5-best-apps-guide
    -local-season-produce.

World Wide Opportunities on Organic Farms. http://www.wwoof.org.

Yukic, Thomas S. *Fundamentals of Recreation.* 2nd ed. New York: Harper and
    Row, 1970.

Zimet, David, Timothy Hewitt, and George Henry. "Characteristics of Suc-
    cessful Vegetable Farmers' Retail Markets." *Proceedings of Florida State Hor-
    ticulture Society* 99 (1986): 291–93.

INDEX

Page numbers in *italics* refer to illustrations; page numbers with a "t" suffix refer to tables.

JENNIFER META ROBINSON is Professor of Practice in the Department of Anthropology at Indiana University, where her scholarship in food studies includes *The Farmers' Market Book: Growing Food, Cultivating Community* (Indiana University Press, 2007).

JAMES ROBERT FARMER is Assistant Professor of Recreation, Park, and Tourism Studies in the School of Public Health at Indiana University, where he focuses his scholarship and service on community food systems and natural resource sustainability.